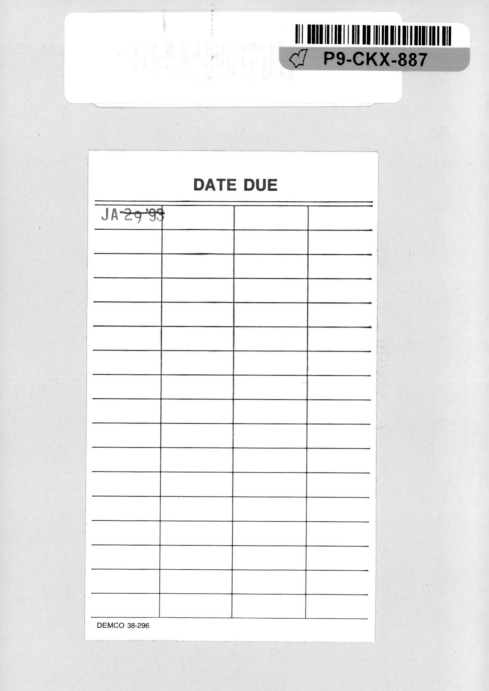

DATE DUE

JA 29 '95			

DEMCO 38-296

COMPARATIVE EUROPEAN POLITICS

General Editors: Hans Daalder and Ken Newton

Multiparty Government

COMPARATIVE EUROPEAN POLITICS

Comparative European Politics is a series for students and teachers of political science and related disciplines, published in association with the European Consortium for Political Research. Each volume will provide an up-to-date survey of the current state of knowledge and research on an issue of major significance in European government and politics.

Multiparty Government

The Politics of Coalition in Europe

MICHAEL LAVER
and
NORMAN SCHOFIELD

OXFORD UNIVERSITY PRESS

1990

Oxford University Press, Walton Street, Oxford OX2 6DP
Oxford New York Toronto
Delhi Bombay Calcutta Madras Karachi
Petaling Jaya Singapore Hong Kong Tokyo
Nairobi Dar es Salaam Cape Town
Melbourne Auckland
and associated companies in
Berlin Ibadan

Oxford is a trade mark of Oxford University Press

Published in the United States
by Oxford University Press, New York

British Library Cataloguing in Publication Data
Laver, Michael, 1949–
Multiparty government: the politics of coalition in
Europe.—(Comparative European politics).
1. Western Europe. Coalition governments
I. Title   II. Schofield, Norman, 1944–   III. Series
321.8043
ISBN 0-19-827292-8

Library of Congress Cataloging in Publication Data
Laver, Michael, 1949–
Multiparty government: the politics of coalition in Europe
Michael Laver and Norman Schofield.
(Comparative European politics)
Includes bibliographical references
1. Political parties—Europe.   2. Coalition governments—Europe.
3. Comparative government.   I. Schofield, Norman, 1944–
II. Title.
JN94.A979L38 1990   321.8'043'094—dc20   89-71133
ISBN 0-19-827292-8

Text Processed by Oxford Text System
Printed in Great Britain
by Biddles Ltd.,
Guildford and King's Lynn

Preface

Our key objective in this book is to explore one of the richest, most fascinating, and most important features of European politics: the politics of coalition government. While several edited collections of country studies have appeared since 1980, few authored books have treated coalition government as a general theme in comparative politics. The early days of coalition studies did generate such books,[1] but most recent work on the subject is to be found in the journal literature. We set out to remedy this situation and in doing so have drawn upon the work and ideas of many others. Since we have both been involved in the field for the best part of twenty years, we have come to know personally most of those who have written on coalitions and have had stimulating discussions with many of them. Many of the arguments that we put forward in this book are the indirect product of such discussions, which means that their precise lineage is often difficult to determine. We should therefore claim credit for very little of what follows, except for the mistakes, and offer our warmest thanks to all of the friends and colleagues who have helped us over the years. They know who they are!

It is invidious to single out for special thanks any other than those who have contributed very directly to this book. First and foremost thanks go to Kay Donohue, of University College Galway, who tirelessly and cheerfully deployed her incomparable keyboard skills on a number of early drafts and redrafts. Members, too many to mention by name, of the Party Manifesto Research Group of the European Consortium for Political Research, of which both of us are members, discussed many bits and pieces of our arguments along the way. They also generated some of the policy data used in Chapter 5. Some of the material was presented at a conference on European cabinet coalitions at the European University Institute, Fiesole, Italy in May 1987. Comments and suggestions by David Austen-Smith, Jeff Banks, Ian Budge, Eric Browne, John Ferejohn, Bernie Grofman, Richard McKelvey, Bill

Riker, Ken Shepsle, and Kaare Strom were very helpful. Students in Laver's 'Coalition Building in Politics' seminar at Harvard were subjected to the cruel and unusual punishment of having to read and discuss the entire penultimate draft as a required text. They were Jonathan Berman, Curtis Chang, Michael Gaouette, Alexandra von der Gablentz, Eric Rosenzweig, Stephen Simon, and Bret Williams; each contributed considerably, possibly in ways that they did not realize, to making the exposition a little clearer.

We should not overlook the politicians and political parties whose activities generated all of our raw material. We have referred to political parties throughout by using the names and abbreviations that are most commonly to be found in the English-language literature. There is no standard convention on this matter. Some parties, for example the VVD in The Netherlands, tend to be referred to by initials derived from their native language names. Others, for example the Social Democrats in Sweden, tend to be referred to by English translations of their names. Others again, for example Fine Gael in Ireland, are referred to by their full native-language names (the latter party would be referred to in English as 'the People of the Gael' only with a very heavy dose of irony). We have thus followed customary usage, suppressing, in order to avoid ambiguity and possible insult, the inevitable desire of political scientists to standardize.

The book could not have been completed without the assistance of the University College Galway sabbatical leave programme, which freed Laver to work on it, and without the good offices of Jim Alt and Ken Shepsle of the Political Economy Program at Harvard, who provided him with such a congenial sanctuary in which to get the work done. Funding from the Mellon Foundation made this possible, and the final pieces of the jigsaw were put together under the auspices of a grant from the National Science Foundation (SES 88–22307). Schofield's contribution to this book is based on research which has been generously funded over a number of years by the National Science Foundation (SES 84–18295, SES 85–21151, BNS 87–00864, SES 88–20845). Sabbatical leave from Washington University gave him the opportunity to work on the book while he was a fellow at the Center for Advanced Study in the Behavioral Sciences, Stanford.

We have tried very hard in presenting our arguments to

eliminate unnecessary formalism and obscure notation, feeling strongly that these alienate many of the very people who might otherwise be most interested in the politics of coalition. There is a price to pay for this, in a degree of rigour that is sacrificed, but we feel that it is a price worth paying in exchange for accessibility. We would none the less welcome comments from readers about passages which they feel should be less obscure, more rigorous, or both; and we encourage people to write to us with suggested improvements. We are also developing more formal exposition of some parts of this argument, which will be published in a forthcoming volume. The most important thing for us is neither rigour of argument nor elegance of prose but a desire to impart a real 'feel' for what is involved in the fascinating process of coalition bargaining. We sincerely hope that we have succeeded.

M. L.
N. S.

Harvard University
Center for Advanced Study, Stanford
March 1989

Contents

Tables

Figures

I

The Politics of Coalition in Europe

WHAT ARE THE POLITICS OF COALITION?

For most of Western Europe, the politics of coalition lie at the heart of the business of representative government. Every West European state has been governed by a coalition for at least some time this century; many have been governed by coalitions for most of this time. Even in European states such as Britain that have no tradition of coalition government, there have been a few quite explicit coalition governments as well as a number of minority governments that have had to hustle for 'outside' support in the legislature in order to remain in office.

The politics of coalition are even more pervasive, however, than the frequency of actual coalition governments in Europe might lead us to expect. The special forms of bargaining and negotiation that characterize the politics of coalition can be found after nearly every election that does not produce an unassailable 'winner' in the shape of a single party that controls a majority of the seats in the legislature. Even in this apparently cut-and-dried situation, it is not unknown for political parties to bargain and for a coalition administration to be formed. Leaving aside actual coalitions and minority governments, furthermore, the perspective of coalition bargaining is a useful one from which to view much of what goes on inside political parties. In the US two-party system, in which talk of executive coalitions is alien, the day-to-day business of politics is intimately concerned with the development, maintenance, and destruction of legislative coalitions, many of which show scant respect for formal party lines.

Coalition, therefore, is a general phenomenon with profound implications. In this book we resist the temptation to apply the perspective to every potentially interesting political interaction, however, and concentrate on the politics of forming a government. In particular, we look at government formation in those constitutional systems, typical of Western Europe, in which the executive is sustained in office on the basis of winning key votes in the legislature. One special, theoretically trivial, and, in European terms, not particularly common type of case arises when one or other of two parties wins a legislative majority and takes office as a single-party government. Once we take account of the potential for party splits, of course, even two-party systems become potential coalition systems; they are certainly conditioned by the politics of coalition. We will not dwell long on two-party systems, despite all the bargaining that goes on within the parties in such cases. What concerns us is every other potential link between a legislature and an executive that must retain the support of the legislature if it is to continue to govern. It is the interaction between legislative and executive power when no one party wins a majority of seats that defines the subject matter of this book. This interaction, for us, is the essence of the politics of coalition in Europe.

THE POLITICS OF COALITION IN THE REAL WORLD

In order to get a feel for the real-world politics of coalition, consider events in Ireland between January and March 1987. A minority Fine Gael caretaker administration, led by Garret FitzGerald as Taoiseach (Prime Minister), was formed on 20 January 1987 after the collapse of a coalition between Fine Gael and Labour. Labour ministers had walked out after the failure of the coalition parties to agree on the shape of the 1987 Budget. The Labour Party, facing a catastrophic slump in its opinion poll ratings, had earlier made a categoric public commitment to enter no further coalition governments for the foreseeable future, save in the most exceptional of circumstances. Following Labour's withdrawal from office, an election was called for 17 February. Fianna Fáil was the main opposition party and fought the election, as it had often done in the past, on the issue of strong, single-party, majority government. Fianna Fáil refused absolutely, as it had always done in the past, to consider anything but governing alone and campaigned as the only party able to deliver the country from 'weak and indecisive' coalition government. As the results in Table 1.1 show, however, the election returned another 'hung' Dáil.

TABLE 1.1. Distribution of seats in Dáil Éireann, 10 March 1987

Party	Seats
Fianna Fáil	81
Fine Gael	51
Progressive Democrats	14
Labour Party	12
Workers' Party	4
Democratic Socialist Party	1
Independent Fianna Fáil	1
Tony Gregory (*left-wing independent*)	1
Sean Treacy (*ex-Labour centrist independent*)	1
TOTAL	166

When Fianna Fáil had last found itself in this position, in 1982, extended negotiations had taken place between the party leader Charles Haughey and representatives of the Workers' Party and the various independent deputies (TDs). These negotiations had resulted in the now infamous 'Gregory Deal' under which Tony Gregory, a left-wing independent TD representing Dublin Central, had extracted promises of major government expenditure on projects of interest to his constituents, in exchange for his legislative support of the Haughey administration. In February 1987 the mood of the times was different. Haughey, acting the role of Taoiseach-in-waiting, announced that there would be no deals, no compromises. Party spokesmen announced that the only alternative to a minority Fianna Fáil administration led by Charles J. Haughey was another election. While there was some public debate as to the constitutional accuracy of this claim, there were few who contested its political realism. Provided that Fianna Fáil remained rock-solid behind its leader, it was clear that they were in a very strong position to dictate the terms of the debate.

Most of the independents and small parties quickly made public declarations of their strategies. The Workers' Party, Labour and the Democratic Socialist Party announced that they would vote against Haughey. Despite promises that had been made by Garret FitzGerald, in the hurly-burly of electoral defeat, to be helpful to a Fianna Fáil government that pursued the 'right' policies, and despite the fact that Fianna Fáil were effectively going to introduce a lightly edited version of the Fine Gael Budget, Fine Gael were assumed to be unlikely to pass up an opportunity to vote against the man disliked so much by so many of them. Neil Blaney of Independent Fianna Fáil was assumed to be a Haughey supporter, however much he might hold out for a deal. The independent Sean Treacy was also assumed to be a Haughey man. Tony Gregory steadfastly refused to declare his position and gave every impression of waiting for a deal or, in the language of the times, of waiting to be 'reassured' on certain matters.

This left Fianna Fáil with 83 votes out of 166. One of the 166 would have to be Ceann Comhairle (Chairman) of the Dáil and Haughey's opponents announced that it would not be one of them. The Fianna Fáil choice was independent Sean Treacy, who had done the job before. This left them with 82 votes out of 165 and a sympathetic Ceann Comhairle, whose casting vote would decide the issue in the event of a tie. On the morning before the vote, Fine Gael announced that they would vote against Haughey, which made 82 votes against him. Gregory still made no declaration and was still 'available for discussions'. His final statement to the press was that he was 'amazed' that Fianna Fáil might be taking his support for granted.

Fianna Fáil headquarters was put on a full election footing, there were no deals and the inauguration debate began. The outgoing Taoiseach, FitzGerald, brought two speeches into the chamber, knowing that he would only need one of them but having no real idea which it would be. After the more boring formal business was transacted and each of the main party leaders had been nominated as Taoiseach, Gregory rose to speak. He began by being very critical of Fianna Fáil but then, two thirds of the way through his speech, said that he felt that it was in the interests of those who had supported him in the election to give Haughey a chance. To whoops of delight from Fianna Fáil TDs and groans from the others, he announced that he was going to abstain. This meant that the vote on Haughey's nomination for Taoiseach was tied 82–82 and that Haughey therefore won on the casting vote of the Ceann Comhairle. A single-party, minority

Fianna Fáil government took office and, given the deep ideological divisions between the parties that opposed it, maintained a secure grip on power for over two years. The Irish newspaper, the *Sunday Tribune*, of 15 March 1987 best summed up the showdown between Haughey and Gregory: 'It was eyeball to eyeball and Gregory blinked.'

We make no apologies for recounting some of the finer details of this fascinating example of the politics of coalition so early in this book, for it illustrates many facets of the process with which we are concerned. We see, in the Irish Labour Party, a party paying a very heavy electoral price for participating in a government that enacted policies with severe consequences for its supporters. So catastrophically had Labour support slumped in the opinion polls as a result of this that the Labour leadership saw itself as having no choice but to leave the coalition and bring down the government. Only then could Labour fight the inevitable subsequent election on a policy platform that held out some hope of winning its old support back. Labour's plight shows quite clearly what happens when a gap opens up between the policies with which a party is associated when it is in government and those its voters want at election time.

We see, when we look at the strategic implications of the 1987 Irish election results, an example of the way in which the distribution of bargaining power produced by an election can be quite, quite different from the distribution of seats in the legislature. Fine Gael might have won fifty-one seats in the election and the Workers' Party only four, but the Workers' Party had just as much power as Fine Gael when it came to making or breaking a government.

This Irish case also provides some very clear examples of the way in which public bargaining commitments can tilt the balance of power in a particular situation. Most dramatically, the concentration of public attention on the 'pivotal' position of Tony Gregory, one of four single-vote actors in the game, arose solely because Gregory was the last to commit himself to a voting strategy. This was a position into which he had manoeuvred himself precisely in order to exert some leverage. It was one that backfired, of course, when his bluff was called.

Another interesting strategic facet of this Irish example concerns politics within political parties. The refusal of the other parties, and in particular of Fine Gael and the Progressive Democrats, to vote for Haughey or even to abstain in the vote when neither clearly had any hope of forming a government itself, was a tactic designed to split Fianna Fáil. The hope was that dragging Fianna Fáil TDs who had just fought a gruelling election campaign to the precipice and forcing them to look over at what would happen in the event of a stand-off would frighten them into ditching Haughey and installing a leader more congenial to Fine Gael and the PDs. Fianna Fáil, clearly sensing this, held firm; we will never know what would have happened if there had indeed been a stand-off and Fianna Fáil TDs had been invited to follow their leader over the edge.

This particular case also highlights the impact of the precise formal rules of the coalition game. These rules deal, among many things, with what should happen in the event of a stalemate. They concern matters such as how a chairman should use his casting vote, whether an immediate election should be called if the legislature cannot agree on an executive, whether the President takes an active or merely a ceremonial role in government formation, and so on. Differences in these rules of the game might well throw up different governments in otherwise similar circumstances.

Finally, and very significantly, we see in this Irish example an episode of the politics of coalition that did not produce a coalition. Instead, the outcome was a relatively secure single-party minority government, an outcome that only becomes comprehensible once we take into account the policy differences dividing the opposition. Minority governments have been rather neglected by political scientists. With one or two notable exceptions they have tended to be treated as pathologies, as deviations from the 'norm' by which government parties control a majority of legislators. We will argue below, however, that minority governments in Europe are simply one among several perfectly 'normal' European manifestations of the politics of coalition.

Any other detailed example of the politics of coalition would have generated as rich and interesting a set of possibilities as this particular Irish case. Coalition is a fascinating political process. In order to allow ourselves to understand this process in a reasonably systematic manner, however, we must move beyond examples to look for general underlying patterns. This is the role of theory, and 'coalition theory' is something that has interested political scientists for a number of years. It has developed within two broad traditions which are sketched out in the following section, after which we describe how we will set about looking at the most important facets of the politics of coalition. It is important to bear in mind, however, in the discussions that follow, that this does not set out to be a book on coalition theory. While we will use particular theoretical concerns to give a structure to our discussions, the heart of the matter, for us, will be real coalition bargaining. We will use examples wherever we can to illustrate this, and we hope that readers will be more inclined, when they are in doubt about something, to resort to the details of particular episodes of coalition bargaining than to the content of particular coalition theories. None the less, coalition theory is indubitably important, for without it we could not even begin to think about the problem.

TWO TRADITIONS IN COALITION STUDIES

Coalition government is an area of political activity which has been both the object of careful empirical analysis and the foundation for an elaborate superstructure of theory. The fact that coalitions are at the same time so important to those who are interested in European politics and so central to the understanding of bargaining in general has meant that the politics of coalition have typically been approached from at least two quite different directions at the same time. On the one hand there is the 'European politics' tradition; on the other, there is the 'game-theoretic' tradition.

The 'European Politics' Tradition

The study of European coalition governments comprises an obvious sub-field within the general study of European politics. It is an area of specialization within an increasingly self-confident body of academic work that we might think of as the 'European politics' tradition. This approach is best illustrated in the workshop sessions and research groups of the European Consortium for Political Research. It is reflected in the style of many of the articles published in journals such as the *European Journal of Political Research*, *West European Politics*, and *Electoral Studies* and in the work of eminent European political scientists such as Arend Lijphart, Giovanni Sartori, Hans Daalder, Jean Blondel, and, perhaps above all, the late Stein Rokkan. This tradition pushed the study of European politics beyond the binding together of collections of single country studies within a single set of covers to the cross-national analysis of particular interesting components of the political process. 'Coalition government' has evolved as one of those components.

The European politics tradition is above all a tradition of empirical theory and research at a cross-national level. Coalition studies within this tradition, therefore, have been essentially empirical attempts to fit the experience of European coalition government to an inductive theory. This has meant that practitioners of this approach have tended to have few qualms about modifying their theoretical assumptions in search of a better fit with reality. In some ways this has been a rather incestuous process. There is, for example, really only one universe of data on European coalition governments—the set of governments that were actually formed. This is a universe which has by now been very thoroughly picked over. The original data on coalition governments were collected to test early coalition theories. As a result of these tests they were used to nurture new theories, theories which the same data were in turn used to test. This is not the fault of the practitioners, of course, for there only can possibly be one universe of European governments, typically confined to those that have been formed in the post-war period. New data can be added to this universe only with the passage of time, which means that the application of the normal scientific process, by which modifications to theories are tested on new data rather than reapplied to the data that gave birth to them in the first place, has proved to be a problem for coalition studies. (We might note here as an aside that the study of coalitions in local government is very much in its infancy. Local government coalitions, however, generate many more cases within a single political system, allowing variables such as political culture and party system to be controlled much more rigorously and above all providing a large, fresh database on which to test new theories.

As yet, little has been done along these lines, but the potential of local coalition studies is clearly enormous.)

The fact that each empirically based coalition theory developed hitherto has addressed the same rather small fixed universe of post-war European governments means that it is far more sensible to assess the academic worth of such theories in heuristic terms, looking for the insights that they can give us into the coalitional process rather than for rigorous 'scientific' 'tests'. Notwithstanding this, there can be no doubt that the European politics tradition has provided us with an immense body of information about the politics of coalition, together with some occasional excellent examples of those unexpected insights into the political process which remind us that the practice of political science is a worthwhile activity.

The Game-Theoretic Tradition

The major alternative approach to analysing the politics of coalition has been that of game theory. Some game theorists, indeed, have argued that the coalition is one of game theory's most fundamental concepts, 'the only . . . one corresponding at least roughly to the anthropological or sociological concept of a group'.[1]

Early game-theoretic approaches, such as that to be found in the genuinely seminal *Theory of Political Coalitions* by William Riker,[2] tended to view the politics of coalition as a constant sum game played for the fixed prize of holding office. (In a constant sum game, everything that is 'won' by one actor must, because of the structure of the game, be 'lost' by another; the payoffs of all actors taken together thus always sum to a constant.) Payoffs tended to be denominated in cabinet seats. The politics of coalition was seen simply as a particular logical type of social interaction, one forcing a subset of the actors to strike a particular type of bargain with each other before they could 'win'. Coalition games could equally be played, and indeed often were played, by groups of paid graduate students winning payoffs denominated in dollars and cents.

European coalition governments, therefore, have by no means been an essential part of the enterprise of the game theorists; their theories could easily be tested on university campuses in the

United States. Most game theorists, however, thrill to the smell of the real political world. The possibility of providing an account of real government coalitions in a down-and-dirty real political environment has usually proved irresistible. In all of this, however, we should never lose sight of the fundamental objective of game theorists. They are motivated by the desire to elaborate upon a particular body of theory. The interpretation of European coalition bargaining helps them to do this, but it is a means, not an end. They are, when push comes to shove, interested in game theory rather than in government coalitions.

The Two Traditions Grow Apart

While two academic traditions have been busy studying different aspects of the coalitional process, an intellectual tragedy has been developing. The European politics and game-theoretic approaches are by now so far apart in their styles of analysis that they have almost nothing to contribute to one another. This tragedy has developed by accident, in large part a product of the fact that most of the game-theoretic work has been conducted by people working in the United States and expressing themselves in a mathematical notation that is incomprehensible to nearly all European politics specialists. Furthermore, as the sub-field has developed, its notation has become more cryptic, often referring back to earlier work and thereby requiring an increasingly arduous initiation process for the neophyte. This has had the practical consequence that European politics specialists have effectively cut themselves loose from the game-theoretic approach, increasingly and understandably treating it, because they cannot understand it, as irrelevant to their interests. On the other side of the Atlantic, as the solution concepts developed by game theorists have become more powerful, there has been a tendency for them to 'let go' of the real world of European coalition government, except when this can be operationalized neatly in terms of the concepts at issue. This growing apart of the two traditions is a tragedy that has recently become especially apparent as game theorists increasingly acknowledge the theoretical importance of particular institutional details of the coalition formation process, together with all sorts of other empirical matters that have long been the concern of the European politics people. It more and more seems to be the case that both groups of scholars are talking about almost precisely the same thing but that they are simply using different languages to do so.

PLAN OF CAMPAIGN

The gap between the two traditions is by now almost certainly too big to be bridged by a single book. It is our intention, however, to begin building the bridge with this book. In other work we plan to build from the game-theoretic tradition. In the present book we build primarily from the European politics tradition, treating the politics of coalition as a crucial theme for cross-national research and relying for the most part upon empirical and inductive arguments. Our main intention is to review and consolidate the existing body of work on the politics of coalition, and to set it in a more comprehensive context, recognizing that coalition formation is a fundamental part of the process of democratic government in most Western societies. While we approach the study of government coalitions primarily from the perspective of European politics, this does not mean that we take the easy way out when it comes to theory. We also evaluate the usefulness of the main strands of game-theoretic coalition theory, setting out to provide a non-technical introduction to this important field to European politics specialists, who increasingly need to know about it.

We did not intend, when we started to write this book, to present new data or new theory, since one of the problems of coalition studies is that there is already more than enough of both to go around. However, we have been unable to resist the temptation to engage in a little new theorizing from time to time. Our main purpose, nevertheless, remains to marshal the existing body of theory and research on government coalitions in Western Europe, much of it of quite excellent quality.

We deal with a rather simple agenda of basic concerns. We begin by looking at the actors who play the coalition game. Traditional game theory has viewed political parties as unitary actors, a matter of assumption rather than an empirical statement and an assumption, what is more, that has often aroused the scorn of the European politics people. We review the empirical evidence on this assumption and consider the theoretical implications of violating it.

We move on to consider the stakes for which the coalition game is played. While early formal theories concentrated solely on the battle for control of the cabinet, viewed as a prize in and for itself, almost everyone now agrees that policy payoffs are also important. They disagree, of course, on how to deal with policy in theoretical terms, while a considerable body of data on the policy preferences of coalition actors has now been built up within the European politics tradition.

Having established who is playing the game and what they are playing for, we move on in Chapter 4 to look at how the game is won. In this chapter we throw away the idea that 'winning' means having a majority of the seats in the legislature, working with the notion of a 'viable' government rather than a majority one. This allows us to bring the study of minority governments into the mainstream of political science, rather than treating these very common phenomena as deviant cases, as many have done up until now.

Once we have established the identity and the motivations of the players and the rules of the game that they are playing, we look at the process of coalition formation, the focus of most existing studies of the politics of coalition. Obviously, who, precisely, gets into government and how, precisely, this is related to past and future elections is a matter of vital concern to all who are interested in representative democracy.

After a coalition has formed, the next question concerns whether it will stay formed: the question of cabinet duration. This is of considerable practical political significance, since many of those who attack coalition government (often those who also criticize electoral systems based on proportional representation) treat coalitions as inherently unstable. A moment's perusal of the evidence shows this to be untrue, but a consideration of the processes that lead coalitions to break up is one of the least developed and most interesting areas of the entire field of study.

We will have considered the stakes for which the coalition game is being played earlier in the analysis. We now look at the related matter of coalition payoffs. Accounts of the coalitional process are inevitably predicated upon assumptions about what the actors are playing for. When we analyse the distribution of payoffs, we find out who were the winners and who the losers. This is another fundamental question, since many casual critiques of the politics of coalition charge it with being perverse, with rewarding the 'wrong' people (be they tiny centre parties, hard-line extremists, or whoever), and with thereby in some sense being undemocratic.

Finally, we look at the effect of the particular constraints on coalition bargaining that can be found in each political system. Each has a different written constitution, a different set of historical conventions and precedents, and all of these things can have profound effects on the final outcome. Sometimes the constraints can be so restrictive, for example, that only one coalition is viable. (Such was the case with the Irish example elaborated above.) This is the item on our agenda at which the essential concerns of the European politics tradition (which spends a lot of time on the particularities of a given system) are approaching those of the game-theoretic tradition (which is increasingly aware of the role of particular institutional factors in bargaining).

Notwithstanding everything that has gone before by way of an intellectual justification for our enterprise, however, it is a simple fact of political life that coalition lies at the very heart of European politics. In this crude but important sense, our book needs no further justification.

2

Who Plays the Coalition Game?

Real political parties consist of real politicians. These may be party leaders or cabinet ministers. They may be people who would like to be party leaders or cabinet ministers. They may be rank-and-file legislators, famous political has-beens, unsuccessful parliamentary candidates, local councillors, well-paid party professionals or voluntary party activists. Political parties have the chance to bargain for a place at the cabinet table because some, at least, of the electorate have voted for them at the most recent election, so there are also party supporters to be considered. These days, voters form an image of who they are voting for as a result of information, interpretation, and analysis purveyed by people working in the mass media. Any or all of these actors can influence the coalitional process. Each of them may well have quite distinct preferences about possible coalition outcomes.

All of this, of course, is saying no more than that coalitional behaviour is an inherent part of politics, that it is as rich and complex, as subtle and fascinating, as politics in general. Our problems arise when we must decide which actors, in particular, to focus our attention upon. This is especially a problem for formal coalition theorists, since an assumption about the identity and nature of the actors is one of the foundation stones upon which most formal theories are constructed. In practice, most theories operate on the assumption that political parties can be treated as 'unitary' actors. This rather neatly leaves open the matter of precisely who makes the key decisions within a particular political party, but it does none the less imply that decisions will be adhered to once they have been arrived at by the whole party, whatever its method of arriving at them. This carries the implication that coalition theories based on the unitary actor assumption will not be able to cope with situations in which one part of a particular party is in a particular coalition and the other part is outside it. Indeed, in political systems in which this type of behaviour is endemic—arguably, for example, in the French Fourth Republic—coalition theorists often abandon any attempt at prediction altogether and exclude the entire class of cases.[1]

The nature of the actors in the coalition game is a feature of the political process that is treated quite differently by the empirical European politics tradition and the game-theoretic tradition. Furthermore, it is something that has been used most effectively by empirical coalition theorists to criticize game theorists.[2] It is, after all, a matter of common sense and easily observable fact that decisions about whether to go into or to stay out of a particular coalition can cause deep divisions within a political party, and that such divisions can have a major impact on the makeup of the government eventually formed. On the other hand, it is also the case that party discipline in Europe is generally very high. If we choose to regard intraparty decision making as a black box, the contents of which we do not need to get involved with before we analyse coalition bargaining, then we can comfort ourselves with the reflection that, in recent times, at least, *parties do in practice tend to go into and come out of government as single actors*, however painful the wounds inflicted upon them inside the black box might have been.

Before moving on to consider the politics of coalition in greater detail, therefore, we must consider the extent to which it is plausible to regard parties as unitary actors. If we decide that we must indeed take intraparty politics into account, we must think about how we might do this.

ARE PARTIES UNITARY ACTORS?

The simple answer to this question, of course, is that they are not. As with most simple answers to complex political problems, this one is not very useful. It is true but trivial, in precisely the same sense as it is true that the chair you are sitting on as you read this is not really a solid object at all but a collection of molecules with vast areas of open space in between them. While this indisputable fact may be of immense importance to those who are interested in molecules it is none the less the case that you, interested as you are in other things, will not come too badly unstuck if you persist in treating it as a chair and sit on it. Thus, to sweep away one very unproductive line of argument without further ado, of course it is true that political parties are made up of many different types of actor with different and potentially conflicting interests; but this is not the point. The real question is, do parties behave as if they were unitary actors as far as the coalitional process is concerned?

We must be careful, however, not to define the problem out of existence. If we wish to go to the opposite extreme and argue in a determined fashion that parties are unitary actors, then we may do so by adopting some rather tough operational definitions. We might reasonably argue that, as far as coalition bargaining is concerned, what we are interested in are the things that go into and come out of coalitions, whether they are political parties or anything else. In this case we can get away with treating parties as if they are unitary actors as long as we do not find too many cases in which it is difficult to decide whether a particular party is in or out of a particular coalition, because some of it is in and some of it is out. We know that such situations are in practice rather rare, notwithstanding some notable exceptions in the French Fourth Republic and in Iceland during the 1980s. Almost all empirical analyses of the politics of coalition have implicitly adopted this relatively trouble free working solution; we are, if we stick to this line of defence, on reasonably solid ground.

We might well, however, be on solid ground in the middle of nowhere. The reason for this is that the politics of coalition could well transform the party system in ways that affect both the configuration of parties in the system and the internal politics of each party. In particular, as far as the argument about whether parties are unitary actors is concerned, the politics of coalition may split parties, while even the threat of such splits may constrain party decision makers. Particular forms of internal party organization, furthermore, may make it much more difficult for some parties to participate in coalitions than for others. Intraparty tensions such as these can have quite systematic and generalizable effects on the process of coalition bargaining, strengthening some parties and weakening others. In the rest of this section, therefore, we shall be looking for evidence on the probable effect of intraparty politics on interparty bargaining.

We must begin by reiterating the point that the legislative

behaviour of European parties is very disciplined. This means that the initial outcome of the politics of coalition, the formation of a coalition cabinet, tends to be brought about by legislative parties voting as unified blocks on the investiture of a government. Even Klaus von Beyme, someone who rarely passes up an opportunity to attack the application of formal coalition theory to European politics, does not demur from this conclusion.[3] Von Beyme is very sensitive to internal divisions within parties, arguing that 'the image of parties acting as monolithic units is a fiction which cannot be sustained . . . The united will of the party is a variation of the older fiction of the uniform will of the people . . . .'[4] Notwithstanding this, he points out, having reviewed evidence on internal party politics from a wide range of systems, that 'although nearly all the Western democracies assume that a member of parliament is free to vote as he wishes, even if they lay varying stress on this, the parties have increasingly strengthened the mechanisms whereby they can exercise control on their members of parliament'.[5] The result is that 'even in fragmented party systems party discipline in Europe is now between 80 and 90 per cent'—this latter conclusion being based on a review of roll call analyses.[6] Von Beyme thus leaves us with the clear impression that, even though intraparty decision making may be a process riddled with conflict, the eventual strategies that emerge are based on the assumption that the party functions as a unit. Certainly, no strong evidence is presented that might force us to reconsider this assumption, and this from an author who would not flinch from doing so if the evidence was there.

Even if parties behave in a unified manner in vital investiture votes, however, it may still be the case that intraparty politics affects the politics of coalition. The reason why most theorists to date have been able to get away without taking intraparty politics into account is precisely because they have homed in on the moment of coalition formation, the very moment when high levels of legislative party discipline may mean that intraparty politics matters least. Hans Daalder, another very experienced commentator on the politics of coalition in Europe, expresses this point quite clearly.

In most formal approaches the party is retained as a unitary actor. This is acceptable in a theoretical model. It is also politically relevant whenever a party does act as one actor; e.g., when it presents an election programme, or decides to enter a cabinet on the basis of a decision that commits the entire party. . . . However, in the actual world of politics, it is hardly defensible to regard a party as a unitary actor . . . Even in the examples just given . . . there is bound to be disagreement before the decision is taken, as well as on its later application in practice . . . a decision on the *investiture* of a new coalition cabinet does not pre-empt a need for continuous decision making on concrete decisions to follow. . . .[7]

Daalder thus accepts that parties may behave as if they are unitary actors at the moment of entry into a coalition; but he argues that much of what is really interesting and important about coalition government, indeed, most of what happens after this moment of entry, may be left out by theories that cannot accommodate themselves to the processes of intraparty decision making.

Daalder raises the matter of what goes on inside the government. To this we might add the matter of what goes on outside the government. Parties that have been excluded from office may well consider the extent to which they are prepared to change policies, leaders and/or bargaining strategies in order to talk their way into a coalition. Particularly in circumstances in which party activists are more policy oriented than party leaders, a scenario that we will explore in greater detail below, such deliberations, an integral part of the overall politics of coalition, are likely to be divisive. This means that opposition parties, too, can be split asunder by the scent of power.

Empirical evidence on these matters can be gleaned from various collections of qualitative case studies of governmental coalition behaviour, in particular those edited by Browne and Dreijmanis, Bogdanor, and Pridham[8]. Browne and Dreijmanis edited their collection from a perspective that was very sympathetic to coalition theory. While they did not explicitly ask each of their authors to comment upon the assumption that the parties are unitary actors, they did ask them to comment on 'the actors' and some authors did provide information on the impact of intraparty politics on coalition bargaining. Bogdanor is a critic of formal theory, which he dismisses rather curtly: 'the achievements of formal theory have been very limited'.[9] In his short and sweeping critique, however, he does not home in on the assumption that parties are unitary actors; nor were his authors given any guidelines on the matter, though some do discuss it. Pridham's more recent collection, however, places intraparty politics at centre stage and each of his authors was explicitly asked to comment on this particular assumption. (Being political scientists, of course, only some of them do.) Drawing on these and on a range of other sources, we have attempted a review of some of the issues that relate to the unitary actor status of political parties in each of the nineteen European party systems from which empirical analyses of the politics of coalition typically select their material. This review is presented in Appendix A; for now we are concerned with the general points it throws up. These relate to 'vertical' divisions between party factions, to 'horizontal' divisions between different levels of the party hierarchy, to actual party splits, and to partial fusions of parties into electoral coalitions.

'Coherent' versus 'Factional' Parties

The first conclusion to be drawn from a general review of the bargaining status of European political parties reinforces the conclusion that almost no party can be considered a unitary actor in terms of every potentially interesting facet of party competition. Notwithstanding this, however, some parties clearly behave much more like unitary actors than others.

The most unified actors in bargaining terms are without doubt the Communist parties, many of them still practising a form of intraparty decision making that is based on the traditions of democratic centralism. For some Communist parties this intra-party discipline may be possible precisely because it has not been necessary for them to take the difficult decisions that face a party forced to choose whether or not to compromise basic principles in order to get into office. The Luxemburg Communist Party, for example, is significant in electoral terms but has not been considered seriously as a potential coalition actor; it therefore appears to remain remarkably united, a product in part of the absence of those dilemmas with which the genuine prospect of office might have presented it. In contrast to this, the Communist parties of Spain, Portugal, Italy, France, and Finland have all at some time been forced to balance the ideological purity of their policies against the consequences of political expediency. Rifts opened up by such debates may well, indeed, have had much to do with the decline of the Spanish Communist Party from its high hopes in the immediate post-Franco period. In general, however, European Communist parties present good examples of one of the general types of coalitional actor that we will be considering: the party that may well face internal strife when deciding upon coalitional strategies but which, once it has decided, acts in a unified and unambiguous manner. We can think of such parties as 'coherent' actors in coalitional terms.

This general category of coherent coalitional actors is by no means the exclusive preserve of Communist parties. Many of the Scandinavian bourgeois parties can also be seen in this light, together with parties such as the VVD in The Netherlands, the Conservatives in Britain, and the FPD in West Germany, as well as Fianna Fáil and Fine Gael in Ireland. There are, of course, several types of intraparty decision making structure that may lead to coherent coalitional behaviour. The democratic centralist traditions of the Communist parties allow for strategy to be debated at various levels in the party hierarchy but demand absolute adherence to the party line once strategy has been determined. More authoritarian party decision making systems, such as those of Fianna Fáil and Fine Gael in Ireland or the FDP in Germany, may simply place the power to decide in the hands of a small party elite and maintain discipline by the enforcement of severe sanctions against dissenters.

In the starkest contrast to the set of coherent coalitional actors we find a type of 'party' that may well be no more than '. . . a coalition of mini-parties run by an oligarchy of factional leaders . . . a ship whose crew is in a permanent state of mutiny', to take Irving's characterization of the Italian Christian Democrats (DC).[10] 'The party as a coalition of factions' is a category that includes many of those with generally Christian Democratic orientations. We might include here as examples, the Austrian People's Party (ÖVP), the Democratic Centre (UCD) and the Allianza Popular (AP) in Spain, the Social Democratic Centre (CDS) and the Social Democratic Party (PSD) in Portugal and, of course, the Gaullists in France. Such parties tend to see themselves as parties of government. The need to distribute the more valuable trophies of office within semi-permanent parties of government may encourage factionalism based around major party personalities. It may also mean that such parties are held together by no more than a mutual desire to cling on to power almost at any cost. Conversely, we might speculate that such parties, located as they tend to be at some pivotal position in the configuration of possible coalitions, can afford the luxury of factionalism. Since they are often so hard to dislodge from office, splits and factions may be far less damaging to their bargaining position and may therefore be more tolerable. One way or the other, even in government, there is a tendency for the factions within such parties to attempt to outmanœuvre each other by forming outside alliances. Classic examples can be found in the machinations of senior DC politicians in Italy. In Belgium, alliances between factions of different parties have even been formalized in explicit groupings, such as Démocratie Chrétienne, that have linked one PSC faction with members of other parties and pitted these against the other PSC factions.

Very rarely does it make sense to regard factionalized parties as having a single unambiguous policy position on any one issue. Parts of such parties often tend to be closer to 'rival' parties in the system than they do to other parts of their own party. Forced out of government for some reason, such coalitions of factions may fall apart once their *raison d'être* is destroyed—the single most spectacular example of this being the almost total collapse of the Spanish UCD after it lost power in 1982, when its seat total fell from 168 to 13.

TABLE 2.1. *Differences between unitary and factionalized coalition actors*

	Party as unitary actor	Party as coalition of factions
Policy	Single policy position (hence policy affinities with other parties are also unambiguous)	Range of policy positions (hence policy affinities with other parties are ambiguous)
Coalitional preferences	Single set of preferences concerning the range of potential coalitions	Internally conflicting sets of preferences concerning range of potential coalitions
Bargaining style	Bilateral negotiations between party leaders and leaders of other potential coalition parties	Multilateral negotiations by faction leaders with other faction leaders both inside and outside party

Parties, therefore, can vary in the extent to which, for bargaining

purposes, they can be considered to be unitary actors or coalitions
of factions. Some of the main dimensions of this variation are
summarized in Table 2.1. Stated even at this very crude level, it
is clear that there will be major differences in the style of
coalitional behaviour between different parties within the same
political system. One of the clearest examples of this can be found
in the politics of coalition in Italy during 1986–8. The Socialist
Party, having moved away from a period of factionalism, was
more or less united behind its leader, Bettino Craxi. In contrast,
the Christian Democrats (DC) could justifiably be regarded as
being any one of a number of different parties, depending on who
was the Prime Ministerial candidate at the time. For the whole
of this period, it was more or less taken for granted that the same
set of five parties, the *pentapartito* formula, would form the
government. Most of the politics of coalition in Italy, therefore,
revolved around which particular DC politician would be Prime
Minister, once it had been decided that the Socialists under Craxi
had taken their turn at this. Coalitions formed and fell as different
DC politicians attempted to forge a stable government based on
the five-party formula. Only by identifying the various DC
factions and looking at these as separate coalitional actors does
this series of cabinet 'crises' make any sense. Accounts of the
coalitional process in Italy which ignore such matters simply see
the same five-party coalition falling and reforming over and over
again and thereby miss most of the point of what was actually
going on.

For particular parties that are best represented as coalitions of
distinct factions, therefore, accounts of the coalitional process
must take intraparty politics into account. Such parties will have
ambiguous policy positions and internally conflicting sets of
preference orderings over different potential coalitions, and will
tend tó engage in multilateral multilevel coalition bargaining.
Such phenomena are without doubt capable of influencing the
outcome of the coalitional process and, provided that they can be
specified in advance in a reasonably general manner, can and
should be considered.

The Party as a Whole versus the Parliamentary Party

The second general point that emerges from the review of the unitary actor status of parties in Appendix A is the clear distinction between the parliamentary party and the rest of the party. The bottom line in most coalition negotiations is a vote of confidence in the legislature. Both in theory and in reality, most parliamentary parties can exert considerable autonomy in legislative votes, a situation arising from the tradition that public representatives cannot be told how to vote by anyone, even those in control of the party to which they belong. Article 38.1 of the constitution of the Federal Republic of Germany puts this most clearly with its provision that 'deputies . . . shall be representatives of the whole people, not bound by orders and instructions, and shall be subject only to their conscience'. Article 11 of the Parliament Act in Finland contains a similar provision.[11]

All of this means that the level of voting discipline within a parliamentary party is a very important aspect of its unitary actor status for coalitional purposes. Even parties that are seriously split may behave as unitary actors on key votes. The Irish Labour Party, for example, was very deeply divided on coalition during the period of its participation in the 1982–7 government with Fine Gael, yet the Labour Parliamentary Party (which included a leading anti-coalitionist as chief whip) was always whipped to vote for the coalition government. To vote against the whip meant expulsion from the party, as several Labour TDs found out after those rare occasions when the party did not vote as a united bloc.

A situation such as this may cause grave divisions between a party's parliamentary body and its rank-and-file members. It is obviously much easier for the rank-and-file membership to bring a parliamentary party to heel when the party is in opposition; indeed, it may even be impossible to do this when the party is in government, given the constitutional obligations of party leaders who are ministers to abide by collective cabinet decisions. This means that the prospect of going into government can create a severe conflict of interest between the parliamentary party and the rest of the party. The actual moment of going into government, furthermore, may represent the point at which the rank-and-file loses control of the parliamentary party. When the party is in opposition, it is governed by its own constitution. When members of the party form part of a cabinet they are governed by the constitution of the state itself. This forces the rank-and-file to extract all they can during formation negotiations, a factor that might well operate to exclude the British Labour Party from entering a coalition, for example, even if its parliamentary leadership decided that it wanted to do so.

The general rule is that the rank-and-file, more concerned with ideology and less in line for the other spoils of office, tend to resent the policy compromises necessary to enter coalition and hence to oppose them. The parliamentary leaders, at least some of whom will become cabinet ministers, are more inclined to see the virtues of policy compromises if these increase the chance of the party going into government.

Party Discipline and Party Splits

Related to the distinction between the more or less disciplined parliamentary wing of a party and its rank-and-file membership is the phenomenon of the party that is well disciplined yet liable to split. As the Danish party system illustrates quite clearly, rigid party discipline can lead to a propensity for splits. Within a very disciplined party no option exists for the expression of dissenting views other than the formation of a quite distinct breakaway party. This may well then itself be very disciplined until it in turn splits.

Parliamentary party discipline is in general very high in Scandinavia, a situation that means that, if we confine ourselves to snapshots of coalitional politics at particular times, the parties indeed appear as unitary actors. Only when we look at the longer-term interaction between coalitional politics and the party system, and specifically at the way in which coalition bargaining encourages party splits and fusions, can we see what we miss by viewing the parties as unitary actors. Within the terms of most existing coalition theories, therefore, the unitary actor assumption is not a bad one for the Scandinavian 'iron discipline' party systems. What this serves to highlight, of course, is not the accuracy of the assumption but the current lack of any genuinely dynamic model of the coalitional process.[12] Parties only seem to be unitary actors because existing theoretical accounts do work with snapshots of the system at particular moments, in the sense that the elections held in February and November 1982 in Ireland, for example, might as well have been held on different planets for all the difference they made to most theories. If that is all we do, then we will not be forced to concern ourselves with party splits and fusions and it is very hard not to see the party as a unitary actor for coalitional purposes. It is only when we look at developments over time that the effects on the system of splits and fusions begin to show up.

Electoral Coalitions and Electoral Systems

The fourth conclusion that emerges from the general review in Appendix A concerns electoral coalitions. What is clear is that there are no simple distinctions to be drawn between electoral coalitions, parties, and coalition governments. One can shade into another far more easily than most existing approaches presume. A very good example is the formation of the Democratic Alliance (AD) between the CDS and PSD in Portugal. This began as an electoral alliance, but 'assumed the form of a coalition of electoral, parliamentary and governmental scope'.[13] The government became known as the Democratic Alliance Government; but after the AD split in early 1983, the PSD subsequently returned to government in coalition with the Socialists and the CDS went into opposition.

Another very clear example of an electoral alliance that has had an impact far beyond election time is the CDU/CSU in West Germany. There is considerable disagreement even among German politics specialists about whether the CDU/CSU should be regarded as an electoral arrangement between two parties who agree not to compete against each other in particular geographic areas or as what amounts to a single party. The CSU did once break its formal links with the CDU, albeit for a very short period, and the main factor that reactivated the alliance was a fear on the part of the CSU that the CDU would campaign against it in Bavaria. This incident illustrates that the potential for each of the two parties to pursue an independent coalition strategy exists even if the current practice of coalition politics in Germany gives no serious indication that one day one partner might find itself out of a government that includes the other.

Some electoral systems positively encourage electoral coalitions by giving a seat bonus to larger parties. We return to a more detailed discussion of this in Chapter 8, when we deal with structural constraints and influences on coalition bargaining. In the meantime, however, it is worth noting that the formation of electoral coalitions may be as much a product of electoral necessity as of any real affinity between the parties concerned. The electoral system, of course, also has a bearing on party splits. Very proportional systems make splits more attractive since they enable even tiny breakaway factions to gain parliamentary representation. Certainly, in Israel and The Netherlands, the two countries typically held to have the most proportional electoral systems, party splits are endemic. At the other extreme, electoral systems that give a substantial seat bonus to big parties, such as those in Britain and Greece, discourage party splits. Thus the electoral system may well be a key factor in the unitary actor status of the parties. Even in systems with no history of major party splits, a PR electoral system keeps at least the possibility of splits on the bargaining agenda.

Summarizing the Main Deviations from Unitary Actor Status

Putting all of this together, it is clear that, while no party is a unitary actor in the strict sense, many parties can be treated as if they were unitary actors for coalitional purposes. It is possible for coalitional purposes, furthermore, to identify four very general categories of party.

In the first place there are what we have called 'coherent' parties, especially the Communist parties and those run on personalist authoritarian lines. These tend to function as unitary actors both when viewed at a single point in time and when their interaction with coalitional politics is considered over a period of years. This is not, of course, to say that such parties are unaffected by the politics of coalition. Far from it. Many Communist parties in the 1960s and early 1970s, for example, were torn by debate over whether fundamental ideological principles should be sacrificed in a 'historic compromise' designed to get the party into government, typically in coalition with socialists. In this way, the coalitional possibilities on offer have a fundamental effect on the internal life of a party. For our purposes, however, we must draw the line somewhere. While the impact of coalition on intraparty politics is a fascinating and integral part of the politics of coalition, it is one that we will consider further only when it feeds back into the system as the impact of intraparty politics on coalition. We will not lose too much, therefore, provided that we bear all of the above qualifications in mind, by treating coherent parties as unitary actors for coalitional purposes.

In the second place there are parties which, while prone to splitting as a result of the stresses and strains imposed by coalition bargaining, are disciplined enough to be treated as unitary actors at least at the point of coalition formation or, indeed, at any other fixed point in time. These parties, however, may well not be unitary actors when viewed over time, given their propensity to split and refuse. The Danish parties provide good examples of this category, as do some of those in Belgium and The Netherlands. In terms of existing coalition theories, therefore, which do tend to concentrate exclusively on a series of disconnected snapshot views of the party system, it does not cause too much of a problem to treat these parties as unitary actors. The problem is not so much that the assumption is empirically wrong in its own terms as that the theories are excessively limited in their scope. When a more genuinely dynamic approach to the analysis of coalition bargaining is developed, the splitting potential of such parties must become an integral part of any account of the politics of coalition.

In the third place there are parties which are clearly not unitary actors in any sense of the word, the Italian Christian Democrats being the classic example. Such parties do not behave as one, even at a single point in time. Any snapshot that we might take of them will find different factions of the same party wanting different things, talking to different people, and making informal alliances with factions of other parties. Coalition crises involving such parties are as likely to be crises of intraparty politics as they are to be crises of interparty politics. To treat such parties as unitary actors will clearly miss the point of much of what is going on in the coalitional process, a caveat that is especially important for France, Italy, and Spain.

In the fourth place we find electoral coalitions of parties. These, of course, we know not to be unitary actors—indeed, the problem for coalition theories in this case is rather the reverse of the usual one. Sets of actors that are taken to be completely independent coalesce in the run-up to an election and announce that they will behave as if they are unitary actors in coalition negotiations. The question here is one of whether it is reasonable to regard each group as a separate actor in such circumstances, as empirical coalition theories generally do. The alternative is to take the electoral coalition at its word and regard it as a single bargaining actor. There are a number of significant examples of this strategy of electoral protocoalition formation. There is the British Liberal/SDP Alliance in 1983 and 1987, the Dutch PvdA/D66 alliance in 1971 and the PvdA/D66/PPR alliance of 1972, the Dutch CDA alliance of CHU, ARP, and KVP between 1975 and 1980, the Fine Gael/Labour alliance in Ireland in 1973, the Democratic alliance between PSD and CDS in Portugal, and even on some interpretations, the CDU/CSU alliance in Germany. It is certainly safer to regard electoral alliances as protocoalitions of separate actors rather than as unitary actors in their own right, but there is no doubt that more attention should be devoted to them than they currently receive. When the coalition formation strategies of electoral coalitions are publicly announced—as they must be, since a more powerful legislative bargaining bloc is precisely what electoral alliances set out to offer the electorate—then the extent to which the alliance can subsequently be abandoned is a significant empirical matter. Certainly, when two or more parties promise to go into government together if they are able, such promises tend only rarely to be broken.

Overall, our general conclusion on the matter of whether or not we can treat parties as unitary actors for coalitional purposes is that we can indeed do so if we confine ourselves to analysing individual episodes of coalitional behaviour at given time points and if we make a few significant exceptions for parties that really are no more than coalitions of factions in every sense. If we wish to develop a more dynamic approach to coalitional behaviour, however, we have no option but to take account of the possibility that we are *not* dealing with a fixed set of unitary actors. There are simply too many examples of party splits and fusions induced by the politics of coalition to ignore this problem. Since the development of a dynamic account of the coalitional process is probably the most important outstanding task facing coalition theorists, the unitary actor status of the parties will in future be a far more important matter than it has been up until now.

WHAT HAPPENS IF PARTIES ARE NOT UNITARY ACTORS?

While coalition theory (with the exception of the work of Luebbert[14]) has had little to say on what happens if parties are not unitary actors, there is a considerable general literature on the internal politics of parties. While much of this has no direct bearing on coalitional behaviour, there are some notable exceptions. Hirschman, for example, discusses the impact on interparty competition of the divergent views that are likely to be held by party workers and party voters, while Robertson considers the impact of the divergent views of campaign contributors and voters.[15] In more recent times, increasing stress has been placed on rational choice accounts of intraparty politics.[16] Most significantly of all, however, Luebbert proposes a theory of coalitional behaviour that is based fundamentally upon assumptions about intraparty politics. He assumes that party leaders are motivated above all by the desire to remain party leaders and considers the role played by policy in the light of this. The really central features of party policy are selected by leaders so as to minimize dissent within the various sections of the party, who are implicitly assumed to be more policy motivated than the leadership. 'From this perspective, the leader's task is to insist on preferences that are sufficiently focussed that they generate the widest possible support within the party, but sufficiently vague and opaque that they do not engage in government formation the disagreements that are a constant feature of any party'.[17] This leads party leaders to restrict the issues on which they will take a stand in coalition negotiations to a very limited number that command widespread support within the party. If they succeed in this, then the party will be saddled with few policy positions that present leaders with the prospect of a public and damaging climbdown if they are conceded in negotiations. Those positions that do represent sticking points in negotiations are selected as the ones which generate sufficient unity within the party that a refusal to participate in government if they are not conceded does not split the party or undermine its leadership.

On Luebbert's view of the role of policy in party competition, coalition formation negotiations are in fact mainly about intra-party politics.

What makes the talks so long, difficult and complex is generally not the lack of goodwill among the elites, but the fact that negotiations must appear the way they do in order to satisfy the members whose orientations are still largely attuned to the vocal, symbolic, and ideological aspects characteristic of each respective political culture. It is wrong to assume that, because interparty negotiations take a long time, much is being negotiated among the parties. *Most negotiation in cases of protracted government formation takes place between leaders and their followers and among rival factions within parties . . .* In parties in which factional competition is intense, government formation provides an often ideal occasion for one faction to seek to sabotage another.[18]

Luebbert goes on to generate an account of coalition formation by superimposing these assumptions about intraparty politics on a classification of political systems into broad structural types, such as those which are consensal, those which are competitive, and so on. These classifications, and the 'testing' of the theory that is based on them, are far more contentious than the general idea of placing intraparty politics at centre stage in coalition theory, but they need not concern us here. The important point is that Luebbert was one of the very few people theorizing about the politics of coalition to take politics within parties seriously. His approach, which is indeed fundamentally based on the dynamics of intraparty competition, clearly does have the potential to expand our understanding of the politics of coalition. To take two vital examples, both minority governments and surplus majority governments (those which carry 'dummy' parties whose votes are not needed for a legislative majority) can be far more easily assimilated by Luebbert's account than they can by most others. Each of these types of government, both of which are typically regarded as pathologies by conventional theories, can offer attractions for party leaders motivated above all by the desire to remain party leaders.

It is certainly not our intention to develop an entirely new body of theory based on the impact of intraparty politics upon coalition bargaining. We do, however, want to put the matter very firmly on the agenda. For the time being we must content ourselves, having cast at least some doubt on the unitary actor status of political parties, with considering the rather more modest question of which basic decision making unit we should use as the most appropriate building block when constructing an account of coalitional behaviour.

The Party as a Coalition of Politicians

The most radical solution is to regard parties as coalitions of individual political entrepreneurs.[19] This approach has the advantage of returning to first principles and establishing the individual politician as the fundamental unit of analysis. It allows cliques, factions, parties, electoral coalitions of parties, and governments all to be regarded as protocoalitions of actors, formed at various levels of the decision making hierarchy.

The main disadvantage of this approach for the study of government coalitions is that it is both unrealistic and impossibly unwieldy. It either fails to acknowledge at all that some protocoalitions of politicians are far more enduring than others or does so only on the basis of *ad hoc* empiricism. If politicians have party or factional loyalties, for example, we need specific information on just how strong these loyalties are in order to assess how they might make some protocoalitions much more durable than others.

What is remarkable is the enduring stability of most cliques, factions, and political parties, given the utterly fantastic number of theoretically possible combinations of politicians in a legislature. Indeed, this very basic point forms the basis of a good argument against the use of the individual politician as the fundamental unit of analysis in studies of coalitional behaviour. Quite apart from anything else, the systematic practical evaluation of all of the theoretical coalition possibilities is not merely unwieldy but computationally impossible, as a simple practical example will show quite clearly. Table 2.2 shows the results of the 1983 election in Iceland and the 1984 election in Luxemburg, to what are far and away Europe's two smallest legislatures. If we see parties as coalitions of politicians, then the number of different possible coalitions of politicians each compatible with these election results is phenomenal. In the case of Luxemburg in 1984, the number of different ways in which the 64 legislators could have combined to produce the given configuration of parties was about 459,154,630,000,000,000,000,000,000,000,000,000. In the somewhat more complex result produced in the rather smaller Icelandic legislature in 1983 the number of possibilities for coalitions of politicians consistent with the final party configuration was several thousand times higher at about 9,813,276,800,000,000,000,000,000,000,000,000,000.

These may seem large numbers, but they are small compared to the numbers of possible coalitions of politicians in the more typical European legislature, a number that increases in a factorial

TABLE 2.2. Election results in Iceland, 1983 and Luxemburg, 1984

Country	Year	Party	Seats
Iceland	1983	Independence Party	23
		Progressive Party	14
		People's Alliance	10
		Social Democrats	6
		Social Democratic Federation	4
		Womens List	3
		TOTAL	60
Luxemburg	1984	Christian Social Party	25
		Socialist Workers Party	21
		Democratic Party	14
		Green Alternative	2
		Communist Party	2
		TOTAL	64

relationship with the number of legislators and is, for mere mortals at least, effectively infinite. Set against this range of theoretical possibilities, legislative behaviour in the real world shows an amazing stability, a stability brought about by the existence of enduring factions and political parties. There can be little doubt that, if we are forced to choose between a reliance on the individual politician or on the party as our unit of analysis, then the party is the only practical alternative.

The Party as a Coalition of Factions

We might, however, seek a level of analysis between politician and party, focusing, say, on the party faction as the basic bargaining unit. The dangers that we face here are those of *ad hoc*-ery, the dreaming up of a particular explanation for each particular problem that faces us. In certain cases 'factions' may be very clearly and uncontentiously identifiable by all concerned. A good example is the separation of the German CDU/CSU into its regional component parts. When factions are as enduring and clear-cut as this, it often makes sense to treat them as separate bargaining entities. Even if they have yet to behave independently in practice, the potential for them to do so clearly exists. Moving beyond such clear-cut cases, however, any particular configuration of factions that we might choose to recognize is bound to be arbitrary. Worse, if we recognize two or more cross-cutting dimensions of factionalism, then we will be forced to deal either with the problem of overlapping factions or with a rapidly expanding set of subfactions. In the absence of unambiguous empirical referents, there is no logical stopping point in the division of parties into factions and subfactions. We quickly approach once more the level of the individual deputy and the attendant problems that we have just considered.

The Party as a (*Fissiparous*) Party

The final possibility is to retain the party as our unit of analysis but to consider its splitting potential. Many of the potential dimensions of cleavage within parties with which we may be forced to deal, of course, will be entirely *ad hoc*. One recurring basis of cleavage, for example, is a personality difference between party notables, a matter that will be impossible to explore in terms of anything other than particular local details. If we concentrate on policy as a basis for intraparty politics, however, there remains none the less considerable scope for systematic empirical analysis. Using various independent measures of the policy positions of party members (with roll call analyses, elite surveys and content analyses of politicians' speeches being obvious sources), the potential lines of policy based cleavage are in principle easy to identify.

In this way the policy based coalition theories that we shall consider in subsequent chapters might well be modified to take account of the splitting potential of parties. This can be measured in terms of one or more of the policy dimensions under consideration and we should note that the splitting potential of a party can be quite different on different dimensions. A party may behave as a unitary actor on one policy dimension, but be schizophrenic on another. The case of the Rassemblement Wallon (RW) in Belgium shows quite clearly how a party used to fighting elections on one basic issue, in this case the language problem, can find itself open to splits when other issues must be faced. The

socioeconomic policy dimension became much more important
for the RW once it went into office, causing internal problems
that gravely weakened the party. The extent to which a party is
fissiparous in policy terms, therefore, depends upon the relative
salience of different policy dimensions, an argument that will
come as no surprise to seasoned party hacks who will know full
well that a large part of practical party competition concerns the
continual search for issues that will split the opposition.

Whether or not a party can function as a unitary actor, therefore,
depends upon the bundle of issue dimensions on which it must
express a position. The bundle can change and be changed as a
result of the hurly-burly of day-to-day party competition. Since
the fact that party splits are relatively frequent in the real world
of coalition politics provides one of the strongest reasons not to
regard parties as unitary actors, it seems worthwhile to make at
least some attempt to consider the impact of actual and potential
splits in an account of the politics of coalition.

SUMMARY AND CONCLUSIONS

There can be no doubt that parties are not unitary actors for
many of the purposes for which political scientists may be
interested in them. For the purposes of coalition theory, however,
this assumption turns out to be not quite as serious as it appears
at first sight. This is because European political parties are, by
and large, well disciplined—going into and coming out of coalitions
as a single bloc. Nevertheless, European party systems are in a
continuous state of flux, with old parties splitting and merging
to form new ones, and a dynamic approach to the analysis of
coalitions and party competition must take account of this. An
approach based on the individual legislator as the fundamental
unit of analysis would be impossibly unwieldy, both in theory
and in practice, while one based on the party faction runs the
risk of *ad hoc*-ery. Keeping the party as the unit of analysis, we
could look at each party's splitting potential and investigate the
implications of this: but once more, many of the factors that
encourage party splits lend themselves only to *ad hoc* treatment.
A key exception to this, however, concerns policy based intraparty

politics, which does offer the possibility of systematic empirical and theoretical treatment.

In short, the reasons for treating the party as a unitary actor are part empirical, part theoretical. The empirical reality of legislative party discipline means that, at least for the static approaches to be found in most existing theories, the assumption is valid. Moving to a dynamic approach, though, the empirical reality of party splits presents a problem. The reason for retaining the unitary actor assumption is in this case theoretical, a product of the fact that many of the reasons why parties split can only be dealt with on an *ad hoc* basis. There is no doubt, however (and Luebbert's work points the way in this regard), that some consideration of the impact of politics within parties will be one of the directions in which the study of coalitions will develop in years to come.

3

What are the Stakes?

Before we go on to explore the process of bargaining that leads to the formation of a government, we must pause to consider what it is that the various actors are bargaining about. Only if we have an idea of what they are trying to achieve can we hope to make sense of their behaviour.

For some time, theorists of party competition and coalition bargaining tended to assume that the driving motivation of the actors was above all else to get into office. This led to the development of a theory of electoral behaviour based on the assumption that parties strive to maximize their popular vote so as to win as many seats as possible and thereby to increase their chance of controlling the executive. It follows from this that, if no party controls a majority of legislative seats after the election results have been declared, then the parties will attempt to bargain their way into the cabinet using their stock of legislative seats as resources. Since bargaining power tends to go up (and at the very least does not go down, all other things being equal) as a party's legislative seat share goes up, the prospect of subsequent coalition bargaining did not affect vote maximizing theories of electoral behaviour. The policies of the parties were a central feature of this account of party competition, though policy packages were seen as the store fronts that parties set up to attract voters rather than as something that politicians care about in and for themselves.[1] This general approach is expressed most clearly in a well known quotation from Anthony Downs's seminal account of party competition: 'Parties formulate policies in order to win elections, rather than win elections in order to formulate policies'[2] This is as succinct a statement as we are likely to find of what has become known as the 'office-seeking' assumption about the

motivations of politicians. At about the same time that Downs'
office-seeking view of electoral competition was exerting its
strongest influence on political scientists, William Riker proposed an analysis of coalition bargaining that was based on the
same fundamental assumption. Riker, furthermore, viewed the
gaining of office as the capture of a fixed prize to be divided
among the members of the 'winning' coalition.[3] No mention whatsoever was made of policy, even as an instrumental factor, in
this very influential early approach to the study of coalition
formation.

While the work of both Downs and Riker stimulated an intense
flurry of intellectual activity, no serious attempt was made
until much later[4] to marry office-seeking theories of electoral
competition to office-seeking theories of coalition bargaining and
thereby produce an integrated theory of party competition; and
this despite the fact that, as any experienced voter in a multiparty
system knows quite clearly, the policies offered by parties at
election time will almost certainly be modified by the process of
coalition bargaining before anyone even attempts to put them into
practice. Calculating voters must thus anticipate the process of
coalition bargaining when deciding how to vote rather than naïvely
taking the package on offer at its face value. Similarly, the
behaviour of parties engaged in coalition bargaining (even those
which could not give a hoot about policy) must surely be modified
by the knowledge that both past and potential future supporters
in the electorate are watching their performance in the negotiations
that lead to the formation of a government and are recalculating
their decisions about how to vote at the next election on the basis
of what they see.

Notwithstanding this failure to integrate analyses of coalition
bargaining with those of electoral behaviour into a comprehensive
theory of party competition, it was not long before the policy
positions of political parties became an important element in
theories of coalition bargaining. The introduction of policy
concerns into accounts of the politics of coalition was an attempt
to enhance both the realism and the predictive power of the
theories, since coalition cabinets in the real world, whatever else
they must do, must agree a package of proposed government
policies. Thus, even when member parties could not care less
about policy, they do face the need to generate particular outputs

while in office, if only in response to unavoidable circumstances or impertinent questions from journalists. It is just not possible for a government minister to sit around in a permanent pink cloud of euphoria, simply enjoying the sheer delight of being a government minister. The job description includes an obligation to pretend, at least, to run the country. This means that a politician driven only by the purest of office-seeking motivations must to a certain extent camouflage these, even after having succeeded in getting into office.

When party policy was first incorporated into coalition theory, however, the assumption was made, explicitly or implicitly, that policy is an intrinsic end valued in and for itself rather than an instrumental means used by politicians to gain office. (This distinction has continued to distinguish theories of electoral behaviour from those of coalition bargaining.) De Swaan, for example, one of the best known early proponents of this view with his 'policy distance' theory, states bluntly that 'considerations of policy are foremost in the minds of the actors . . . the parliamentary game is, in fact, about the determination of major government policy'.[5] One of the main arguments that we will develop in this book is that very few who have written on coalitions (not even de Swaan, for example) have fully digested the profound implications of this fundamental assumption, which carries the clear implication that membership of a coalition cabinet is no more than an instrumental means to affect policy. If major government policy can be influenced by playing the parliamentary game from a position outside the government coalition then this should be just as good, for an actor concerned only with policy, as doing precisely the same thing from the vantage point of a seat at the cabinet table. This means that we must fundamentally revise our view of what it is to 'win' the coalition game, together with our view of minority governments, of 'surplus majority' governments and of a whole range of other crucial features of the politics of coalition. It is, in short, difficult to over-emphasize the impact on coalition theory of assuming that politicians are motivated by the intrinsic desire to influence policy. Some years ago, Schlesinger drew attention to the consequences of different motivational assumptions for theories of electoral behaviour.[6] In the rest of this chapter we explore in greater detail the various goals that might be assumed to motivate actors engaged in coalition bargaining. We look at both office-seeking and policy-seeking motivations, viewing these both as means and as ends.

OFFICE AS AN END IN ITSELF

As we have just seen, the gospel according to Downs is that 'parties formulate policies in order to win elections' while the gospel according to de Swaan is that 'the parliamentary game is . . . about the determination of major government policy'. Within the same game-theoretic tradition, we find two quite different views of why politicians seek office. On the one hand, office is an end in itself; on the other, it is a means to affect policy. In reality, of course, most of us can think of some politicians who fit one description, some who fit the other, and some who fit both.

If office is an end in itself then getting into the government is the only way to win. When this is the case we need to very be clear about what, precisely, is involved in 'getting into the government'. We could, for example, regard simply being one of the parties in the government coalition as the crucial payoff. Given the way in which governments are quite often described in terms of their party membership, we might assume that parties simply seek the public recognition provided by having their name on the list of government members, regardless of anything else. We do, after all, hear of the Fine Gael/Labour coalition in Ireland or the CDU/FDP coalition in Germany. Perhaps getting the party name up in lights is enough of a reward in itself. Putting it another way, perhaps all that really counts is parking the party leader's rear end on a seat at the cabinet table. If simply getting into the government is all that is important then a party that is in, once it is in, has no incentive to exclude a party that is out. Coalition formation, on this assumption, is a highly co-operative game and it is hard to see why political life would not involve a perpetual round of grand coalitions designed to keep everyone happy by parking every party leader's rear end on a seat at the cabinet table. This is not, however, the way in which office-seeking coalition bargaining is usually portrayed; neither is it an interpretation that bears much relationship to reality.

Typically the yearning for office is seen, as it was seen by Riker, as the desire to control some sort of fixed prize, a prize captured by the winning coalition and divided among its members. Viewed thus, coalition bargaining becomes a competitive process of determining how this prize will be carved up. The assumption that the rewards of office are fixed in this sense can be seen, very crudely, as the product of a feeling among politicians that to be one of only a few parties in government is in some way more glorious, offering a bigger share of the limelight, than to be one of a large number of parties in the same government. And, after all, while we do talk of the CDU/FDP coalition in Germany, mentioning the members explicitly by name, we talk in more general terms of the *pentapartito* coalition in Italy. The less well informed may need reminding that the five parties concerned are the PSI, DC, PRI, PSDI, and PLI. Thus, if it is intrinsically satisfying to be in power, it may be intrinsically more satisfying to share power with only one other party than it is to share power with four others. This view regards 'incumbency' as a fixed prize that is shared in equal measure by all incumbents. If there are more incumbents then each gets a smaller share. Coalition bargaining then involves deciding who gets to be one of those who shares the prize.

Going one stage further again, we may assume that parties feel that there are degrees of incumbency, so that some incumbents are more incumbent than others. The Prime Minister, after all, tends to get far more of the limelight, to consume far more state dinners in interesting and exotic places and to be driven around in the back seats of bigger cars than other members of the government. Thus the party that controls the premiership might well think itself to be the senior incumbent, with a higher payoff than other incumbents. Other key government posts may have their own attractions. The Minister for Foreign Affairs, for example, gets to travel widely, to gather quite a lot of the limelight and to risk less of the odium that attaches, say, to a Minister for Social Welfare forced to cut old age pensions in a budget crisis. There may, in this way, be a pecking order of goodies to be distributed between the incumbents as the spoils of office. The bargaining game, rather than being one of win-or-lose, becomes one in which each of the winners can win more, or less, depending on the outcome of the negotiations among them. On this view, the winning coalition in effect captures a sack of trophies of unequal value, the contents of which sack are to be shared out among its members.

This raises a galaxy of interesting possibilities, though the most generalizable ones can be grouped under two headings. In the first place, the spoils of office may be taken to have a greater or lesser 'scope'. At the one extreme they may be seen as being confined to the premiership and a few really senior government ministers; at the other extreme, patronage may extend deep into the political and social system, providing very extensive spoils for winning parties. In the second place, the spoils may be valued equally by all parties or particular spoils may be valued differently by different parties. The latter possibility reintroduces a co-operative element into the coalition bargaining game as the players can attempt to allocate particular trophies to those who value them most. Some allocations thereby become worth more than others of the same spoils.

The scope of the spoils of office will obviously vary from country to country, depending on the pervasiveness of the patronage system in operation. It is certainly conventional to take the set of cabinet portfolios as one of the key pieces of booty to be redistributed, while bargaining over who gets which cabinet portfolio does seem in practice to be at least one of the components of coalition formation negotiations. It is not even an invariable rule, however, that all members of the 'government' take cabinet seats. Some Israeli government parties, for example, have on occasion forgone the right to cabinet office, as did the CRM in the 1974 Rabin administration.[7] The precise constitutional provisions and conventions that deal with appointments to cabinet portfolios vary a very great deal from system to system. By and large, however, it is reasonable to assume that the allocation of cabinet portfolios is, in terms of practical politics, something that is both within the control of the prospective coalition partners and a matter upon which they must all agree before they can take office and receive the payoff.

Moving beyond the cabinet, however, we typically find a whole series of non-cabinet ministerial appointments, as deputies to senior ministers, for example, or as heads of more obscure goverment departments. Such positions may not strictly be formal parts of the government but they are without doubt in the gift of the government and are equally without doubt valued by those who receive them. De Swaan explicitly notes that, in The Netherlands, these junior government appointments form 'part of the overall cabinet balance' and are a significant factor in coalition bargaining.[8] It is almost certainly the case that the same situation obtains elsewhere.

Empirical accounts of the distribution of portfolio payoffs among coalition members, as we shall see in Chapter 7, typically confine themselves to cabinet portfolios. The implicit justification for this is that what really counts in coalition bargaining is a vote in cabinet. It is true, of course, that only the cabinet can commit the government, though this carries the implication that a cabinet vote must be valued for what it can do, presumably because of its effect on policy outputs, an argument that takes us away from intrinsic office-seeking motivations. To confine our attention only to cabinet portfolios, therefore, is implicitly to admit that instrumental policy motivations are important. Browne and Franklin, for example, in their well known study of portfolio payoffs, confine themselves to accounting for the distribution of cabinet portfolios but quite explicitly justify this in terms of the instrumental desire of politicians to control portfolios in order to influence policy.[9] Notwithstanding the citations that the Browne and Franklin findings often receive, their fundamental concern is with the outcome of bargaining among policy-seeking politicians.

If we wish to model the behaviour of politicians who are concerned solely with the intrinsic benefits of office, it does not make much sense to confine ourselves to cabinet portfolios as the denominators of the spoils of victory. Many other patronage appointments should also, presumably, be considered. Indeed, if we equate intrinsic office-seeking with the quest for patronage-based office payoffs, we could look well beyond the legislature to all sorts of other appointments which are controlled by the incumbent government and which might form part of a looser definition of the executive. Our search might extend to the judiciary and to the civil service, senior appointments to both of which typically require at least formal executive approval. Probably the most important sphere of patronage, however, can be found in the parastatal agencies, such as the many nationalized industry boards; water, electricity, and other service authorities; health boards; development authorities, and so on. These have mushroomed in nearly every Western political system during the post-war period. More and more, semistate bodies of one form or another have taken on roles that would formerly have devolved upon the core civil service. Typically, senior appointments to the administration of such agencies are in the hands of a particular government minister, so that these appointments provide scope for rewarding those who might be felt by members of the administration to deserve rewarding.[10] This, to the best of our knowledge, is a largely unresearched area, and one that offers considerable promise if we wish to develop a broader interpretation of the payoffs attaching to a place at the cabinet table.

One theoretical consequence of viewing the payoffs of office as being more than the sack of cabinet and other ministerial trophies is that we are forced to deal with rewards that will typically be dispensed to people outside the legislature. Returning to the discussion in the previous chapter, this forces us to reconsider what we understand to be a 'party'. We can be quite clear about what is meant by a parliamentary party. Parliamentarians have legislative votes, and we may observe how particular parliamentarians are rewarded for using their votes in particular ways. Extraparliamentary party members and supporters, however, are harder to identify and to keep tabs on. They may perform services for the party that are much less tangible, or at the very least much less likely to be applauded from the roof-tops, even if these are at least as valuable as voting in the legislature when it comes to keeping a government in office. We may regard patronage appointments distributed beyond the parliamentary party as being no more than 'points' that are won and enjoyed by the party as a result of its bargaining endeavours; they may, in effect, be a way of keeping the score. Alternatively, we may regard the need to gain control over patronage appointments as an essential feature of party competition in general, as a means to reward backroom supporters who cannot or will not assume legislative responsibilities but who nevertheless need powerful incentives if they are to work their hardest for their party at election time.

In general, extraparliamentary patronage appointments can be a significant set of trophies in the sack of booty to be shared out by a winning coalition cabinet interested only in the spoils

of office. To consider them within cross-national analyses of
office-seeking coalition bargaining, however, presents us with
severe empirical problems, not only because their scope varies
considerably from system to system, but also because they are
not nearly as neatly defined as the explicit set of cabinet portfolios.

The precise evaluation of the spoils of office is another matter
that may well vary from actor to actor. It is clear that, when
cabinet ministries are divided up among the coalition partners,
some will be regarded as more valuable than others. If all parties
agree on the degree of importance to be attached to each ministry
then this will imply that, when they carve up the cabinet, they
will be carving up a fixed prize. The premiership may be worth
four times as much as the Ministry of Sport, the Foreign Ministry
twice as much, and so on; but, if everyone agrees upon what each
is worth, then the total collection of portfolios will have a fixed
value. In this case parties will, in a sense, be able to a score their
payoffs on the basis of the mutually agreed values of the portfolios
that they capture. On the other hand, different parties, as we have
suggested above, may value different ministries to a different
extent. One of the main reasons for this might be their desire to
influence policy in particular spheres, since holding a portfolio
typically gives executive power over a particular government
department. This assumes an intrinsic desire to influence policy
and thereby moves beyond the pure office-seeking hypothesis. It
is therefore a matter to which we will shortly return.

It may be the case, however, that parties differ in their evaluation
of portfolios for other reasons, though this phenomenon is more
difficult to generalize. A particular senior party politician, for
example, may see herself as the elder stateswoman of the legal
profession and yearn to be Attorney General. Foreign affairs can
assume the proportions of a vocation for particular politicians,
who want to be Foreign Secretary above everything else and
would actually turn down the premiership in order to fulfil this
ambition. These factors are entirely *ad hoc* with reference to a
particular set of party politicians; while they might be used to
interpret unexpected quirks in a particular distribution of portfolios, they cannot form the basis of a general explanation. Indeed,
it is difficult, within a model based on the assumption that
politicians are motivated by the desire to get into office in and
for itself, to see any generalizable theoretical justification for the

differential evaluation of the same cabinet posts by different parties.

POLICY AS AN END IN ITSELF

Instead of following Downs and taking the view that office is an end in itself for politicians, we may follow de Swaan and take the view that parties are motivated by the desire to influence policy. In the extreme case, we may consider parties to be concerned with nothing else but policy outputs, caring not at all about whether or not they hold office. This particular version of party strategy is probably the one that is most frequently put forward for public consumption by politicians, few of whom are willing to admit to voters that they promote policies merely in order to get into office. From the perspective of practical political analysis, furthermore, it is quite common to assume that parties are more or less motivated by the strength of their policy preferences. Communist parties, for example, are often seen as being relatively inflexible on policy when compared with, say, Christian Democratic parties. The implication is that the Communist parties have the stronger policy motivation. Such characterizations are typically based on accounts of party competition in systems where Communist parties seem to be outside the political mainstream, apparently refusing to adopt more centrist policy platforms when this appears likely to maximize either electoral support and/or coalition prospects. It is instructive, therefore, to use the behaviour and apparent motivations of the Communist Party in post-war Italy (PCI) to illustrate some of the points that we must consider when attempting to assess the relative importance of policy- and office-seeking motivations for a particular set of politicians.

Typically viewed, at least in the immediate post-war period, as a programmatic party, the PCI has explicitly and publicly confronted the need to balance policy and office in the development of its strategy of *Compromesso storico*, or 'Historic Compromise'. Hellman describes this dilemma as follows:

The PCI, DC and PSI (with the emphasis on the first two) could together effect serious change in Italy. This could obviously not be a Socialist transformation of the country—hence the 'compromise'. But since these parties were viewed as the political embodiment of Italy's most progressive forces, their collaboration would guarantee a consolidation of democracy and significant inroads into the country's worst structural problems.[11]

While the explicit public image of the 'compromise' neatly sums up the dilemma facing a policy motivated party deciding to modify its programme in order to achieve power, Marradi argues that the result was nothing new: 'Since its establishment in 1921, the two bulwarks of PCI's policy have been allegiance to the Soviet Union regarding international alignments, and great flexibility as regards Italian politics.'[12] Most authors stress the PCI's continuing desire in the post-war period to avoid being left isolated on the fringes of Italian politics. Pasquino, for example, sees the Historic Compromise as a period during which 'the search for legitimacy took precedence over other claims'.[13] This leaves open, however, the question of whether PCI politicians were motivated primarily by policy concerns, while accepting the instrumental need to participate in coalition governments in order to implement policy and the consequent policy compromises need to achieve this. The alternative view is that their policy motivations were more secondary, the product of an intrinsic desire to get into office from time to time. Pridham, in a sensitive analysis of precisely this point, concludes that policy is indeed the PCI's driving motivation:

On the important question of its willingness to govern and share power, the PCI has on the one hand linked its own legitimation with being accepted as a governing party and it has actively sought this role, both in demanding national government participation during the 1976–79 parliament and in leading or participating in coalitions regionally or locally. Yet, the PCI has at the same time insisted on its radical aims and long-term revolutionary goals . . . In short, the PCI has linked its governmental co-operation to the question of basic policy objectives, thus suggesting that policy comes before power as such, which fits with what we know of the PCI as a distinctly programmatic party (a category happily accepted by PCI interviewees).[14]

Whether this accounts for the PCI's non-participation in post-1947 Italian coalition *cabinets*, however, is a moot point, since there is a good chance that their opponents would have kept them out of office whatever happened. Their main opponents, the Christian Democrats (DC), may be seen as an office-seeking party *par excellence*—'over time the DC's desire to maintain power for its own sake has overwhelmed other considerations'.[15] The politics of coalition in Italy are none the less keenly influenced by the traditionally intense anti-Communism of the DC and of the Catholic Church in general. In 1949, for example, followers of the PCI were excommunicated by Pope Pius XII, who was 'almost pathologically anti-communist'.[16] This means that, as Pridham notes, 'to some extent "ideology" is in the eye of the beholder,'[17] with the DC consistently attempting to portray the PCI as a bunch of fanatical ideologues. This may stem in part directly from intrinsically valued Catholic beliefs held by members of the DC. It is also significant, however, that the exclusion from office of the PCI on policy grounds has allowed the DC to maintain an absolutely pivotal position in all post-war Italian coalition cabinets. Pragmatically, the DCs' refusal to deal with the PCI has done it no harm at all.

The post-war history of the PCI, therefore, illustrates quite a range of the arguments that can be made about the role of policy-seeking party motivations in the politics of coalition. In practical terms it can be very difficult to decide, when a programmatic party modifies its position in an attempt to get into government, whether this is being done for the sake of power in and for itself or simply in order to influence policy. At the very least, pretending to be concerned with policy is one of the rules of the political game in most systems, while accusing opponents of being cynical power-seekers is an equally standard political tactic. At the same time, centre parties, often in a pivotal position in the coalition system, like to portray their political rivals as members of some lunatic fringe, typically alleging an obsession with extreme policies and thereby attempting to marginalize them from the political process.

In general terms, when parties are genuinely motivated to an overwhelming degree by the intrinsic desire to influence policy, then this motivation has a fundamental impact on the entire process of coalition bargaining, as we shall see in Chapter 4. This is primarily because most policy outputs are public goods that apply to all—for better or for worse, for richer or for poorer. They apply whether or not the actors concerned have participated in the policy process, whether or not they are in cabinet; whether or not, indeed, they are politicians at all. In most democratic systems a Farmers' Party that pushes for an increase in agricultural subsidies, for example, will increase agricultural subsidies for everyone if it is successful. It will not (at least, not legally) be able to increase subsidies only for members of the Farmers' Party. It is important to note that this is not at all to argue that substantive policy outputs will necessarily involve the production of public goods. Rather, it is to argue that policy outputs, whatever they might involve, apply equally to all. This is true even when the policy in question involves the abandoning of a more public 'good', for example that of broadcast TV signals, in favour of a more private good, for example that of pay-as-you-view cable TV. The policy *as a policy* remains a public good, in the sense that it applies in the same way to all.

Using Policy 'Dimensions' to Describe Policy Motivations

It is nowadays conventional to describe the preferred policy positions of politicians, parties, or voters, as well as the agreed policy packages of coalitions and the actual policy outputs of governments, in terms of one or more general 'dimensions' of policy or ideology. Thus, when we talk about economic policy, we describe particular economic policies as being more (or less) right- (or left-) wing. We think of one policy as being to the right or to the left of another. We think of particular parties as shifting their policies to the right or to the left. At any particular time each party in the system we are talking about is typically assumed to have a policy that is located on this 'left–right' scale of economic policy. Aspects of party policy that cannot be described in these terms can be represented on similar scales using other policy dimensions, which may deal with social policy, with church–state relations, with ethnic minorities, and so on. We can take all of the salient policy dimensions in a given system together, to define a 'policy space' in which any salient policy package can be located—whether it is a package that is offered by a politician, desired by a voter, or enacted by a government.

For example, if the major themes of policy debate in a given system can be well enough expressed in terms of two policy dimensions, say an economic left–right dimension and a clerical vs. anti-clerical dimension, then these dimensions can together be used to define a two-dimensional policy space such as that shown in Figure 3.1. This hypothetical example shows a Christian

Social Party (CSP) and a Social Democratic Party (SDP) having the same position on the left–right dimension, but shows the CSP to be significantly more pro-clerical than the SDP. On the other hand, the CSP has the same position as the Christian Democrats on the clerical vs. anti-clerical dimension—but is quite far apart from them on the left–right dimension.

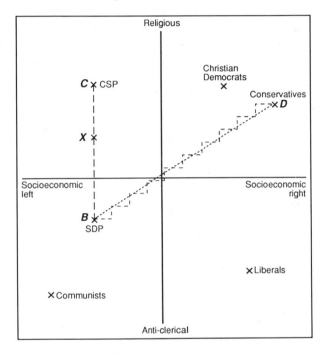

Fig. 3.1. Party positions in a hypothetical two-dimensional policy space

Expressing policy motivations in spatial terms, policy-seeking parties are assumed to be striving to create a set of public policy outputs that is located as close as possible in the policy space to their own preferred position. Any deviation of public policy from this 'bliss point' produces a related cost for the politician concerned. Politicians engage in policy bargaining, it is assumed, in order to minimize the size of these deviations, expressed as the policy distance between actual and preferred policy points. Policy bargaining, in short, can be seen as a process of policy distance minimization. We should remind ourselves that, since the policy outputs of a government apply to everyone, this specification of bargaining strategy holds regardless of whether or not the actor in question is a member of the 'winning' coalition. If for some reason or another policy distance is minimized by a strategy that involves the actor in question staying out of office, then this should none the less be the strategy selected, if policy is the overriding motivation.

Thus, in the example shown in Figure 3.1, if a coalition forms between the CSP and the SDP with an agreed policy package located at X, the policy distance between the SDP and coalition policy is BX. The SDP, it is assumed, will be continually striving in its bargaining to reduce the size of this policy distance. If the CSP, instead of dealing with the SDP, forms a minority government on its own and continues to enact a policy package at point X (perhaps because it needs SDP support in the legislature) then the policy distance between the SDP and the government will still be BX. Considering only policy motivations, the SDP will be just as satisfied with this result as it would have been had it gone into government.

The notion of 'policy distance' is a seductively simple one that conceals a range of complex issues. One issue concerns the metric, or measure, that we should use to capture the 'distance' between two points. We are accustomed in everyday life to the Euclidean maxim that 'a straight line is the shortest distance between two points'. The application of this notion to policy bargaining means that, if we consider the policy distance between the SDP and the Conservatives in Figure 3.1, for example, we are assuming that diagonal movement between the two parties has some meaning— and that the distance between the two parties would be the straight line BD. Most game-theoretic accounts of coalition bargaining, grounded as they are in the traditions of economic theory, do indeed make such assumptions and deal in Euclidean distances. An alternative view is that the bargaining between parties that drives such movement in policy space must take the form of a series of observable movements defined on each dimension under consideration. Thus 'diagonal' movement in the space is in practice achieved by a series of steps of finite size. On this view, the distance between the SDP and the Conservatives is the length of the step-like path between B and D in Figure

3.1, in other words the distance between B and D measured using the 'city block' metric. Relatively little consideration has been given by coalition theorists to such matters, but they do, as might be expected, have a fundamental bearing on the account that is given of coalition bargaining.[18]

While spatial representations of policy bargaining are powerful, suggestive, and elegant from the point of view of the theorist, they present serious problems in practice. This is because establishing the preferred policy positions of real political actors can be a difficult and elusive process. Several approaches have been attempted, including the use of 'expert' judgements, the analysis of legislative roll calls, the content analysis of party manifestos and the use of mass survey data. One way of deriving expert judgements of party positions is on the basis of a good old-fashioned literature review. The researcher dives into the literature on a particular political system and eventually emerges clutching a picture of its policy space, drawn on the basis of a more or less systematic sifting of data and opinions culled from a range of published sources. This is the approach used, for example by Taylor and Laver, de Swaan, and Dodd, in their early tests of coalition theories.[19] A rather more systematic approach is to apply a version of the 'delphic' technique. This proceeds by explicitly asking a wide range of country specialists to provide information about the policy positions of the actors and is the approach used by Morgan and by Castles and Mair.[20] This latter technique, of course, considerably spreads the risk associated with asking experts for their views of party positions, though there is always the danger that these views will in part be conditioned by the coalitions which actually formed. They must thus be used with care, though there is simply no other way of getting some of the information that can be derived from expert judgements.

Another empirical technique for deriving policy positions, and one that quite definitely cannot be used for coalitional analysis, is the multidimensional scaling of legislative roll calls. McCrea, for example, used this technique to bring some order to the apparent chaos of party competition in the French Fourth Republic.[21] For other purposes, the assumption that those actors who vote together also think alike can be used to tap a rich lode of information through the dimensional analysis of legislative voting records. Since a typical executive coalition tends very frequently to vote as a bloc in legislative roll calls, however, and not only in the case of confidence votes and other key divisions, roll calls are in a very real sense outputs of, rather than inputs to, the politics of coalition. They can certainly not be used, therefore, as independent variables that might explain coalitional behaviour. In this case the objection seems to us to be so fundamental as to be absolutely overriding.

An entirely independent fix on party policy positions is provided by the policy programmes issued by the parties themselves at election time. Even these documents may, of course, anticipate possible coalitions, perhaps dropping particular policy proposals that might prove repugnant to a likely coalition partner. However, the official policy programme of a party is much closer to being an independent and authoritative source of its policy than is anything else that is on offer. A recent large-scale research project conducted under the auspices of the European Consortium for Political Research has conducted a detailed content analysis of the policy emphases of the programmes of most parties in most European systems since the war.[22] These published electoral policy positions do retain a high degree of analytical independence from the coalition bargaining process, and it is on data such as these that we will tend to rely most heavily in subsequent empirical discussions.

A final technique that can be used to estimate party policy positions is the dimensional analysis of mass survey data. More and more these days, voters are asked by survey researchers to locate themselves on a left–right scale and possibly on other policy scales too. They may also be asked to locate the political parties in their system on the same scales. While voters' perceptions of party policy positions may not seem to have any bearing on coalition bargaining if we ignore anticipations of the next election, such perceptions will become increasingly central to accounts of the politics of coalition as integrated models of coalition bargaining and electoral behaviour are developed. For this reason we report estimates of such perceptions in Appendix B, which summarizes a series of published data sets dealing with the policy positions of parties in the main West European coalition systems. When all is said and done, a rather comforting conclusion can be drawn on the basis of scanning the scales in Appendix B, namely, that different techniques, used by different researchers, tend to yield rather similar placements of the parties on the main policy scales. There is thus a reasonable consensus in the field about what the policy positions of the main coalition actors actually are.

Achieving Policy Objectives

Since policy outputs apply to those outside government as much as to those in government, we need to consider the extent to which those outside government can affect policy before we can determine the incentives for them to get into office.

There are several ways in which a party can influence policy from a position on the opposition benches. First, it may have a direct effect on legislation as it passes through parliament. Bills may be defeated, if the government is in a minority position or if members of the government defect on specific issues. The opposition may be able to delay a bill, and thereby to extract concessions from the government in exchange for its speedy passage. Second, a party may be in a position to make or break a government by supporting it or opposing it in key legislative votes, particularly in votes of confidence. This possibility can be exploited in threats to put the future of the government on the line. Legislative strategies such as this can force the government to change tack on policy outputs that do not require legislation (which of course comprise the vast bulk of real-world policy outputs). A party's ability to make such threats depends upon the extent to which it is pivotal in the legislature, which in turn depends upon on the distribution of seats. If a party is pivotal, given the seat distribution, then it will be pivotal whether it is in or out of government; if it is not pivotal, then government membership can make no difference to its legislative voting power.

The third way in which the legislative game can be played in order to influence government policy is by using committees and the other institutional mechanisms of influence that are available to all legislators, whether they are in or out of office. The strength of the committee system, the power of the opposition in these committees, and their impact on key policy outputs are matters that vary dramatically from system to system. Strom, who lays great stress in his account of minority government on the role of committees in giving influence over policy to those out of office, develops an index of the extent of oppositional influence over the government.[23] This index takes account of the number of standing committees, whether these have fixed areas of specialization, whether they shadow ministerial portfolios, whether there are procedural constraints on assigning committee positions, and whether committee chairs are proportionally distributed among all parties. All of these factors, Strom argues, enhance the power of the opposition to affect government policy and thereby both reduce the incentive of a policy-seeking party to bargain its way into office and increase the relative attractiveness of opposition.

For each of the three reasons outlined above, and considering only parties motivated exclusively by the desire to influence policy, government membership may well be irrelevant. The incentive for policy-seeking parties to join coalition cabinets may emerge, however, once we consider the business of detailed policy implementation, a matter that goes beyond the concerns of most coalition theorists. The nitty-gritty of public policy is typically carried out by a government department headed by a cabinet minister. Control over a government department may be particularly important for a policy-seeking actor once we recognize that the policy implementation process is the cumulation of a vast number of minor decisions, each of which is in itself of insufficient importance to force a government crisis. When parties value several dimensions of policy at the same time, furthermore, legislators may well be unwilling to bring down a government that is enacting favoured policies on a more salient policy dimension in order to force policy changes on a less salient dimension. Policy-seeking politicians, in short, may want to participate in the executive in order to exert an influence on the particulars of policy, reserving for broad generalities and key policy areas the flexing of bargaining muscle based on the cataclysmic threat to bring down the entire administration.

We may conclude from all this that, when policy is an end in itself, membership of the government assumes secondary importance, with the big policy questions being settled by the balance of forces in the legislature. If they are not settled at the government formation stage (and it will rarely be the case that all of them are settled at this stage) then pivotal parties may have a direct impact on legislation or an indirect impact on the executive via threats to the future of the government. The desire to affect more detailed matters of policy, however, may provide a strong incentive for parties concerned not at all with the intrinsic rewards of office none the less to slug it out for a seat at the cabinet table, the matter to which we now turn.

OFFICE AS A MEANS TO INFLUENCE POLICY

Membership of the executive provides at least some opportunities to influence policy, though we should not forget, as we have just seen, that the threat to bring down the government, the major threat that can be deployed against a government over policy outputs, depends only upon the configuration of parties in the legislature.

Executive influence over policy takes place at several levels. First and without doubt most importantly, the cabinet makes many key policy decisions which are not subject to direct legislative review. On issues which are not matters of life or death for the government, membership of the cabinet may offer considerable control over policy outputs. This means that one of the main elements of value in the package that makes up a cabinet portfolio is the possession of a vote in cabinet decision making. Excepting the Prime Minister's control over the general agenda of cabinet meetings, this gives all cabinet portfolios equal value, since each confers a single cabinet vote. The Minister for Finance and the Minister for Foreign Affairs have no more power than the Minister for the Arts, provided that all have a seat at the cabinet table. This forces us into a consideration of intracabinet decision making, a matter considered explicitly by de Swaan in developing his policy distance theory. He assumes that cabinet decisions are based on majority voting, which leads to the conclusion that cabinet policy on a single dimension should be that preferred by the median cabinet member on that dimension. This enables de Swaan to conclude that the policy position of the median cabinet member is the 'expected' policy of the coalition.[24] Grossman suggests that de Swaan's assumption of majority decision making renders the minority portion of the coalition completely powerless.[25] However, the minority in cabinet may retain some power if its party is pivotal in the legislature, namely, if the withdrawal of its support is able to bring down the government. Once more, we see a way in which intracabinet decision making can be affected by the balance of power in the legislature.

The second type of influence over policy that is provided by a cabinet portfolio was introduced in the previous section. It is the power of a minister to influence detailed policy outputs. When Browne and Franklin conducted their analysis of the distribution of cabinet portfolios, as we have seen, it was the ability of ministers to exert a detailed adminstrative influence over policy that they assumed to motivate politicians in their quest for portfolio payoffs, not a desire to hold office in and for itself.

> The most important policy payoff, however, is the distribution of public offices among the various governing parties. Here, each party is awarded one or more of the government ministries (and/or sub-ministerial posts) in exchange for bringing its parliamentary support to the government, thereby establishing its formal responsibility for and primary influence over individual policy areas. Government ministries are the most tangible manifestations of policy payoffs to governing parties in that they give parties an institutional base from which to attempt to influence the entire flow of public policy . . . the control of a given set of ministries confers upon a party a particular set of institutional resources which it can manipulate in an effort to advance its policy goals.[26]

The power to influence policy in this way obviously extends far beyond the cabinet to a range of other appointments that may be under the control of the government. (The most obvious examples include senior posts in the judiciary, the governorship of the central bank, and many of the other patronage appointments that we have already mentioned in our earlier discussion of the intrinsic rewards of office.) If parties want to control portfolios in order to affect policy, furthermore, it is likely that different parties with different policy concerns will value different portfolios to a different degree. Agrarian parties, for example, are likely to set special store by the agriculture portfolio, socialist and social democratic parties by the welfare portfolio, parties that lay a heavy emphasis on defence on the defence portfolio, and so on. There is some limited evidence to suggest that there are in practice consistent relationships between particular parties and particular ministries.[27] This has the implication that some allocations of a given set of portfolios to a given set of parties (those that give particular portfolios to those who most want them) may be more 'efficient' or 'valuable' than others, with the very important consequence that even the allocation of a fixed set of government portfolios is not a constant sum game.

Instrumental Office-Seeking and the Party Hierarchy

In general terms, the pursuit of office as a means to influence policy is a matter that may open up serious divisions within political parties. Senior politicians often argue in favour of compromising basic policy objectives so as to be able to get into office and thereby to have at least some influence on real policy outputs. The alternative, they typically claim, is to retain a pure policy position, to stay out of office and thereby to have little effect on policy. Since it is the senior politicians in a party who hold the offices, such arguments allow for a happy coincidence of self-interest and idealism on their part. Down at the grass roots, however, party activists who have little chance of holding major office may distrust those who tell them, often from the back seat of a chauffeur-driven Mercedes, that policy compromises are necessary so that the party can to get into office in order to fulfil at least some of its basic policy objectives.

Policy-based instrumental office-seeking depends for its ultimate justification on the heavy use of counterfactual arguments of the 'if we were out of office things would be much worse' variety. In Ireland, for example, Labour leader Dick Spring often defended in precisely these terms his party's continuing participation with a monetarist Fine Gael party in a coalition that enacted several rounds of severe cuts in public spending. Stretching the doctrine of collective cabinet responsibility as far as he could (though able to shield himself with it when convenient), Spring and his Labour ministerial colleagues were wont to drop hints about the atrocities that would have been committed by Fine Gael if Labour had not been there to hold them back. Indeed, Spring was careful to ensure that the break-up of the 1982–7 coalition followed directly from Fine Gael's refusal to move on yet another proposed tough Budget. This allowed him to make the vital argument that Labour had stayed in the coalition only while it was able to do some good and withdrew as soon as it was not. We will never know, of course, what Fine Gael would have done had it been able to govern without Labour, so we can never really evaluate the impact of Labour participation on coalition policy in Ireland. It was certainly true in this case, however, that the main anti-coalition pressure came from Labour's grass-roots activists, who did not enjoy the luxury of ministerial appointments and remained singularly unimpressed, throughout the lifetime of the coalition government, by their party leader's protestations about all the good he was doing.

What is clear from the preceding discussion is that the neat analytical distinction between the desire for office in and for itself, and the desire for office as a means to influence policy, can easily become blurred in practice. This is especially true given the additional benefits of office that are enjoyed by senior party figures, even by those who are genuinely concerned about policy. We have also seen that the broad thrust of government policy can be influenced as easily by flexing legislative muscle as it can by working within the executive, thereby removing one of the main incentives for policy-seeking parties to bargain their way into office.

POLICY AS A MEANS TO GAIN OFFICE

Unlike theories of party competition, theories of coalition bargaining tend to assume, if they consider policy at all, that politicians value policy outputs for their own sake. In contrast, most of the analyses of electoral competition that have been based on the work of Downs assume that party policy is something used by politicians solely to help them win elections. While one of the recent growth areas of political science has been in the development of theories of electoral behaviour built on assumptions of intrinsic policy-seeking,[28] and a few authors have considered the impact of instrumental policy-seeking on coalition bargaining,[29] there remains a considerable gap between theories of electoral behaviour and theories of coalition bargaining on this matter.

If we regard a party policy package as something that is put forward solely in order to win elections, then we must expect policy to have an impact on coalition bargaining only to the extent that parties have an eye on the next election when they consider entering a particular coalition. In other words, only a theory of coalitional behaviour that assumes some form of dynamic interaction between coalition bargaining and electoral competition, along the lines suggested by Austen-Smith and Banks or Laver,[30] is able to accommodate instrumental policy motivations in coalition bargaining. The problem for coalition theory, therefore, is that it has up until now been essentially static, assuming implicitly that politicians do not look forward to the next election when they bargain. Coalition theory, in short, has failed to take heed of Schlesinger's dictum that 'office-seekers must be future oriented'.[31] This makes it difficult for the theories to accommodate the notion of 'instrumental' office-seeking. Even those models that claim to be dynamic such as those of Grofman or Laver and Underhill,[32] tend to be only locally dynamic in the sense that they look at the process involved in a single coalition formation rather than at the more global interaction between coalition bargaining and electoral competition over a series of elections.

Austen-Smith and Banks, however, have recently made a determined attempt to set this situation to rights, developing an integrated model of coalition bargaining and electoral competition that is based very firmly in the Downsian tradition of assuming politicians to be concerned with policy only for instrumental reasons. 'Parties' ex ante policy preferences will be a function only of the *difference* between their electoral policy positions and the final policy outcome . . . Even if parties are only concerned with winning elections . . ., *future* benefits will be a function of the current difference between the electoral position of the party and the formal policy outcome of the legislature.'[33] Office-seeking parties are concerned with policy outputs, on these assumptions, solely because future voters will vote on the basis of the gap between what was promised at the last election and what subsequently happened in the legislature. The authors then go on to construct a 'simple' three-party model of coalition bargaining and electoral competition that illustrates quite clearly how complicated even simple dynamic models can be. They ignore many of the factors that we might want to bring into play in a full consideration of policy manipulation designed to fulfil longer-term office-seeking objectives, including the discounting of future costs and benefits, the credibility costs of changing policies, the extent to which parties are 'tainted' with the policies of coalitions to which they have belonged in the past, and so on. None the less, the Austen-Smith and Banks model, discussed in greater detail in Chapter 5 below, serves to illustrate very clearly that the development of an integrated model of coalition bargaining and electoral competition, driven by the instrumental manipulation of party policy to gain office, will force a fundamental re-evaluation of the theory of party competition.

A full consideration of the impact of instrumental policy-seeking, then, demands a dynamic theory of party competition; and a dynamic theory of party competition requires an extension of our assumptions about the motivations of the actors to cover how they feel about the future. Unless we take account of such longer-term motivations and explore how they affect party competition over a sequence of elections and governments, we are reduced to treating each round of coalition bargaining as an entirely independent event, proposing no more of a relationship between politics in Germany in 1983 and 1987 than, say, between politics in Germany in 1987 and politics in Iceland in 1947. This is clearly unrealistic.

Taking a longer-term view of the motivations of politicians, however, we see why an office-seeking party may engage in vigorous policy bargaining, a matter that is only beginning to surface in existing theoretical treatments of the politics of coalition. When an office-seeking party bargains over policy with an eye to the next election, however, there is no 'ideal' policy point that determines its payoffs. Coalition policy outputs, in this case, are no more than weapons in the war between the parties.

SUMMARY AND CONCLUSIONS

We can generate quite different accounts of coalition bargaining by making different assumptions about what motivates the key actors. Office-seeking parties may bargain over policy, if that is what they are attempting to sell to the electorate. Policy-seeking parties may scramble for office, if that is how they hope to influence the flow of government outputs. On the other hand, policy-seeking parties may not care whether they are in government at all, if they are confident of being able to dictate policy to the cabinet from a pivotal position in the legislature. Actors with a longer-term time perspective will use their experience of previous interactions between coalition formation and electoral politics to gauge the impact of one coalition on subsequent elections and balance the impact of one election programme against subsequent coalition prospects.

Above all, it is clear that the simple notion of 'winning' the coalition game can only be defined in the context of a set of explicit assumptions about the motivations of the actors, a point made very clearly by Schlesinger.[34] Until we know what the stakes are, it is hard to know which game is being played and how to win it. Yet many of the existing theoretical accounts of the politics of coalition are remarkably vague, when we really get down to it, about the precise assumptions that they make about the motivations of the actors. In particular, coalition theories often fail to distinguish between the valuation of either office or policy in and for itself, and the instrumental valuation of office or policy as elements in a broader strategy of party competition.

4

How Do You Win?

One of the key characteristics of European parliamentary democracy is that the executive is responsible to the legislature. In
practice this means that the chief executive (an office quite distinct
from the altogether more formal position of head of state) is
selected or approved by the legislature and can be dismissed by
it. The only exceptions to this are the French Fifth Republic (in
which the Prime Minister is also responsible to a powerful and
independently elected President) and Switzerland (in which the
executive, once selected, cannot be dismissed by the legislature).
These cases, therefore, lie outside the West European mainstream
and are difficult to fit into conventional accounts of government
formation. In all other cases, the overriding requirement for a
government to form and to stay formed is that it have the support
of the legislature. This requirement is fundamental to the practice of parliamentary democracy in Europe and it is solely as a result
of it that West European voters can be said to choose their
governments.

The support of the legislature is crucial at two key stages in
the life of an executive. In the first place it is often necessary for
a prospective government to be able to demonstrate its legislative
support before it can take office. We may think of this as a
requirement for a formal investiture vote. In the second place it
is always necessary for a government to be able to muster
legislative support if challenged. Typically, such a challenge is
formalized in the parliamentary procedure of a vote of no
confidence tabled by opponents, or a vote of confidence tabled

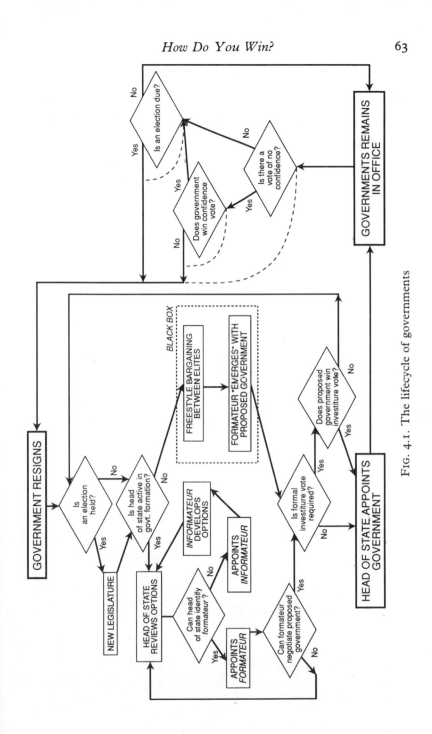

FIG. 4.1. The lifecycle of governments

TABLE 4.1. Constitutional factors in government lifecycles

Country	Does head of state play active role in formation?	Is formal investiture vote needed?	Must government resign if it loses confidence vote?	Can government dissolve legislature?	Can legislature dissolve legislature?	Maximum time between elections
Austria	No	No	Yes	Yes	Yes	4 years
Belgium	No	Yes	Yes	Yes	No	4 years
Britain	No	No	No	Yes	No	5 years
Denmark	No	No	Yes	Yes	No	4 years
Finland	Yes	No	No[a]	No	No	4 years
France	Yes	No	Yes[b]	Yes[c]	No	5 years
Germany	No	No	Yes[d]	Yes	No	4 years
Greece	No	Yes	Yes	Yes	No	4 years
Iceland	No	No	Yes	Yes	No	4 years
Ireland	No	Yes	Yes	Yes	No	5 years
Israel	Yes	Yes	Yes	No	Yes	4 years
Italy	Yes	Yes	Yes	Yes	No	5 years
Luxemburg	No	No	Yes	Yes	No	5 years
Malta	No	No	Yes	Yes	No	5 years
Netherlands	Yes	No	Yes	Yes	No	4 years
Norway	No	No	Yes	No	No	4 years
Portugal	Yes	Yes	Yes	Yes	No	4 years
Spain	Yes	Yes	Yes[e]	Yes	No	4 years
Sweden	No	Yes	Yes[b]	Yes	No	3 years
Switzerland	No	Yes	No	No	No	4 years

[a] President 'may' accept resignation in the event of a no confidence vote.
[b] Absolute majority of legislature required to pass no confidence vote.
[c] After one year.
[d] No confidence vote must designate new Federal Chancellor

by the government itself. An executive that loses a confidence vote, according to the principles of European parliamentary democracy, must resign.

The set of interacting decisions and events that describe the lifecycle of a government is outlined in Figure 4.1. This shows the various constitutional provisions that affect the lifecycle of governments in particular political systems, listed in Table 4.1. These relate to the role played by the head of state in the formation process; the requirement for a formal investiture vote; the requirement that the government resign if it loses a vote of confidence; the ability of the cabinet to dissolve the legislature; the ability of the legislature to dissolve itself; and the maximum period between elections allowed under the constitution. We will return to various aspects of this lifecycle in later chapters. For the moment, we note that the proposed government is required to win an investiture vote in some systems, such as Belgium, Ireland, Israel, and Italy, though not in others, such as Denmark, Finland, and Norway. Any government in any system, however, may be required to win a confidence vote, save for the exceptions that we have already noted. The loss of other legislative votes may be very serious indeed for the government but, unlike the loss of a confidence vote, no other loss is automatically fatal. In practice, a serious legislative defeat (such as the defeat of a budget) may immediately be followed by a confidence vote or may provoke a government resignation in anticipation of the loss of a confidence vote. But it is perfectly possible, and indeed it is not uncommon, for a government to suffer a serious legislative defeat but to go on to win the subsequent confidence vote. Parliamentary forces that can agree on their opposition to a particular legislative proposal may well not be able to agree on the need to replace an incumbent government, together with its entire legislative programme.

Just as governments can sometimes extricate themselves from catastrophic legislative defeats by winning a subsequent confidence vote, so they can raise the stakes of the legislative game by making a particular vote a matter of confidence. They may choose to do this even when the issue involved is quite trivial. In 1988 Charles Haughey, leading a minority Fianna Fáil administration in Ireland, made an issue of confidence out of an opposition amendment concerning which of two Limerick hospitals would be closed in a round of public spending cuts. He stated firmly that the government would resign and an election would be called if the opposition amendment was carried. The opposition had lined up a legislative majority on the amendment and had already defeated the government on a number of other minor matters. However, sections of the opposition believed Haughey's threat and, fearing an election because of their low standing in the opinion polls, backed down and did not vote against the government. The government won the vote and Haughey was never called upon to act on his threat. There is every reason to believe that he would indeed have resigned had he lost the hospital amendment, but the important point is that he was under no formal obligation to do so. He would have lost face, of course, but he would have been perfectly entitled to remain in office.

Governments may resign 'voluntarily' for all sorts of reasons. They may carry out threats that have been made to, and called by, the opposition. They may anticipate legislative defeats or electoral victories. They may simply fall apart. All of these possibilities are captured by the dotted curved lines on the right-hand side of Figure 4.1. Such voluntary resignations, however, are all underpinned by the constitutional bottom line. This is that a government *must* resign if it loses a confidence vote.

THE VIABILITY AND EFFECTIVENESS OF GOVERNMENTS

The ability of a government to win votes of confidence is thus the key to its ability to remain in office. We may think of a government that can do this as a viable government. While a viable government can, as we have seen, suffer a range of legislative defeats, it is clearly the case that it must be able to enact at least some of its legislative programme if it is to be in any sense effective. A viable government, therefore, need not be an effective government, an important distinction elaborated by Strom.[1] Technically, a government can remain viable, in the sense of being able to win votes of confidence, yet be quite unable to win any other legislative vote and thus be totally ineffective. Politically, of course, this is unlikely; but only once the subsequent electoral penalties of being a part of an ineffective government are taken into consideration. If we do not assume that politicians take at least some account of anticipated future election results, then we will be forced to contend with the possibility that a totally ineffective yet viable government will cling to office while at the same time being unable to pass any legislation.

It is very important to keep in mind that it is the balance of forces in the legislature that determines whether or not a particular government is viable. Put another way, while the executive coalition comprises the set of parties who control positions in the executive, the coalition which determines the viability of a government is a legislative coalition. It is almost invariably the case that members of parties in the executive coalition will support it in the legislature. It is by no means certain, however, that members of parties that are not in the executive coalition will oppose it in the legislature. The legislative coalition supporting the government may thus be bigger than the executive coalition forming it. Parties which are in the legislative coalition over a period of time but which are not in the executive coalition are usually called 'support parties'. It is not at all necessary, however, for an executive to be supported by the same legislative parties from vote to vote. In other words, while the executive coalition must remain stable during its life (a change in the executive coalition always signals a change of government), the same executive coalition may be maintained in office by an ever-changing legislative support coalition.

Sometimes, parties which could vote against a government do not do so but instead abstain. This may be thought of as a more half-hearted form of support. For cases in which the difference between an abstention and a vote against the government is crucial to its viability, however, the effect of abstention is the same as outright support and can be treated as such, since abstention in these circumstances is typically a strategy undertaken with a clear foreknowledge of its effects.

In the period of bargaining that leads up to the investiture of a viable government, the period upon which most conventional accounts of coalitional behaviour tend to concentrate, there is no clear distinction between a legislative coalition and a proposed executive coalition. Everything focuses upon the ability of the proposed executive coalition to win the actual or implicit investiture vote in the legislature. After the investiture of the new government, however, there is a very clear distinction between legislative and executive coalitions. An executive that is determined to remain in office can from this moment on be brought down only by particular types of legislative defeat, the opportunities for which will present themselves only now and again. Legislative and executive coalitions thus maintain a more or less independent existence after the investiture debate, being linked only by the periodic need of the executive to generate a winning coalition of supporters in the legislature in order to win actual or anticipated confidence votes.

The full impact of this distinction between legislative and executive coalitions has not always been appreciated by coalition theorists. The most obvious consequence of this has been the reverence that has been accorded to legislative majorities in some accounts of the behaviour of coalition executives. In particular, there has been a strong tendency to assume that a 'winning' coalition is one whose members between them control a legislative majority. This in turn has had the consequence that, whatever the precise details of particular theories, most theoretical prediction sets contain only majority coalitions. Before policy became such a central feature of coalition theories, this was quite understandable; any other solution generates considerable confusion in office-seeking theories. If minority coalitions can 'win', for example, this allows for the possibility that two, or even more, minority coalitions—each with quite exclusive memberships— might simultaneously claim the prize with equal justification. In such cases there is no basis for deciding who is the real 'winner'. Majority coalitions, of course, have the comforting property that, if two rival coalitions both claim the same prize at the same time, then they must overlap on at least one member: this pivotal member can thus choose which coalition is actually to win the prize. Since coalition theorists now profess to be concerned to a great extent with policy, however, the majority criterion for winning has become an anachronism, albeit a ubiquitous one. What is quite clear, however, is that the policy outputs of a government can be enjoyed by politicians whether they are in or out of office. It is also clear, as we showed above in our discussion of policy motivations, that legislative parties outside the executive coalition can retain some control (sometimes considerable control) over government policy making. They may do this by threatening legislative votes of no confidence, by using parliamentary committees, or by exploiting other, even extra-parliamentary, mechanisms of influence. This means that even opposition parties retain full enjoyment of and some control over government policy outputs. This in turn may well lead them to support minority executives, which may therefore be quite viable.

A related consequence of equating winning with having a legislative majority is the implication that any coalition containing more members than are needed to control such a majority will tend to jettison members until 'minimal winning' status is achieved. Minimal winning coalitions are coalitions which have the property that, if any member leaves, then the coalition ceases to control a majority in the legislature. Once more, when theorists were not concerned with policy motivations, this approach was understandable. If there are only the fixed rewards of office to be shared out, why share these with people whose legislative support is not needed in order to secure them? On these assumptions, what became known as 'surplus majority' coalitions were treated as pathologies that deviated from the norm in the same way as minority governments. If we take policy seriously, however, then the logic of the minimal winning coalition evaporates. Since policy payoffs are public goods (see Chapter 3 above), then nothing is lost if more, rather than fewer, people enjoy them. Indeed, larger coalitions, all other things being equal, may possibly have more legitimacy and authority than smaller ones. There is, on these assumptions, no cost to a coalition in carrying passengers and no reason to suppose that legislative majorities will tend to be minimal.

In contrast to formal theories, which have tended to treat minority and surplus majority governments as deviations, empirical discussions of European coalition cabinets have for some time highlighted their role.[2] There can be no doubt from such analyses that both minority and surplus majority executive coalitions are in practice as much the norm in European politics as minimal winning coalitions.

From both the empirical and the theoretical perspectives, then, it is clear that minority governments can be viable in the right circumstances. Viewed either way, there is nothing magic about a majority when it comes to forming a government in Western Europe. The game can be 'won' with fewer than a majority of seats in the legislature, just as it can be 'lost' with more than a majority. In the rest of this chapter, therefore, we look first at minority government and then at surplus majority government in Western Europe. We will be looking for what appears in practice to be the bottom-line requirement for a prospective government to 'win' the coalition game, bearing in mind that winning, in its broader sense, involves forming a viable government and sustaining it in office.

THE POSSIBILITY OF VIABLE MINORITY GOVERNMENT

The Frequency of Minority Government

Quite a few authors have catalogued the frequency of minority governments and all come to very similar conclusions.[3] The

TABLE 4.2. Frequency of European coalition cabinets, by type, 1945–1987[a]

	Number of cabinets	% of total	% of cabinets in minority situations
Majority situations[b]			
Single party	14	6	–
Surplus majority coalition	8	4	–
Minority situations[c]			
Surplus majority coalition	46	21	24
Minimal winning coalition	77	36	39
Minority government	73	33	37
TOTAL	218	100	100

[a] For list of countries covered see Table 4.3.
[b] A majority situation is where one party controls more than 50% of legislative seats.
[c] A minority situation is where no party controls more than 50% of legislative seats.

situation is summarized in Table 4.2, which shows the frequency of various cabinet types in twelve European systems. About one third of all governments are minority governments, while another

TABLE 4.3. Frequency of coalition cabinet types, by country, 1945–1987

	Majority situations		Minority situations			Total
	Single party	Surplus majority coalition	Surplus majority coalition	Minimal winning coalition	Minority government	
Austria	4	2	–	6	1	113
Belgium	1	–	4	15	2	22
Denmark	–	–	–	2	18	20
Finland	–	–	17	5	10	32
Germany	–	2	–	10	–	12
Iceland	–	–	2	10	2	14
Ireland	4	–	–	3	5	12
Italy	–	4	14	3	14	35
Luxemburg	–	–	1	9	–	10
Netherlands	–	–	8	6	3	17
Norway	4	–	–	3	8	15
Sweden	1	–	–	5	10	16
TOTAL	14	8	46	77	73	218

quarter have surplus majorities. Only 40 per cent of governments which form when no single party controls a majority are minimal winning coalitions. Table 4.3 shows the distribution of different cabinet types in each of the twelve political systems and shows that the incidence of both minority and surplus majority governments varies considerably from system to system. There are countries, such as Denmark, that almost always have minority governments. There are countries (Luxemburg and Germany) that never do. There are others, such as Finland and Italy, in which surplus majority governments are very common. There are even three systems—Austria, Germany, and Italy—in which majority parties have on occasion formed coalitions with others to create surplus majority governments. (These were for the most part governments of national unity formed immediately after World War II. No such government has formed in recent times.) There can be no doubt, considering the combined evidence of Tables 4.2 and 4.3, that minority government is as much the norm in Western Europe as any other type of government, and that some systems are more disposed towards it than others.

Theoretical attempts to account for this phenomenon can take on\` of two general paths. In the first place, empirical theorists have attempted to modify the office-seeking approach to government formation, viewing majority government as the norm and looking for systematic patterns of observed deviation from this. In the second place, theories that put policy at centre stage can, if they choose to do so, provide a more comprehensive account of minority government in Western Europe.

Accounts of Minority Governments as Deviations from a Norm

One of the first systematic considerations of minority government was provided by Herman and Pope, who offer 'five reasons why majority governments do not form'.[4] It should be clear at once from this attitude to the question that these authors regard majority government as the norm and set out to explain minority government as a 'deviation' from this. The particular explanations that they offer for minority government confirm this general impression, suggesting that minority governments arise in one of five broad types of situation.

1. 'When elections usually can be expected to provide one party with a legislative majority but, on those occasions where the post-election one-party majority government is not present, a one-party minority government comes into office';[5]
2. 'in *immobiliste* situations when certain structural features inherent in the party system severely handicap the formation of majority coalitions';[6]
3. 'caretaker' administrations [which] . . . come to power on those occasions when the normal political differences between parties are temporarily forgotten . . . they are deliberately established for only a short period of time—for example, until a constitutional amendment can be passed and/or a general election held';[7]
4. 'when a tradition of co-operation between coalition parties collapses and one or more of the parties continues in office until the previous coalition can be reconstituted or until a coalition with a different partner (or partners) can be established';[8]
5. 'in situations in which the party forming the government is only a small number of seats short of a legislative majority'.[9]

These explanations of minority government can be characterized as the 'waiting for a(nother) majority government' thesis (1,3, and 4 above), the *'immobilisme'* thesis (2 above) and the 'almost a majority government' thesis (5 above). Each quite clearly characterizes majority government as the norm and minority government as an aberration.

The same style pervades Taylor and Laver's treatment of minority government, which lays most emphasis on the 'almost a majority government' explanation.[10] 'The presence of a party with almost an absolute majority and with support from other parties appears to be the most important single "explanation" for the formation of minority governments'.[11] Taylor and Laver proceeded by progressively lowering what they assumed to be the effective winning threshold in each system from 50 per cent of the seats to 49 per cent, 48 per cent, 47 per cent, and so on. They looked for the effective winning threshold that best explained the incidence of minority governments in each country, analysing 132 governments in 12 states between 1945 and 1971, of which 45 (that pervasive proportion of just over one third) had minority status. Table 4.4 shows the overall distribution of the sizes of the minority governments analysed in that study and shows that many of them were indeed only a whisker short of a majority. In many legislatures, the political reality may well be that these minority governments, at least, can govern 'as if' they controlled a majority of seats.

Both the Herman and Pope and the Taylor and Laver accounts of minority government, however, offer no more than a description, at best a taxonomy. They do not provide any real explanation, for example, of why some governments seem to able to get by with just short of a majority of seats in the legislature while others cannot. This lacuna is a consequence of the fact that minority government is more or less impossible to explain on the basis of office-seeking assumptions. Neither of these accounts of minority government pays attention to the configuration of policy positions in the party system. Implicitly, each offers an office-seeking account of minority government, something which is almost a contradiction in terms. Office payoffs go only to government members and those who are out of office get nothing. They must therefore want to get into office at any opportunity. Every minority government faces a majority opposition. If this majority opposition

TABLE 4.4. Distribution of government seats in the Taylor and Laver
study, 1945–1971

Government size (% seats)	No. of governments
0–29.9	5
30–39.9	6
40–44.9	12
45–47.9	6
48–48.9	3
49–49.9	13
TOTAL	45

Source: Taylor and Laver.

is motivated solely by the desire to gain office it is difficult to
imagine why it might refuse to take power when it has the
ability to do so. It is hardly surprising, therefore, that more
comprehensive accounts of minority government had to await
the development of policy-driven interpretations of government
formation.

Policy-Seeking and Minority Government

Policy payoffs go to those outside the government as well as to
those within it. Even more to the point, policy outputs can be
influenced by those outside the government. Since government
membership is not the sole key to the distribution of policy
payoffs, we need not necessarily suppose that a majority opposition
is going to seize every opportunity that it can find to evict a
minority government. This argument has most recently been
expounded in the work of Strom and Luebbert.[12]

Strom develops 'a rational choice theory of minority government
formation' based quite explicitly on the assumption that 'the
underlying motivation [of parties] is to influence policy-making in
the national assembly'.[13] To this is added the assumption 'that
parties seek to maximise their longer-term as well as short-term
utilities'.[14] These assumptions drive two explanations of minority
government. The first is based on the benefits of governing, seen
in terms of the '*policy influence differential* between government

and opposition. The greater the opportunities for parliamentary opposition to influence legislative policy-making, the lower the benefits of governing.'[15] The second explanation is based on the costs of governing, seen in terms of anticipated electoral losses. 'Government incumbency tends to result in subsequent electoral losses . . . a decision to remain in opposition temporarily implies no lack of interest in governing in the long run, but rather a willingness to wait for more favourable circumstances.'[16] The second explanation of minority government advanced by Strom is thus a refinement of the office-seeking model to introduce the idea that the actors may be trying to maximize their payoffs over the longer, rather than the shorter, term. One of the reasons why the members of a majority opposition might not force a minority government into immediate defeat, on this account, is that they may be biding their time, waiting for the most auspicious moment to do so. This explanation remains, therefore, in the office-seeking tradition. Putting matters rather crudely, it sees minority governments merely as losers awaiting defeat.

Strom's argument about the policy influence of the opposition, however, can be used to show how minority governments may have a more or less permanent role in particular political systems and thereby allows minority governments to be viewed in the same light as majority governments. There are number of ways in which opposition parties may have an impact on government policies, including the deployment of affiliated interest groups, such as labour, employers', or farmers' organizations. These may be used to put direct pressure on the executive on the basis of threats of extraparliamentary sanctions. The legislature itself, however, offers avenues of opposition influence over policy and Strom concentrates upon these. He operationalizes the 'influence of the opposition' in terms of explicit legislative structures and norms. In particular, Strom concentrates upon the role of the opposition in the legislative committee system. He looks at the number of standing committees, at their areas of specialization, at the extent to which committees shadow cabinet portfolios, at the norms governing the assignment of committee places to legislators and especially at the extent to which committee chairs are proportionately distributed among parties in the legislature. Strom's estimations of the relative influence of the opposition in

TABLE 4.5. Influence of opposition, by country

Country	No. of committees	Specialization	Shadow cabinet	Membership	Chair	Aggregate value
Belgium	+	+	+	−	+	4
Britain	−	+	−	−	−	1
Canada	+	+	+	−	−	3
Denmark	+	+	+	−	+	4
Finland	+	+	−	−	+	3
France	+	+	+	+	−	4
Iceland	+	+	+	+	−	4
Ireland	−	−	−	−	+	1
Israel	−	+	−	+	−	2
Italy	+	+	+	−	−	4
Netherlands	+	−	+	−	−	2
Norway	+	+	+	+	+	5
Portugal	+	+	+	−	+	4
Spain	+	+	+	−	−	3
Sweden	+	+	+	−	+	4

Source: Strom.

selected political systems are reported in Table 4.5. The results of this type of analysis are at least partially persuasive and the availability of formal institutional structures that allow the opposition to influence policy seems to help us account for the frequency of minority governments in Norway, France, Italy, and Sweden. As Strom measures the influence of the opposition, however, he does not help us to account for the endemic nature of minority government in Denmark, or its frequency in Finland, both systems in which, according to Strom, the opposition is accorded only moderate influence over policy. Conversely, we might be led to expect a greater role for minority government in Belgium, Iceland and Portugal, all systems which Strom scores high on opposition influence but which do not in practice have many minority governments. Indeed, Strom himself concludes, having contrasted opposition influence with electoral decisiveness as explanations of minority government, that the influence of the opposition is the less significant factor.

Given the theoretical elegance of policy-driven explanations of minority government, however, these initial results should not discourage further analysis. It is worth pursuing the idea a little. There are at least two avenues of potential development: the first is to look for other ways in which the opposition can influence policy; the second is to look more closely at strategic legislative behaviour that might influence the policies of the executive.

The first path is chosen by Luebbert, who develops a general theory of coalitional behaviour that is driven by the desire of party leaders above all else to protect their positions as party leaders.[17] The approach is based on Luebbert's own classification of the impact upon party leadership strategies of certain structural properties of each political system. For the purposes of understanding minority government, the important group of systems are those classified by Luebbert as 'consensual democracies'. He places Norway, Sweden, and Denmark in this category, while Finland is treated as an 'unconsolidated' system because of its 'rough transition to democracy'.[18] Consensual systems are characterized by 'extreme corporatism', the 'institutionalised pattern of cooperation between interest groups and the executive of the central government in the formulation, implementation, and administration of public policy'.[19] Corporatist systems offer powerful extraparliamentary mechanisms for influencing policy outputs. This provides the opposition with the potential opportunity of having an effect on government policy and thereby increases the chance of minority governments. In Luebbert's words,

the existence of well-developed consensus-building mechanisms and the normative commitment to their use means that ultimate policy outcomes will be generally satisfactory, whether reached in cabinet, parliament, or outside of both; the leaders of the party forming a government have little incentive to create majority governments, if they must do so at the cost of policy sacrifices . . . Because [policy] concessions will not then be party-to-party concessions, and therefore highly risky for party leaders, but will . . . be concessions among the interest groups . . . [they will be] consequently much less threatening to party leaders.[20]

The argument, in short, is that policy bargaining in consensual systems takes place outside the legislature. The leaders of legislative parties prefer to hold firm on policy while allowing a minority government to negotiate directly with interest groups. Minority governments are more likely in consensual democracies, to put the argument rather crudely, because legislatures in such systems are less important. The real action is taking place elsewhere and the leaders of the opposition parties in particular prefer to let their associated interest groups do the dirty work of policy bargaining, and of making the inevitable policy concessions that this will entail. This argument can be used to account for the coincidence of corporatist decision making and minority government in the Scandinavian states (including Finland, even if Luebbert does not classify this as a consensual system), though it runs into serious problems with Austria. Austria has very strong corporatist decision making structures by almost all accounts but has no history of minority government. Luebbert excludes Austria from his analysis altogether because 'it became a multi-party democracy for the first time as a result of the 1983 election . . . it is only at this point that it comes within the scope of the theory'; prior to this it was effectively a two-party state, and another that had experienced a 'rough transition to democracy'.[21] Arguments such as this, of course, cast doubt upon the nature of the causal linkages of Luebbert's theory (a point also made in a rather different context by Strom[22]). There seems to be a danger that political systems might be classified into particular categories so that they can be made to fit a particular theory. Notwithstanding

this ambiguity over Austria, however, the association that Luebbert points out between corporatist extraparliamentary policy
bargaining and minority government in Scandinavia is both
striking and suggestive.

An alternative method of understanding minority government
is to explore further the potential strategic avenues of legislative
influence over policy. Rather than downgrading the role of the
legislature, as is the case with the 'corporatist' account of minority
government, this approach keeps the parliament at centre stage
and concentrates upon the interaction between legislature and
executive. In particular, it looks at the way in which particular
legislative strategies may be used to force the government's hand
over policy. This is the approach used by Budge and Laver, who
exploit the distinction between majority government and viable
government.[23] As we saw above, many minority governments may
be viable governments once we take the policy preferences of the
government and the opposition parties into consideration. Certain
governments which control much less than a majority of seats
may be effectively unbeatable. This leads Budge and Laver to
replace the majority winning criterion with a viability criterion.
'A protocoalition V will form a government if there is no
alternative coalition A which is supported by parties controlling
more legislative votes than those supporting V and which all
supporters of A prefer to form rather than V.'[24] Expressed
in these very general terms, the notion of viability can even
accommodate the occurrence, as in Finland or Portugal, of
non-party cabinet coalitions of public figures. Such coalitions are
viable if they cannot be beaten on the basis of patterns of support
in the legislature. (Non-party coalitions, of course, are the ultimate
minority governments, controlling zero per cent of the total
legislative weight. Carried to the extreme, this means that even a
coalition of frogs, or of turkeys, would be viable, provided that a
legislative majority was prepared to support it.)

Such a general criterion of government viability is too vague
to be of any real theoretical or empirical use. Further assumptions
must be made about the motivations of the actors for it to acquire
a cutting edge. If we assume that politicians are motivated solely
by the desire to affect policy, however, we can refine the viability
criterion to enable us to predict stable minority governments in
quite a wide range of situations. We might think of governments

that are viable, given the policy constellation of parties in the legislature, as 'policy viable'. Many minority governments may be policy viable, and many policy viable minority governments may control far less than a majority of legislative seats, a possibility that takes us well beyond the 'almost majority' approach to minority government. In the hypothetical case described in Figure 4.2, for example, the locations of the parties on the left–right scale mean that party B will be very difficult to exclude from office and might well be able to form a viable minority government on its own, a government based on 20 per cent of the seats in the legislature, if it chose to do so. If party B forms a government which sets a policy located at B, then there is no coalition of the 'out' parties that can defeat party B on the basis of an alternative policy which they can not only agree upon but which they both also prefer to policy B. Party A can beat party B single-handedly but only if party C fails to support party B. But party C, fearing policy A if party A beats party B, has every incentive to keep party B in office. The reverse argument applies to any potential challenge of party B by party C. (We will be returning in Chapter 5 to a much more general version of this argument, which deals with the 'core' of the bargaining game.)

Party	A	B	C	
L				R
Seats	40	20	40	

FIG. 4.2. A hypothetical example of bipolar opposition

Party	PCI	PSI	PSDI	PRI	DC	PLI	PDIUM	MSI	
L									R
Seats	140	84	23	6	273	14	25	25	

FIG. 4.3. The Italian party system 1958–1963

Rather more complex real-world examples of this process at work can quite often be found in Italy, the classic example of a party system of 'bipolar opposition'. Figure 4.3 shows the situation that arose after the 1958 election; the parties are ranked on a left–right scale taken from Appendix B and the seat distribution is the outcome of the election. There were 596 seats in all, six going to 'others' and minor parties. The majority winning threshold was therefore control over 299 seats in the Chamber of Deputies. It can immediately be seen that it was impossible for parties motivated only by policy to keep the Christian Democrats (DC) out of office. It is also clear that the DC needed to take no one else into government with it, since it could have been defeated neither by a coalition of the left nor by a coalition of the right. In our terms, a single-party DC minority government was policy viable. In practice, a succession of DC single-party minority governments did indeed rule Italy for most of this period.

What these examples illustrate quite clearly is the basic point that a minority government may be viable, given its policy package, because no coalition of the 'out' parties can agree on a replacement. The key to this argument is that policy motivations can divide the opposition. If we consider only office-seeking motivations, then all of the parties who are out of office get nothing. They are thereby united by a desire to get the government out and get themselves in. Minority government thus becomes incomprehensible, except as a deviant case in particular local circumstances or in terms of much longer-term electoral considerations.[25] If policy is important, it becomes necessary for a coalition of 'out' parties to be able to agree upon a policy package that is preferred by more legislators than the policy package of the government. This enables governments to divide the opposition by putting forward policy packages at the 'centre' of the policy space, making it impossible for the opposition to agree on an alternative and thereby allowing the government to manage with much less than a majority.

SURPLUS MAJORITY GOVERNMENTS

If political parties are motivated only by the desire to get their hands on the spoils of office, then coalitions, as we have seen, must control a majority of seats in the legislature. Furthermore, there should be a tendency for coalitions to shed 'surplus' members until they include no more members than are absolutely necessary in order to control a legislative majority. These are the minimal winning coalitions predicted by office-driven coalition theories and discussed in greater detail in the next chapter. This means that, within the office-seeking approach, surplus majority coalitions are as difficult to explain as minority coalitions. Surplus members are no more than 'passengers' who have to be rewarded but who contribute nothing to the success of the government. As we saw from Tables 4.2 and 4.3, surplus majority coalitions are almost as common as minority governments in Europe. Coalitions have even formed when a single party controlled a majority of

the legislative seats. Just as minority governments show a clear
tendency to occur in certain systems and not in others, so we find
that surplus majority governments occur much more often in
Finland, Italy, and The Netherlands, which between them account
for 39 of the 46 surplus majority coalitions referred to in Table
4.3. We also note that Finland and Italy are systems in which
both minority governments and surplus majority governments are
relatively common.

One rather untypical circumstance in which the need for
'surplus' majority governments arises is when special legislative
majorities are needed to enact particular constitutional amendments, a situation that has arisen recently on several occasions in
Belgium, for example. In such cases what happens is that the
winning post is moved so that what is needed for effective
government is not the simple majority of 50 per cent + 1 but
rather some larger, qualified majority that determines effective
control over the legislature on salient issues.

Another situation in which it has been suggested that surplus
majority governments are likely to form is when party discipline
is low, so that party leaders cannot be certain, for key votes, that
they will be able to deliver the full seat total won by the party at
the preceding election. In this case, surplus majorities represent
'insurance' against unauthorized defections by factions of un-
disciplined parties. We can think of what happens in this case as
party strategists unofficially moving the winning post a bit further
down the road, so as to include a few extra seats for insurance
purposes. This type of explanation is the equivalent of the 'almost
winning' explanation of minority governments. We might think
of it as the 'not really surplus' explanation of surplus majority
governments, based on a redefinition of the majority that is 'really'
needed in a particular circumstance. Empirical evaluation of such
propositions can be handled, as Taylor and Laver suggested, by
progressively increasing the size of the winning threshold to
determine empirically the winning threshold in any given system
that is most useful in predicting actual government formations.[26]

To 'explanations' such as these we may add a series of *ad
hoc* criteria that have been used to explain surplus majority
governments, each based on the notion that minimal winning
coalitions are in some senses a norm from which other types of
coalition deviate. Such criteria typically boil down, in some form

or other, to the assumption of a need that is perceived in the political system as a whole for a government of national unity. This, indeed, is almost certainly the explanation for most of the surplus coalitions which formed in the immediate post-war period and included a majority party among other members. The value of 'national unity' was seen in this period by all, including the party with a majority of seats, to override the advantages of single-party majority government. Yet while more recent economic crises have provoked similar calls for governments of national unity, almost none have formed. Indeed, for all of the rhetoric about the need for a policy consensus that tends to emerge at times of economic crisis, governments of national unity are conspicuous by their absence.

What is quite clear from all of this is that the need for special majorities, the lack of party discipline, or the desire to form a government of national unity cannot explain the formation of many of the surplus majority governments which occur in reality, the incidence of which is summarized in Tables 4.2 and 4.3. Some of the best known surplus majority governments in recent times, for example, the series of *pentapartito* coalitions in Italy, cannot plausibly be accounted for in this way. The first of the Italian *pentapartito* governments was formed in 1981, on the basis of a legislative seat distribution generated by the 1979 election. This coalition's membership is summarized in Table 4.6. It can immediately be seen that this coalition carries three 'passengers', the PSDI, PRI and PLI, none of whose seats are needed for a legislative majority. Yet this *pentapartito* coalition formed, fell, and re-formed several times in the period after 1981, becoming a firm fixture on the Italian political scene in the process. It was not justified in terms of any particular crises facing the Italian state at the time that generated a need for national unity, nor in terms of particular constitutional amendments or particular circumstances of party disunity.

Coalitions such as this, as Tables 4.2 and 4.3 show, are quite common. The most satisfactory theoretical interpretation of them is to take policy into account. After all, if politicians are concerned only with policy outputs, then those in government have nothing to lose by allowing additional members into the cabinet. Whereas for office-seekers the fixed stock of trophies represented by the set of cabinet portfolios must be spread more thinly, the more

TABLE 4.6. *Pentapartito* coalition in Italy, June 1981

Party	No. of seats
DC	262
PSDI	20
PRI	16
PSI	62
PLI	9
TOTAL	369
MAJORITY THRESHOLD	315

parties share the government, it is certainly not the case for policy-seekers that there is in some sense less policy to go round, the more parties there are in government. (It may, of course, be more difficult to agree on policies if there are more parties in the cabinet but that is another matter.) In the specific case of the Italian *pentapartito* coalition we note that two of the three 'passengers', the PSDI and the PRI, are ideologically located between the two parties, the PSI and the DC, whose legislative seats are essential to the coalition's majority. If the two key coalition partners are motivated exclusively by policy, then they lose little by allowing at least the PSDI and PRI on board, even as passengers.

When politicians are motivated solely by policy, therefore, there is no reason whatsoever why the process of coalition formation should exclude parties whose legislative seats are not essential to the government's majority, provided that the policy preferences of such 'passengers' are compatible with those of other government members. This general conclusion can be elaborated by building upon the ideas of Luebbert, who offers one of the few comprehensive theoretical accounts of surplus majority government to be found in the literature.[27] He argues that surplus majority governments are more likely in competitive party systems (and he places Ireland, Israel, Germany, Belgium, and The Netherlands in this category) which are 'dominated' by a single party. 'A dominated system is one in which party leaders assume that no majority government is possible in the foreseeable future that excludes a particular party.'[28] The particular case that Luebbert elaborates is Israel, where the dominant position of the Labour Party until 1974 made it an almost inevitable member of all governments. The reason why dominated party systems generate surplus majority governments, according to Luebbert, is that the all-powerful dominant party has an incentive to add surplus members to the coalition in order to protect itself from 'blackmail' by much less powerful coalition partners.

A minimum-winning government would contain no excess parties, and the withdrawal of one party would bring down the government. This situation permits of a kind of blackmail of the dominant party . . . for a party can threaten to leave the government at will, and thus compel the dominant party to choose between making concessions or renegotiating the entire government agreement. The leaders of the dominant party can avoid this dilemma if they can form a government that includes one or more unnecessary parties, none of which can bring down the government by itself.[29]

The extent to which this rather neat argument holds together depends largely upon the empirical validity of the premise that a surplus majority government is not harmed by the withdrawal of a non-pivotal actor. This is by no means necessarily true. Once a government has formed it may well be the case that constitutional provisions and widely accepted norms dictate that the withdrawal of any member, pivotal or not, requires a full-scale government resignation. To return to the Italian example, it has traditionally been the case that any change in government membership, even if this does not threaten the legislative majority of the executive, requires the government to resign and re-form. This process obviously imposes costs upon the government, the very costs that Luebbert alleges the formation of surplus majority coalitions allows the dominant party to avoid. In November 1987, for example, the *pentapartito* coalition that was at that stage led by Goria fell as a result of the withdrawal of the tiny PLI, a party that was in no sense necessary to the government's majority. But the constitutional norms that apply in the Italian case required that the government resign, even though the same government was formed once again within days, by the same five parties and under the same Prime Minister. Even passengers, therefore, can inflict wounds upon surplus majority cabinets, contrary to Luebbert's assertion.

If we shift the locus of the argument to the point at which the coalition is formed, however, we can make the case rather more plausible. If a dominant party deals simultaneously with a cluster of less powerful 'other' parties, offering each of them a place at the cabinet table, then none is able to twist the dominant party's arm in the negotiations that precede government formation since none is essential to the proposed government's majority in the investiture debate. Dumping an awkward passenger by the side of the tracks in the run-up to the investiture debate presumably has few costs for the dominant party and it may thus be useful for it to keep a number of passengers on board to enable this to be done. Dumping the same passenger after the government has formally taken office is another matter altogether and may impose far higher costs on the dominant party.

The second key element in Luebbert's argument concerns why it is that a particular party might be seen by the others to be dominant in the first place. One of the most obvious reasons for this involves the constellation of party policies. If we ignore policy motivations entirely, then even a party with 49 per cent of the seats is not dominant if it faces several other parties which hold 51 per cent of the seats between them. There is nothing to prevent the other parties from ganging up and keeping the dominant party out of office on a more or less permanent basis. Once we take policy into consideration, however, as we saw in the discussion of minority governments, certain parties at the 'centre' of the policy system can prove very difficult indeed to keep out of office. Luebbert himself sees policy position as part of the definition of a dominant party and argues that 'if the dominant party has partners on opposite sides of it on the same [policy] dimensions . . . then these flank parties tend to balance each other out, as neither can get what it wants without the dominant party's support . . . the result is not much removed from what would occur in a government consisting only of the dominant party.'[30]

It may seem rather surprising that Luebbert predicts surplus majority governments on the basis of more or less the same argument that the notion of policy viability predicts single-party minority governments—namely, the exploitation of a central or dominant bargaining position which emerges on the basis of the particular configuration of policy preferences. But it should be remembered that there are some systems, such as Italy and Finland, in which both minority governments and surplus majority governments are common. Thus it may be the case that the same basic processes generate both of these 'departures' from minimal winning status. The key difference between Luebbert's account and the account based upon the notion of policy viability concerns the policy influence of the opposition, the very influence emphasized by Strom in his account of minority governments. Luebbert is very firm on this: 'The first and essential point to appreciate is that in a dominated system the only opportunity a party has for influencing public policy is by participation in a coalition.'[31] The notion of policy viability, in contrast, sees opposition parties as being able to influence a minority cabinet from the outside by threatening it with legislative defeat. There is no reason at all, in terms of the notion of policy viability, why a dominant party would not take a number of additional parties on board and form a surplus majority government. The viability criterion, which to be sure implies that minority governments can be viable, does not in any sense imply that governments will be minimally viable in the sense that they carry no passengers. Indeed, both accounts of government formation concentrate on the role of pivotal actors which are almost certain to be in government. Beyond this, it might well be the case that it makes little difference whether some of the other, much less powerful, actors are in or out of office. They are, after all, equally weak whether they are in or out of office. In this important sense, minority and surplus majority governments are two sides of the same coin and both may be more likely to occur when there is a single dominant party.

SUMMARY AND CONCLUSIONS: WHERE *IS* THAT WINNING POST?

The central purpose of this chapter has been to argue, on the basis of a brief exploration of the processes that lead to the formation of minority or surplus majority governments, that there is nothing magic about a legislative majority. We have seen, both in theory and in practice, that executives can sustain themselves if their members do not control a legislative majority. We have seen, both in theory and in practice, that executives may add surplus members over and above those needed to control a legislative majority. In this sense there is no single winning post that is applicable to all systems and in all circumstances. Despite this, as we shall see in the next chapter, many theories do indeed give a fundamental role to the majority winning criterion, while many empirical accounts persist in treating minority governments as pathologies or deviations. Theories which impose the majority criterion as the be-all and end-all of winning, however, consign themselves, as a quick glance at Table 4.2 will confirm, to no better than about a 40 per cent success rate when they set out to predict which governments will actually form.

The obsession with the majority winning criterion results from giving far too little attention to the precise link between legislature and executive. Since a government must be able to survive key votes in the legislature, a particular legislative party or parties may occupy a pivotal role in its fortunes. This pivotal role, however, is exercised *in the legislature*, not the executive. And such a party will be pivotal in the legislature, whether or not it is a member of the executive coalition. In this important sense, *it does not matter whether or not the pivotal party is in government*. Even if it is in opposition, the fate of the government remains in its hands. This means that a pivotal party can beat all others as a member of a minority government. It also means that it has little to fear, in policy terms, by bringing others into government with it, if this is indicated for some reason or another.

When all is said and done there is one solid piece of ground that we do always find beneath our feet. This is that a coalition executive is winning as long as it is not losing. And it cannot lose as long as it cannot be beaten in a key vote in the legislature. The effective location of the winning post at any given time thus depends upon the constellation of policy preferences of the politicians who among them form the legislature.

5

Who Gets In?

The Membership of Government Coalitions in Western Europe

INTRODUCTION

Attempts to explain which parties will succeed in getting into the government have been at the heart of most accounts of coalition bargaining. Most early coalition theorists concerned themselves with predicting the membership of coalition cabinets, while most early empirical analyses of coalition set out to test these predictions. While we have argued throughout this book that there is much more to the politics of coalition than government membership, there can be no doubt that this is an interesting and important matter. Those who argue, for example, that proportional representation electoral systems and coalition government undermine democracy by taking the choice of government away from the electorate and giving it to politicians in smoke-filled rooms, do so because they presume that the membership of coalition cabinets in some sense does not reflect the wishes of the electorate. There can be no doubt at all that the government formation process, which begins with a particular election result that leaves open many coalition possibilities and ends with the formation of a government comprising a particular combination of parties, is one of the fundamental processes of European parliamentary democracy. Understanding how a given election result leads to a given government is, when all is said and done, simply one of the most important substantive projects in political science.

The membership of coalition cabinets is also important from a scientific point of view, however. Coalition theories typically make unambiguous predictions that the coalition which forms will be one of a limited number contained in a particular 'solution set'. When the theory comes up with a solution set very much smaller than the universe of all coalitions that are arithmetically possible (and this is typically the case), then the theory is making a worthwhile prediction that can be compared in a relatively straightforward manner with the coalition which actually forms. This opens up the possibility of a 'scientific' evaluation of coalition theories in a manner that is not too frequently encountered in other fields of social 'science'.

We should not get too bowled over by the possibility of 'testing' coalition theories on data from European coalition governments, however. As we will argue in Chapter 8, coalition bargaining in Europe is often constrained by a wide range of institutional and behavioural factors. As a consequence, it is simply not the case that all arithmetically possible coalition cabinets may form. Some are likely to be ruled out quite categorically by these external constraints on bargaining. Thus, if a party formally binds itself in some way not to go into any coalition cabinet (as the Irish Labour Party did just before the 1987 election), then should we consider coalitions which include that party in our evaluation of a particular set of predictions, when we know full well that such coalitions are politically inconceivable? Coalition bargaining in Europe, in short, does not take place in the sterile conditions of a laboratory; it takes place in the dirt of a real political world in which all things are never equal. This means that we should not expect too much from the confrontation between theories that deal with coalition formation and the formation of real government coalitions in Western Europe. Such a confrontation is far more productive if it is seen as a heuristic exercise rather than as a scientific test. Theories of coalition formation have much to add to our understanding of the politics of coalition in Europe, while the reality of European coalition cabinets provides an interpretative challenge to coalition theories that could otherwise be arid and irrelevant. Thus, while we do not attempt to 'test' theories of coalition formation in the discussions that follow, we do set out to juxtapose the theory and the reality of coalition bargaining in an attempt to expand our appreciation of both.

This book is organized around the idea that theories which deal with coalition formation can be divided into two broad types, depending upon the assumptions that they make about what motivates the actors as they bargain. In the first place there are 'office-seeking' theories; in the second place there are 'policy-seeking' theories. Among office-seeking theories there are those that are utterly policy blind in the sense that they take no account whatsoever of the policy positions of the various actors. There are also, however, theories that do take account of policy in order to reduce the range of bargaining possibilities that are evaluated, but which maintain as a fundamental assumption the notion that politicians are motivated above all else by a desire to get into office. As we saw in the previous chapter, there have also recently been accounts of coalition bargaining that see coalition formation and electoral competition as parts of an integrated process of party competition. For these theories, coalition bargaining over policy is really to do with subsequent election campaigns. When it comes down to it, therefore, these theories are also driven by office-seeking assumptions.

We first consider interpretations of coalition formation based on office-seeking assumptions; we then consider how these have been modified to take account of the policy positions of the actors, before going on to look at interpretations of coalition formation based wholeheartedly upon the assumption that politicians are motivated above all else by the desire to have an impact on public policy.

OFFICE-SEEKING INTERPRETATIONS OF COALITION FORMATION

Policy Blind Theories

While it is important not to construct straw men out of accounts of coalition bargaining motivated solely by the desire to get into office, it is without doubt the case that the most early and influential coalition theories were 'policy blind'. Riker's classic consideration of coalition formation, *The Theory of Political Coalitions*,[1] took no account whatsoever of the policy preferences of those involved in bargaining. The result, as we have seen above, is a view of coalition bargaining as a constant sum game, a game with a fixed prize. Every bit of this prize won by one actor must be lost by another. It is not necessary to be an expert at game theory to appreciate the type of prediction that policy blind theories will make about which coalition will form. Since everything that is won by one actor must be lost by another it is unlikely, on these assumptions, that coalitions will contain members whose presence is not absolutely necessary. Any 'dummies', actors whose presence is not essential to the coalition, will be kept out, for they consume payoffs while contributing nothing. Arguing in these terms, Von Neumann and Morgenstern proposed that only 'minimal winning' coalitions will form, where a minimal winning coalition is one that is turned into a losing coalition by the subtraction of any of its members.[2]

The prediction that minimal winning coalitions will form is the most frequently cited, best known and most comprehensively tested result in coalition theory. The predictive failures of this proposition, furthermore, provide the most commonly used ammunition against the collection of formal theories taken as a whole, though this information is often misinterpreted: the level of misprediction is not nearly as serious as it might seem on the face of it. Returning to Table 4.2, it can be seen that the *prima facie* evidence is that, of the 218 governments considered, 'only' 77—a mere 35 per cent—were minimal winning. Critics such as Bogdanor, von Beyme, and Pridham cite such figures as evidence of failure, but there is another way of looking at them. Consider the results of the 1971 and 1972 general elections in The Netherlands which have contributed to this pattern of predictive success and which are reported in Table 5.1. There were 16,383 different arithmetically possible coalitions after each of these elections. Of these, 8,192 were winning. Three coalitions actually formed during this period. The first was a minimal winning combination of KVP, ARP, CHU, VVD and DS70 under Biesheuvel. The second was a short-lived minority caretaker government, also under Biesheuvel, comprising the above parties minus DS70. The third was a surplus majority government under Den Uyl, comprising PvdA, KVP, ARP, PPR, and DS70. The 'success rate' of the minimal winning theory, measured very crudely, might seem to be one out of three: 33 per cent. On the other hand, for a theory to make a correct prediction it must pick the right coalition out of 16,383 possibilities. To succeed in doing this once in three trials is by no means a poor achievement.

TABLE 5.1. Elections to the *Tweede Kamer* in The Netherlands, 1971–1972

Party	No. of seats	
	1971	*1972*
KVP	35	27
PPR	2	7
ARP	13	14
CHU	10	7
SGP	3	3
GPV	2	2
PvdA	39	43
CPN	6	7
PSP	2	2
DS70	8	6
VVD	16	22
BP	1	3
D66	11	6
NMP	2	1
TOTAL	150	150

Obviously, if we are to calculate how much better off we are when we use a particular theory rather than picking coalition predictions out of a hat, we must take account of how many coalitions out of the total number that can possibly form are predicted by the theory. This is the approach adopted by Taylor and Laver in their 'tests' of coalition formation theories using data from a wide range of European coalition governments.[3] They found that the minimal winning theory performed much better than picking a coalition prediction out of a hat. In very complicated bargaining situations, such as those that are often to be found in The Netherlands, Israel, or Denmark, theories which predict the precise party membership of a coalition face a pretty steep task. And, faced with such tasks, minimal winning theory does not do all that badly.

In the complicated bargaining situations generated by 'large' party systems, however, a rather unsatisfactory feature of the minimal winning approach is that there are, quite simply, many minimal winning coalitions. In an attempt to reduce the crude number of predictions, Riker suggested a much more precise approach.[4] Using the assumption that each actor expects to receive a larger share of the payoff, the greater the weight it brings to a winning coalition (a more general version of the 'proportional payoffs' norm, typically attributed to Gamson[5] and discussed in detail in Chapter 7 below), Riker predicted that the coalitions that form should be a subset of the set of *minimal* winning coalitions comprising those with the smallest total weight. These are *minimum* winning coalitions. Such coalitions, Riker argued, maximize the expectations of each coalition member. Minimum winning coalitions, sometimes called bare majority coalitions, will command the smallest seat total that is none the less larger than the winning criterion. Quite often this theory yields a unique prediction, even in quite complex bargaining situations, and it is not uncommon for the predicted coalition to control only one or two seats over a bare legislative majority.

In the real political world, however, a bare majority may not be good enough. Politicians often operate in practice with the notion of a 'working majority', a majority that holds out the prospect that the government will be able to govern over most of the expected lifetime of a legislature and thereby reduces the risk of that most unwelcome event in the life of a cabinet member, a surprise election fought on hostile territory. Members of the government are typically assumed to prefer having at least a few seats over and above the bare minimum as a cushion against accidental government defeats arising from illness, stupidity, maverick defections, and other natural or man-made disasters. (Potential mavericks on the back benches of governing parties, particularly those who have given up all hope of high office, may in contrast prefer a very tight result, since this gives them maximum leverage over the party leadership—yet another example of the intraparty conflicts of interest that can be generated by the politics of government formation.) The predicted minimum winning coalition can often be found in the grey area that is above a technical majority but short of a working majority, leaving open the possibility that such minimum winning coalitions are not seen as being effectively winning in the real political world. Unfortunately this possibility has not, to our knowledge, been subjected to systematic empirical analysis. Indeed, the general notion of the working majority has not been explored by coalition theorists to any significant extent.

Another way to reduce the number of coalition predictions that are made is to use the bargaining proposition, suggested by Leiserson.[6] This restricts the set of minimal winning coalitions by concentrating on those with the smallest number of actors. Leiserson proposed that, other things being equal, two-party coalitions are more likely to form than three-party coalitions, three-party coalitions are more likely to form than four-party coalitions, and so on. The bargaining proposition is thus based upon an additional behavioural assumption: that the smaller the number of parties in a prospective coalition, the easier they will find it to reach an agreement. The bargaining proposition tends to make fewer predictions than the minimal winning criterion but more than the minimum winning criterion, since there are typically two or three minimal winning coalitions with, say, only three members, while there tends to be only one winning coalition controlling the smallest seat total.

All three versions of policy blind coalition theory share a fundamental reliance on the minimal winning criterion; they are all, therefore, based on the idea that coalitions will shed surplus members. Notwithstanding this important similarity, it is often the case that each theory generates a different set of predictions about coalition membership in the same situation. Consider, as an example, the situation that arose in Iceland after the 1983 election. There were sixty-three possible coalitions. Of these Table 5.2 shows that there were seven minimal winning coalitions. Of these, two coalitions, each with two parties, were predicted by the bargaining proposition, while the minimum winning criterion made a unique prediction: a four-party coalition that controlled a bare majority of seats. In this case, the minimum winning coalition had the most members while one of the coalitions with the fewest members had the largest weight.

Comparative tests of the performance of these policy blind theories of coalition formation have been conducted by Browne, Taylor and Laver, and de Swaan.[7] While there has been some debate over the different techniques and methodologies employed by these researchers,[8] their general results, synthesized by Franklin and Mackie, tell the same story.[9] The minimal winning criterion

TABLE 5.2. Election results and coalition predictions in Iceland, 1983

	No. of seats
Total seats	60
Bare majority	31
Party	
Independence Party (IP)	23
Progressive Party (PP)	14
Peoples Alliance (PA)	10
Social Democrats (SD)	6
Social Democratic Federation (SDF)	4
Women's List (WL)	3
Minimal winning coalitions	
IP + PP	37
IP + PA	33
IP + SD + SDF	33
IP + SD + WL	32
PP + PA + SD + SDF	34
PP + PA + SD + WL	33
PP + PA + SDF + WL	31
Bargaining proposition	
IP + PP	37
IP + PA	33
Minimum winning	
PP + PA + SDF + WL	31

outperformed each of the others. The minimum winning criterion, by and large, did the worst of the three, with the bargaining proposition somewhere in between.

While these tests show us that the best policy blind theory, minimal winning theory, is more often wrong than right about which coalition will form (making correct predictions in about 40 per cent of all situations in which no party has a legislative majority), it does very much better than we would do by picking coalitions out of a hat. If you were about to bet a substantial sum of money on which coalition would form after a particular election result and had no information to go on other than the distribution of seats among the parties, then you would be well advised to bet only on minimal winning coalitions. This shows us that, even if it does not tell us everything that we would like to know about the process of coalition formation, the minimal winning approach does add significantly to our understanding of what is going on.

Policy as a Means to Simplify Office-Seeking Bargaining

Soon after the appearance of the first policy blind coalition theories, attempts were made to build a role for party policy into accounts of coalition bargaining. The approach that was initially adopted was to treat party policy as another way to cut down the number of predictions made by constant sum coalition theories. Policy was not treated as the motivating force behind the entire bargaining process; rather, one or two prospective minimal winning coalitions were selected as being particularly likely to form as a result of the policy compatibility of their members. Policy compatibility was treated, in short, as another type of bargaining proposition. Just as it was assumed to be easier to forge a coalition agreement between fewer rather than more parties, so it was assumed to be easier to do so between parties closer to each other, rather than farther apart, in terms of policy.

The authors whose work is most frequently cited to illustrate policy based coalition theory include Leiserson, Axelrod, and de Swaan.[10] De Swaan in particular does place policy-seeking motivations at the centre of his set of assumptions about coalition formation, and we will therefore return to his work later. Axelrod and Leiserson, however, are more inclined to see policy compatibility as an aid to bargaining while at the same time retaining a strong implicit attachment to the assumption that office-seeking is the overriding motivation of politicians. Axelrod's 'minimal connected winning' (MCW) theory deals with party policy in terms of a single dimension of ideology and predicts that the coalitions that form will be ideologically 'connected' in the sense that all members of the coalition will be adjacent to each other on this dimension. It predicts that coalitions will be 'minimal connected winning' in the sense that the loss of a member renders the coalition either no longer winning or no longer connected. The approach is based upon general behavioural assumptions, which have recently been challenged, about the role of 'conflict of interest' within coalitions. These imply that prospective coalitions with a lower internal conflict of interest will find it easier both to form and to stay formed and will therefore be preferred to others by each of the members.

TABLE 5.3. Distribution of legislative seats, Italy, 1972

Party	Seats	MCWs	Actual coalition members				
			1	2	3	4	5
L Communists (PCI)	179						
↑ Socialists (PSI)	61	x			x	x	
│ Social Democrats (PSDI)	29	x x		x	x	x	
│ Republicans (PRI)	15	x x			x		x
│ Christian Democrats (DC)	267	x x x	x	x	x	x	x
↓ Liberals (PLI)	20	x x		x			
R Neofascists (MSI)	56	x					
TOTAL	630		267	316	372	357	282

The general ideas behind MCW theory are illustrated in Table 5.3, which shows the bargaining situation following the 1972 election in Italy, with the parties arranged from top to bottom in a left–right ordering. Of 127 different coalitions that could conceivably have formed, there were three MCW coalitions. Out of the five governments which did in fact form, one was an MCW coalition: a success rate of 20 per cent. Making random predictions, picking three coalitions out of a possible 127 over five trials would have yielded a success rate of just under 12 per cent. In this instance, the MCW theory does better than chance, but not spectacularly so. Overall, however, comparisons of the performance of MCW theory and minimal winning theory in predicting the membership of post-war European coalition cabinets suggest that MCW theory is superior.[11]

One reason for MCW theory's ambiguous performance in the Italian example summarized in Table 5.3 is that there is some question as to whether or not it makes sense to exclude 'dummies' from the predicted coalitions. It is quite possible for a party to contribute nothing to the legislative majority of a prospective coalition but for it to have a policy between that of two other coalition members. In that case, the dummy party's inclusion is necessary if the prospective coalition is to be connected. If politics really is one-dimensional and parties really are concerned only with policy, then there is no reason at all to exclude a party whose policy position lies between that of two coalition members. It costs nothing in policy terms and adds to the government's legislative strength, which may have some advantages. If the politics of coalition is concerned solely with the rewards of office, the possibility with which we are now concerned, then while the policy compatibility of coalition members may well be a factor simply because it makes for easier bargaining, there is still every reason to exclude a party whose votes are not essential to the government majority, even if its policies lie within the range of the coalition and thereby render it connected. The excluded party adds nothing to the prospective coalition except bargaining complexity and another demand for a share of the fixed set of office payoffs. If both office and policy payoffs are valued at the same time, then it is again the case that a dummy party adds to the overall demand for office payoffs while contributing nothing. It should thus be excluded, other things being equal.

In other words, the extent to which a role is predicted for non-pivotal parties within the ideological range of an otherwise connected coalition may seem to be a mere detail. In fact, the matter turns quite fundamentally upon the factors that we assume to motivate politicians. If they are motivated only by a desire to affect policy in and for itself, then coalitions should be connected, regardless of whether all parties within the ideological range of the coalition are needed for a legislative majority; 'surplus' majority coalitions will be predicted quite frequently. If there is any degree of intrinsic office motivation among those who bargain, then coalitions should not carry passengers. There will be a tendency for coalitions to drop non-essential members even if this means that they cease to be ideologically connected. Indeed, the frequency with which non-pivotal actors are retained within MCW coalitions should give us some idea, other things being equal, of the relative potency of office-seeking and policy-seeking motivations in any given political system.

In the Italian example summarized in Table 5.3, each of the hypothetical MCW coalitions contains at least one dummy, a party that does not contribute to the legislative majority of the government. The PRI was always a dummy. The PSDI was a dummy in the centre–left coalition and the PLI was a dummy in the centre–right coalition. Of the five governments that formed, two were minority administrations, though we should note that

TABLE 5.4. Frequency of coalition types, by country, 1945–1987

Country	Majority situations	Surplus not MCW	MCW not MW	MCW and MW	MW not MCW	Minority	Total
				Minority situations			
Austria	6	–	–	5	1	1	13
Belgium	1	4	–	7	8	2	22
Denmark	–	–	–	2	–	18	20
Finland	–	17	–	4	1	10	32
Germany	2	–	–	9	1	–	12
Iceland	–	2	–	6	4	2	14
Ireland	4	–	–	–	3	5	12
Italy	4	8	6	–	3	14	35
Luxemburg	–	1	–	8	1	–	10
Netherlands	–	5	3	4	2	3	17
Norway	4	–	–	3	–	8	15
Sweden	1	–	–	5	–	10	16
TOTAL	22	37	9	53	24	73	218

the minority DC–PRI government did comprise adjacent parties. Of the three majority governments that formed, one was an MCW coalition and two were MCW coalitions minus at least some dummies. The evidence from this Italian example is not clear-cut but it does hint at a tendency for dummies to be dropped from MCW coalitions, which is at least consistent with a concern on the part of Italian politicians for the rewards of office as well as for the impact that they can have on policy.

It should be clear from this illustration that the MCW and minimal winning theories are quite distinct. That is, a given coalition may be minimal winning without being MCW, it may be MCW without being minimal winning, or it may be both. Table 5.4 presents a version of the information in Table 4.2, in which surplus majority coalitions (those which are winning but not minimal) are divided into those which are MCW and those which are not. In Italy, for example, of the fourteen surplus majority coalitions that formed in situations with no majority party, only six were MCW while the other eight were not. Across all twelve countries considered in Table 5.4, however, only nine MCW coalitions formed that were not also minimal winning, suggesting strongly, on the basis of the argument above, that office-seeking motivations are significant for most European coalition actors.

A systematic re-evaluation of Axelrod's MCW theory has been undertaken by Browne, Gleiber, and Mashoba.[12] In contrast to earlier tests, these authors assess the extent to which MCW coalitions in a wide range of European contexts have lower levels of conflict of interest than non-MCW coalitions. Their results show little relationship between the level of conflict of interest within a coalition and its MCW status. These results are certainly not encouraging for MCW theory, though it should be noted that an empirical test of the internal consistency of basic assumptions is an ordeal to which few political science theories have been subjected and which many well known theories would no doubt fail. The Browne *et al.* tests do not gainsay the ability of MCW theory to predict actual governments. The possibility remains that MCW coalitions form, not because they minimize conflict of interest within the coalition (a matter to which most who cite Axelrod do not, if the truth be told, pay much attention), but for some other reason associated with policy bargaining. What the

Browne *et al.* tests show quite clearly, however, is the danger of
making exaggerated claims for the scientific status of theories in
this field that are based merely on their predictive success. These
findings raise the clear possibility that MCW theory may predict
the right coalitions for the wrong reasons. This is why we do not
present the empirical findings that we review in this book as
'tests' of coalition theories. Really testing these theories, as the
Browne *et al.* treatment of MCW theory shows, is a much more
demanding task than most authors have hitherto attempted.

When all is said and done, the key thing that must be
kept firmly in mind when evaluating this general approach to
understanding coalition formation is that, notwithstanding its
extensive reference to party policy and notwithstanding its frequent citation in the literature as an example of policy based
coalition theory, it is driven by office-seeking assumptions. The
policy positions of the parties are used to provide information
about the likely outcome of bargaining, but only in the sense that
taking account of policy positions simplifies the range of alternative
coalitions confronting office-seeking parties. If the motivations of
the actors could be ordered into some form of hierarchy, then the
desire to control office payoffs would rank above the desire to
influence policy. Party policy only comes into consideration, on
this logic, when there is a need to choose between coalitions which
are identical in terms of office-seeking assumptions.

The arrangement of bargaining criteria into hierarchical, or
lexicographic, orderings such as this was first suggested by Taylor
as a means of generating unambiguous predictions from otherwise
chaotic bargaining environments.[13] It was put forward by Taylor
as a form of bargaining proposition, a means by which the actors
could reduce bargaining costs by bringing some order to the way
in which they evaluate prospective coalitions. In effect, it is
assumed that bargaining norms may emerge under which the
parties first set out to apply one criterion, such as size, to the set
of prospective coalitions; only when this has been done do they
then set out to identify coalitions that satisfy some other criterion,
such as ideological compactness. The emergence of such norms
is implicitly assumed by Taylor rather than derived from a
sociology of the bargaining process. If it is accepted, then Taylor
shows that it is possible for bargaining equilibria to emerge in

situations where they would otherwise not exist. Taylor represented a series of existing coalition theories in these terms and this view of the coalition formation process forms the basis of the tests conducted by Taylor and Laver.[14]

Another way of arriving at a hierarchical, or lexicographic, set of bargaining criteria is to assume that politicians operate with a variety of different rules of thumb when they evaluate prospective coalition payoffs. Office-seeking politicians, for example, need not be assumed to be utterly indifferent to policy. Rather, they may be assumed to be 'motivated by office above all else', to use a phrase that we have deployed time and again in this book. This might be interpreted to mean that politicians maximize their expected payoffs from office before they bring any other factor into consideration but that, once they have done this, they do take matters such as policy into account to choose between coalitions that offer identical expected office payoffs. Conversely, policy-seeking politicians may take office payoffs into account, but only to help choose between prospective coalitions with identical expected policy payoffs.

Whichever view is taken of the reasons why parties may rank different bargaining criteria in this hierarchical manner, the fact remains that the 'policy based' coalition theories of Leiserson or Axelrod are really office-seeking theories that assume that a concern for policy occupies a lower level in the decision making hierarchy. Their coalition predictions may be steered, in some situations, by policy, but in no sense is their general approach driven by policy in the manner of the theories that we will be considering at a later stage in this chapter. Before we move on to these, however, we must take time to look at a recent approach that is based on the assumption that politicians are driven above all else by the desire to gain office, but which takes policy far more seriously than hitherto since it assumes that politicians must keep an eye, when they form coalitions, on the policy positions that they will be forced to defend at the subsequent election.

Bargaining over Policy as a Form of Electoral Competition

Austen-Smith and Banks have made one of the first thoroughgoing theoretical attempts to explore the interaction between electoral

competition and coalition bargaining for parties which are concerned only instrumentally with policy.[15] In doing this, they
develop a decidedly Downsian model of party competition.

Voters are assumed to be intrinsically motivated by policy and
to act with the aim of influencing the final policy outcome of
party competition, expressed for the sake of simplicity in terms
of a single dimension of ideology. Political parties (of which
Austen-Smith and Banks consider only three) are assumed to be
concerned with their policy positions only to the extent that this
helps them to win elections by encouraging voters to support
them in a sequence of events that runs as follows.

There is an election. (While paying all due homage to chicken
and their eggs, we must start the description of what is going on
somewhere.) At this election, parties win votes (and hence seats)
on the basis of electoral policy positions. No party commands a
legislative majority, so a majority coalition must be formed. (This
is an office seeking approach, so Austen-Smith and Banks do not
consider the formation of minority governments on the basis
of the policy influence of the opposition. The longer-term
office-seeking rationality of minority governments proposed by
Strom is not considered either.) Parties bargain to form a
government, taking account of the expected eventual policy
position of the government. Since parties are not intrinsically
concerned with policy outputs, their approach to coalition policy
is determined solely by the knowledge that they will have to face
the voters at the next election. They will not want to appear to
have been powerless and ineffectual in policy terms and will
therefore fear electoral punishment if coalition policy deviates too
far from party policy.

Austen-Smith and Banks proceed by assuming that a particular
institutional norm governs the sequence of coalition bargaining.
Specifically, they assume that the largest party is first asked to
form a government; if this fails, the second largest party is asked;
and so on.[16] This assumed norm is not a bad approximation to
reality and has the vital theoretical effect that the precise outcome
of the legislative game can be clearly foreseen by voters, for a
given distribution of party weights and policy positions. The
predicted outcome, given these particular assumptions, is a
coalition between the largest and smallest parties, whatever their
policy positions.[17] The interaction between electoral behaviour

and coalition bargaining is modelled by the ingenious technique of assuming that voters can in this way forecast the coalition that results from each particular election result and can calculate back from this forecast to decide how best to cast their vote.

Accounting for the role of policy in an interactive model of electoral behaviour and coalition bargaining is an ambitious task, and vast simplifying assumptions are obviously needed to bring matters under control. In the Austen-Smith and Banks account, the parties' evaluations of future utility flows are not assumed to be discounted, either for time preference or for uncertainty, so that benefits in the future are assumed to be as valuable as benefits now, while politicians are not assumed to be averse to risk. No assumption is made about the credibility costs facing a party that changes policy positions between elections. No assumption is made about the extent to which the electoral policy position of a party at time t_2 is 'tainted' by the policy outputs of coalitions to which it has belonged at time t_1 or, indeed, by any other aspect of its prior legislative behaviour. Instead, the authors assume that voters content themselves with punishing parties when electoral promise and government output differ, regardless of who was in the government or, indeed, of anything else. All of this means that the model cannot address itself to many of the intriguing strategic dilemmas that (at least on the face of it) appear to confront parties engaged in competition with others over the long run. For example, it cannot address itself to the dilemma faced by an office-seeking party that is considering staying out of office at time t_1, paying the short-term price of opposition in order to be better placed to fight the next election from a more commanding position and hence take higher office payoffs at time t_2 and beyond.

It is not strictly fair to evaluate this particular approach in terms of the empirical accuracy of its predictions, since the concern of the authors is much more to demonstrate that theories of voting choice and coalition bargaining can be integrated than it is to predict legislative outcomes in the real world. None the less, their predictions are so categorical, at least for three-party systems, that the temptation to hold them up to the light of the real world is irresistible. We do this in Table 5.5, comparing predicted and actual coalitions for the three European cases that can most plausibly be seen as three-party coalition systems

TABLE 5.5. Austen-Smith and Banks's predictions and actual coalitions in Austria, Ireland, and West Germany

Country	Year	Predicted coalition	Actual outcome
Austria[a]	1949	ÖVP + FPÖ	ÖVP + SPÖ
	1953	ÖVP + FPÖ	ÖVP + SPÖ
	1959	ÖVP + FPÖ	ÖVP + SPÖ
	1962	ÖVP + FPÖ	ÖVP + SPÖ
	1970	SPÖ + FPÖ	SPÖ minority govt
	1983	SPÖ + FPÖ	SPÖ + FPÖ
Ireland[b]	1961	FF + Labour	FF minority govt
	1965	FF + Labour	FF minority govt
	1973	FF + Labour	FG + Labour
	1981	FF + Labour	FG + Labour
	1982(Feb)	FF + Labour	FF minority govt
	1982(Nov)	FF + Labour	FG + Labour
West Germany	1961	CDU + FDP	CDU + FDP
	1965	CDU + FDP	CDU + FDP
	1969	CDU + FDP	SPD + FDP
	1972	SPD + FDP	SPD + FDP
	1976	CDU + FDP	SPD + FDP
	1980	CDU + FDP	SPD + FDP
	1983	CDU + FDP	CDU + FDP

[a] Four parties were pivotal in 1956; the ÖVP had a majority of seats in 1966, the SFÖ had a majority of seats in 1971, 1975, and 1979.
[b] FF had a majority of seats in 1969 and 1977.

(Austria 1949–83, Ireland 1961–82, and West Germany 1961–83). As can be seen, success rates are rather low, and it is difficult to get a sense that predicted and actual coalitions are related to each other. Two of the systems, however, are probably subject to powerful side constraints on bargaining for the periods in question, a problem to which we will return in much greater detail in Chapter 8. In Ireland, the refusal of Fianna Fáil to share office with any other party confounds all predictions since, as the largest party, it is a predicted member of all coalitions. In Austria the era of 'red and black' grand coalitions, during which coalitions were not the product of bargaining in the conventional sense, continued until 1966 and was then followed by a period of single-party government. The red–black coalitions united the two main parties in the system—the Socialists and the Peoples Party—and outlasted all other 'grand coalitions' formed in the era of post-war reconstruction. In the less constrained bargaining environment that obtained in the Federal Republic of Germany between 1961 and 1983, the predictions fare far better.

We should not set too much store by these figures, however, since the Austen-Smith and Banks approach is not really concerned with predicting which coalition will actually form. Rather, it is an attempt to show some of the ways in which a theoretical elaboration of the relationship between coalition bargaining and electoral competition can transform our view of both processes. On this score it must be judged an unqualified success. Reading between the lines, the concern of the authors is more with the role of coalition bargaining as an element in the process of electoral competition than it is with the role of anticipated electoral competition in coalition bargaining. This may account for the rather degenerate 'predictions' about coalition outcomes that Austen-Smith and Banks obtain. None the less, there can be no doubt that their general approach represents a very promising potential line of enquiry.

Policy Bargaining as a Means to Hold on to the Party Leadership

Another instrumental reason for parties to bargain over policy in coalition negotiations has to do with politics within parties. The intraparty politics of coalition is the subject of the informal analysis by Luebbert that we discussed in the previous chapter in relation to both minority and surplus majority governments, and we will return to it only briefly here. None the less, it is worth emphasizing in this context that, as far as those who actually do the bargaining are concerned, Luebbert sees policy as fulfilling a decidedly instrumental role. While we assume voters, party activists, and 'the party' in a very general sense to be concerned intrinsically with policy, he in contrast assumes that

leaders are motivated above all by the desire to remain party leaders . . . They will, therefore, attempt to rest the party's attitude towards participation on preferences that produce the least disunity, so that, if they decide against participation, activists and parliamentarians will endorse this decision because of the policy concessions that would otherwise have been entailed. Or, in the case of participation, so that they will agree that the policy price paid in joining the government was not excessive.[18]

Politicians, on this analysis, also want to get into government and control cabinet portfolios: 'Typically these positions represent the pinnacle of a political career, and their attraction to men who have spent much of their lives striving for them can hardly be overestimated.'[19] But the desire of party leaders to remain party leaders dominates all else and relegates policy to very much a secondary role in the entire process of party competition. This leads Luebbert to conclude, in perhaps his most remarkable observation about coalition bargaining, (quoted in Chapter 2 but worth repeating here), that

what makes the talks so long, difficult and complex is generally not the lack of goodwill among elites, but the fact that negotiations must appear the way they do in order to satisfy the members whose orientations are still largely attuned to . . . vocal, symbolic and ideological aspects . . . It is wrong to assume that, because interparty negotiations take a long time, much is being negotiated among the parties. Most negotiation in cases of protracted government formation takes place between leaders and their followers and among rival factions within parties.[20]

Coalition bargaining, in short, may well be a show put on to impress the ideologues within a particular party, or indeed, may even be an activity that takes place between leaders and ideologues within the same party.

This view of coalition bargaining has a major impact on the type of government that Luebbert predicts will form. As we saw in Chapter 4, his analysis accommodates minority and surplus majority governments in the same terms as minimum winning coalitions. In addition, however, Luebbert argues that the coalition which forms may not always include the parties whose policy positions are closest to each other. Categorizing the differences between the policy profiles of parties into those that are divergent, those that are tangential, and those that are convergent, he argues that

it is self-evident that the leaders of the formateur's party will prefer tangential and convergent preference relationships . . . It is also reasonable to expect that a tangential preference relationship will be preferred to a convergent preference relationship. The reasoning behind this is in the simple need for leaders to preserve the distinctiveness of their parties . . . Insofar as parties who advocate the same preferences tend to compete

for the same pool of voters, cooperation based on convergent preferences . . . will enhance the competitor's image as a legitimate alternative
recipient of electoral support.[21]

Thus, relying on a view of party leaders as instrumental policy-
seekers who also have an eye on the next election, Luebbert
constructs an argument about policy based coalition bargaining
which results in the prediction that ideologically compact coalitions
may be avoided by party leaders who can find partners whose
policy concerns are neither the same as theirs nor competing with
them, but simply different. As far as we are aware, this is the
only policy driven coalition theory that does not predict ideological
compactness in coalitions.

The problem with this approach, however, as elaborated by
Luebbert, is the rather vague definition of most of the key
concepts, and in particular his rather *ad hoc* classification of
polities into those that are competitive, those that are consensual,
and so on. This makes the whole approach difficult to operationalize in a systematic and reliable manner and almost
certainly make it impossible for anyone else to reproduce. Still,
despite the fact that the empirical relevance of Luebbert's
account could have been demonstrated more conclusively and its
elaboration could have been more systematic, it does address itself
to a number of matters that have otherwise been ignored by most
coalition theorists. There is at least the hint of a concern to link
the analysis of coalition bargaining at one time to expectations
about the next election, a hint provided in the the argument that
party leaders may prefer coalition partners with policy profiles
different from their own, though this is never really developed as
a theme. More importantly, and this is Luebbert's distinctive
contribution, there is a consistent concern for the intraparty
politics of coalition. The bottom-line argument here is that the
leaders of different parties often have more in common with each
other, sharing a concern to control the spoils of office and being
prepared to sacrifice almost anything on policy in order to do so,
than they do with the ideologues in their own rank-and-file.
The claim that protracted coalition bargaining is actually about
intraparty politics is one that cannot be found elsewhere in the
theoretical literature on cabinet coalitions, almost all of which
treats parties as unitary actors.

POLICY DRIVEN THEORIES OF COALITION FORMATION

Party policy, as we have already seen, plays an important role in theoretical accounts of the formation of coalition cabinets in Western Europe. However, as we have also seen, policy is often seen as a secondary motivation in coalition bargaining, a motivation dominated by the overwhelming craving for the spoils of office that is assumed to drive most politicians to do what they do. Recently, however, interest has developed in accounts of coalition bargaining that place policy-seeking motivations at centre stage. Most of these accounts have followed in de Swaan's footsteps in retaining the implicit assumption that politicians are also concerned with office. This is manifested by a stubborn use of the majority winning criterion; indeed, some theories even retain some form of minimal winning criterion, in predictions that the smallest and most ideologically compact coalition will form, even though there can be no rationale whatsoever for predicting this as the outcome of bargaining between politicians motivated only by the desire to affect policy.

Accounts of policy driven coalition bargaining can be classified into three general types. The first type comprises analyses based on the assumption that policy bargaining can be described in terms of a single dimension of ideology. Generalizing this account to allow for more than one dimension of policy has proved to be more difficult than might have at first been expected. Of the two other general approaches, one is essentially theoretical, and has been concerned with the elaboration of a multidimensional model of coalitional behaviour; the second is essentially empirical, and has concerned itself with the use of multidimensional data on party and government policy positions to predict the formation of actual coalitions. We deal with each of these approaches in turn.

One-Dimensional Accounts of Policy Bargaining

The first thoroughgoing account of the role of policy in coalition bargaining was published by de Swaan in 1973. De Swaan retains an implicit concern with office-seeking motivations in his very clear assumption that 'an actor strives to bring about *a winning coalition in which he is included* and which he expects to adopt a policy that is as close as possible . . . to his own most preferred policy'.[22] Within this general assumption, de Swaan develops a 'closed minimal range' account of coalition formation. This is a version of minimal connected winning (MCW) theory that takes account of the actual positions (rather than just the ordering) of the parties on the policy dimension in question. The closed minimal range coalition in a given bargaining situation is the MCW coalition with the smallest ideological range. As we have just argued, this is certainly not an account of coalition bargaining that gives absolute precedence to policy motivations, otherwise it would be impossible to exclude minority governments so categorically. None the less, it is an account in which policy motivations are taken seriously, and de Swaan provides a comprehensive empirical elaboration of this approach in terms of a single dimension of ideology. While, in principle, it is not necessary to confine this analysis to a single ideological dimension, de Swaan himself makes very little attempt to develop a multi-dimensional account in his detailed exposition.

The one-dimensional theory of coalition bargaining predicts a more or less dictatorial role for the party that controls the median legislator, an argument that we elaborated in the previous chapter when discussing the policy viability of minority governments. The party controlling the median legislator can form a policy viable minority government, however many (or few) seats it controls. Indeed, it can do this, in the limiting case, even if it comprises only a single legislator. Consequently, the party in this position is effectively a dictator on policy. It makes no difference whether the core party governs alone, in a minority coalition, in a minimal winning coalition, in a surplus majority coalition, or even in a grand coalition. It makes no difference if it goes off on holiday to Bermuda and sits on the beach getting a suntan. If we confine ourselves to one-dimensional accounts of coalition bargaining, then the core position of the party controlling the median legislator implies that its policies should be enacted whatever it does.

The powerful role of the party with the median legislator is illustrated by the situation in Denmark after the 1966 election, as set out in Table 5.6. This election left the Social Democrats in a very strong position. The table orders the parties, from top to bottom, according to their position on the left–right scale. Of

TABLE 5.6. One-dimensional view of Danish party system, 1966

	Party	No. of seats
L	Socialist People's Party (SFP)	20
	Social Democrats (SD)	69
	Radical Liberals (RV)	13
	Liberals (V)	34
R	Christian People's Party (KFP)	35
	Others	8
	TOTAL	179

the 179 legislators, the eight 'others' included four (representing the Faeroe Islands and Greenland) who could not be classified in straightforward left–right terms. The party which controlled the median legislator of the remaining 175, the 86th legislator on the left-right scale, would be in the core position. In 1966, this position was occupied by the Social Democrats. There could be no majority, either on the right or on the left, that could find a policy position to beat that of the Social Democrats. The only way the Social Democrats could be beaten by a vote on an issue located on the left–right dimension would be as a result of an unholy alliance of right and left. Furthermore, even if this had happened, it is very likely that this alliance would have been forced to agree upon a policy position very close to that of the Social Democrats.

It appears, then, that the Social Democrats should have been able to get their way in or out of government, so that other parties would gain nothing by excluding them. If the situation was entirely one-dimensional, furthermore, the Social Democrats were effectively dictators and need include no other party in the government. They could form a policy viable minority government on their own. As it happens, a single-party minority Social Democrat government was formed after this election, even though the Social Democrats controlled only 69 of the 179 seats. This instance was the only time over the post-war period, however, when the Social Democrats occupied the median position on the left–right scale in Denmark. In general, the Radical Liberals (RV) or, after 1977, the Centre Democrats (CD) occupied this position.

In only three of the nineteen governments which formed when either the RV or CD accepted did the small median party formally belong to the government. However, in another six cases, the median party lent explicit support to a minority government, usually a one-party Social Democrat government.

TABLE 5.7. *Typology of European coalition systems, 1945–1987*

Country	Frequency of govt types			No. of non-majority situations	Average effective number of parties	System type
	Single-party majority	Median party included	Largest party included			
Austria	6	5	7	7	2.2	Bipolar
Germany	2	9	6	10	2.8	Bipolar
Ireland	4	3	3	8	2.7	Unipolar
Norway	4	10	4	11	3.2	Unipolar
Sweden	1	14	12	15	3.2	Unipolar
Luxemburg	–	9	9	10	3.4	Unipolar
Iceland	–	10	11	14	3.8	Unipolar
Italy	4	31	31	31	3.4	Multipolar
Belgium	1	16	19	21	4.5	Multipolar
Netherlands	–	17	17	17	4.6	Multipolar
Denmark	–	10	13	20	4.8	Multipolar
Finland	–	31	30	32	5.2	Multipolar
TOTAL	22	165	162	196		

The role in coalition bargaining of the party controlling the median legislator on the left–right scale is summarized in Table 5.7, which ranks parties according to the 'size' of their party system and lists the number of times over the post-war period that the median party belonged to or supported the governing coalition in each of the systems under consideration. Over 80 per cent of the coalitions formed either contained the median party on the left–right scale or were supported by it, which implies that a single left–right scale does indeed give us considerable analytical leverage in explaining coalition formation in these systems. This suggests that one-dimensional representations of coalition bargaining capture many important elements of government formation. In our subsequent discussions we therefore classify bargaining systems according to the pattern of one-dimensional coalition bargaining that they appear to exhibit.

Bipolar systems (Austria, Germany)   Both Austria and Germany are effectively 'two-and-a-half' party systems with two large parties and a much smaller one which may nevertheless hold the balance of power. This tends to lead to a situation in which governments swing from one 'pole' to the other. In Austria (as may be seen in Appendix B) it is usual to rank the parties on the left–right scale from the Socialists (SPÖ) through the People's Party (ÖVP) to the Freedom Party (FPÖ). Until 1970, the median ÖVP belonged to the Red–Black coalition (SPÖ, ÖVP). In 1970, however, the SPÖ formed a minority government with the support of the FPÖ, excluding the median ÖVP. The SPÖ won a majority of seats at each of the next three elections and was thus the median party. It lost its majority in 1983 and this time went into alliance with the FPÖ.

There is some dispute as to the left–right ranking of the main parties in West Germany (see Appendix B). If we follow the scales proposed by Inglehart and Klingemann, Sani and Sartori, or Castles and Mair, however, we rank the three main parties from left to right in the order: Social Democrats (SPD); Free Democrats (FPD); Christian Democrats (CDU/CSU). Until 1965, either the FPD or the CDU/CSU controlled the median legislator and the median party belonged to each government. In 1966 a 'grand coalition' of the SPD and CDU/CSU was formed that excluded the median FPD, but all subsequent coalitions in Germany have included the median party.

Unipolar systems (Luxemburg, Ireland, Iceland, Norway, Denmark 1945–71, Sweden)   Unipolar systems are characterized by a single dominant party that confronts a string of much weaker opponents. There is an important distinction to be made, however, between systems in which the dominant party is located at the median position and those in which it is in an off-centre position, away from the median.

In Luxemburg, for example, Appendix B shows the parties to be ranked by Dodd and Morgan from left to right as follows: Communists (KPL); Socialists (LSAP); Christian Socials (CSV); and Democratic Party (DP). The large CSV has been able to exploit its median position by playing off the LSAP against the DP and has, as a consequence, been in every post-war coalition in Luxemburg, bar one. In Ireland, Fianna Fáil has been in the median position, if a single left–right scale is used, between

Labour on the left and Fine Gael on the right. This has enabled Fianna Fáil to form several single-party minority governments, including the one described in detail in the opening pages of this book. None the less, a Fine Gael–Labour coalition has been formed on several occasions, thus excluding the median party on the left–right scale.

The party systems of Norway, Sweden, and Denmark are each characterized by the dominance of a large social democratic party confronting a collection of smaller bourgeois opponents. In Norway, the Labour Party (NA) faced four small right-wing parties for most of the post-war period and was in the median position until 1965. At the election in that year, the Liberal Party (Venstre) gained enough seats to occupy the median position and a right-wing coalition formed, persisting until 1973 and re-forming after the 1981 election. Similarly, the Social Democratic Party in Sweden (SD) has faced three moderate-sized bourgeois parties on the right and a small Communist party on the left. The Agrarian (renamed the Centre) Party has occupied the median position after about half of the elections and, on these occasions, has formed a coalition either with the SD (in 1951, 1952, and 1956) or with the parties on the right (in 1976 and 1979). In both Norway and Sweden the high frequency of minority governments, reported in Table 5.4, can be interpreted in terms of the positioning of the Social Democrats at the median of the left–right scale. This gives the median party the ability to control policy outputs, whether or not it has been able to form a majority coalition.

The situation in Iceland is slightly different, with a large right-wing party, the Independence Party (IP) confronting a number of smaller and more left-wing rivals. As Appendix B shows, it is usual to rank the four parties on a left–right scale as follows: People's Alliance (PA); Social Democratic Party (SDP); Progressive Party (PP); and Independence Party (IP). The IP has always been the largest, while the PP occupies the median position. The median party has been in government except for the period 1959–71, when a coalition of the SDP and IP formed. While the four coalitions in this period were minimal winning, they were not minimal connected winning. However, Grímsson and Paloheimo have suggested that support or opposition to NATO was relevant at that time, and that the SDP and IP were united in their support for NATO.[23] Thus a second policy dimension must be introduced in order to account for a considerable proportion of coalition governments in Iceland.

Denmark in the period up to 1971 had a political structure which appears similar to those of Norway and Sweden, with a Social Democratic party (SD) facing three or four small right-wing parties—the Radical Liberals (RV), the Agrarian Liberals (V), the Conservatives (KF), and the Justice Party (DRF)—with the Communist Party (DKP) and the Socialist People's Party (SF) on the left. Until 1960 the RV was in the median position, though it was only formally in the government on one occasion—with the Social Democrats. It did, however, support four other minority governments. In 1960 the Socialist People's Party gained eleven seats and the median position moved to the Social Democrats, who formed a minority government, first with the radicals and then alone, from 1964 until 1968. In later elections, the median position has been occupied by the Radical Liberals or by the small Centre Democrat Party that made its appearance in 1973 (see Appendix A).

Multipolar systems (Denmark after 1971, The Netherlands, Belgium, Finland, Italy) Coalition bargaining in these systems is much more complex, a product of their larger and more intricate party systems. We measure the effective 'size' of the party system, for a given actual number of parties, in terms of an index of the 'effective number of parties'.[24] This index is lower when a few parties control nearly all of the seats and higher when all of the parties are more evenly balanced. It thus takes account not only of the actual number of parties, but of their relative weights. Obviously, if one party controls 96 per cent of the seats and another four parties have 1 per cent each, this is much less like a 'five'-party system than one in which each party has 20 per cent of the seats. It is easy to imagine that coalition bargaining in a system with a large effective number of parties is more difficult and complex than it is in one with a smaller effective number of parties. For this reason, we identify 'large' party systems as being multipolar and expect them to generate different patterns of coalition bargaining.

In Denmark after 1971, for example, a number of new parties won parliamentary representation, and the effective number of parties in the system increased to 7.0, before falling back to about

5.5. As we noted above, the median position in Denmark is occupied by a small centre party, located between the larger Social Democrats on the left and the Liberals on the right. These larger parties jockey for control of the government, creating a strong element of bipolarity. In the other four multipolar systems that we consider, on the other hand, the largest party generally holds the median position and is thus able to control government policy. In Belgium, for example, the Christian People's Party (CVP–PSC) has been at the median except for the period 1971 to 1977, when the small Francophone Democratic Front (FDF) occupied this position.[25] The CVP–PSC was in every post-war Belgian government, save for those formed in 1946 and 1958. In The Netherlands, the Catholic People's Party (KVP)—followed by the Christian Democratic Appeal (CDA) after 1973—has occupied the median position and been in every government. In the same way, the Christian Democrats in Italy (DC) have tended to occupy the median position and have been in every government. The median position in the Finnish system is nearly always occupied by the Centre Party, although, on two occasions in 1958 when the left-wing Finnish People's Democratic Union gained sufficient seats, the median position was held by the Social Democratic Party. The only occasion in Finland when the median party was not a member of the government was for a brief period during 1972, when the Social Democratic Party formed a minority administration.

The information in Table 5.7 allows us to assess the performance of the one-dimensional model of coalition formation. The observations made above are summarized in Figure 5.1, which shows the most commonly accepted left–right scale for each country and identifies the largest and the median party in each party system.

As we have noted, in The Netherlands, Finland, and Italy, the largest party typically occupies the median position on one dimension and appears to be able to control coalition building and policy making. As we suggested, the majority status of the coalition that forms is hard to predict, and we observe that surplus majority, MCW, minimal winning, and minority governments all form in these systems. The high effective number of parties generates a complex bargaining system, with coalitions forming and re-forming frequently. We shall return to this matter in the

AUSTRIA (71%)

| 1945–75 | KPÖ | *SPÖ* | ***ÖVP*** | FP |
| 1975– | KPÖ | **SPÖ** | *ÖVP* | FPO |

GERMANY (90%)

| | *SPD* | **FPD** | *CDU/CSU* |

LUXEMBURG (90%)

| KPL | LSAP | ***CSV*** | DP |

IRELAND (40%)

| LABOUR | ***FF*** | FG |

NORWAY (94%)

| 1945–61, 1973–81 | ***LABOUR*** | LIB | Christ. | Con. |
| 1961–73 | *LABOUR* | **LIB** | Christ. | Con. |

SWEDEN (94%)

| 1951–58, 1976–82 | *SD* | **CENTRE** | LIB | CON |
| 1958–76, 1982– | ***SD*** | CENTRE | LIB | CON |

ICELAND (78%)

| PA | SDP | **PP** | *IP* |

DENMARK (60%)

| 1945–71 | SF | | *SD* | **RV** | | V | | KF | |
| 1971– | SF | DKP | *SD* | **RV** | CD | V | FRP | KF | KRF |

BELGIUM (82%)

1946–71	PCB	PSB	RW	VU	FDF	***PSC***	PRL
1971–77	PCB	PSB	RW	VU	**FDF**	*PSC*	PRL
1977–	PCB	PSB	RW	VU	FDF	***PSC***	PRL

NETHERLANDS (100%)

| 1946–77 | CPN | PvdA | D66 | ARP | ***KVP*** | CHU | VVD |
| 1977– | CPN | PvdA | D66 | | **CDA** | | VVD |

ITALY (100%)

| PCI | PSI | PSDI | PRI | ***DCI*** | PLI | MSI |

FINLAND (97%)

| SKDL | ***SD*** | ***CENTRE*** | LIB | SPP | KOK |

FIG. 5.1. One-dimensional models of coalition politics in Europe
The parties are ordered ideologically from left to right on the Figure. The largest party is identified in italic type and underlined; the party controlling the median legislator is identified in bold type. (If one party is both the largest and in control of the median legislator, it is shown in bold italic type.) The percentage of all governments which the median party either joined or supported is shown in parentheses after each country name.

following chapter when discussing the stability of coalition cabinets. Figure 5.1 also highlights the fact that in Norway and Sweden, as we have seen, small changes of electoral support have caused the median position to change from Social Democratic to Liberal or Centre Party positions, causing changes in government. In Luxemburg and Germany, the party centrally located on the single policy dimension has also tended to be in the government. In the other five systems, however, Figure 5.1 suggests that the one-dimensional representation is insufficient to provide a model of coalition formation. In Ireland, the median Fianna Fáil party has been excluded from a number of governments. Moreover, Fine Gael and Labour have been able to form relatively stable coalitions in these cases, which suggests that more than one dimension of policy is needed to capture the dynamics of the government formation process. The same possibility is suggested by the exclusion from government of the median ÖVP in Austria between 1970 and 1983, and by the exclusion of the median IP in Iceland between 1959 and 1971. In Denmark, there is general agreement that the Radical Liberals and Centre Democrats lie between the Agrarian Liberals and the Social Democrats (see Appendix B). The one-dimensional account of coalition formation suggests that these small parties should control the balance of power between the Social Democrats and the Liberals; but as we have seen, they joined or supported about half of the governments that were formed during this period. Finally, almost all accounts of Belgian politics refer to the clear need, as a result of the language question, to consider at least two policy dimensions when representing party politics. All of this suggests that a model involving more dimensions may provide further insights into the process of coalition formation in these systems. Such models are the subject of the rest of this chapter.

Coalition Formation in a Multidimensional Policy Space

Most recent theoretical work on coalition formation assumes that more than one policy dimension must be considered at the same time. Much of this work, however, has been concerned with the interpretation of legislative coalitions in the US Congress rather than government coalitions in Western Europe. This has led to a heavy emphasis on distributive 'pork barrel' policy bargaining

in which it is assumed that when legislators negotiate policy outputs with their colleagues, they are attempting, above all else, to
win specific local projects of particular benefit to their constituents.
Much less emphasis is placed in these models on the 'public
goods' aspects of policy outputs that go to all legislators, not just
to those directly involved in the deals that produce them. On top
of this, there is a major constitutional distinction between
parliamentary government as it is found in Western Europe and
legislative politics under the much more clear-cut separation of
powers found in the USA. The US executive does not, of course,
depend for its legal existence upon the support of the legislature.

Notwithstanding the special factors that condition coalition
building in the US Congress, the theory of legislative coalitions
nevertheless has the clear potential to help us understand the
politics of coalition in Europe. In the sections that follow we first
sketch the key results relating to legislative coalition building in
the USA. We look at the potential chaos in voting behaviour in
legislatures implied by the existing theories and at the structural
factors that may account for the absence of such chaos in the real
world. We then move on to elaborate the theory of government
coalition formation in multidimensional policy spaces, looking

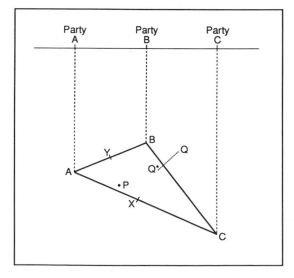

FIG. 5.2. Adding a new dimension to a hypothetical policy space

first at deductive theories. Since deductive theories remain rather intractable when several policy dimensions are salient at the same time, we turn, finally, to inductive empirical accounts of government coalition formation in multidimensional policy spaces.

Coalition Formation in Legislatures with Multidimensional Policy Spaces The backdrop to the entire theory of coalition formation in legislatures is the potential for chaos in multidimensional voting games. The central problem is stated very clearly by Keith Krehbiel: 'simply expanding the dimensionality of the choice space from one to two has profoundly disequilibriating consequences.'[26] This point is illustrated by the hypothetical example in Figure 5.2, the top half of which shows a one-dimensional representation of a three-party system in which no party wins a majority of seats. Party B controls the median legislator and, if we have no other information, we predict that it will be very powerful since it is pivotal in any majority vote on the issue. Imagine that a new policy dimension emerges. The positions of the parties on the first dimension are unchanged but the parties also adopt positions on the second dimension. This generates the two-dimensional policy space shown in the lower part of Figure 5.2. Now, no one party controls the median legislator on both dimensions. Party B retains the median legislator on the old (horizontal) dimension but party A controls the median legislator on the new (vertical) dimension. Not only does party B's dominant position evaporate but, because no single party is in a dominant position, the entire situation becomes much less stable.

Imagine that the leaders of Party B consider themselves still to be in the driving seat and propose a policy package at point B. Parties A and C not only have the arithmetical ability (which has always been there), but also, now, the policy based incentive (which has just arisen), to defeat party B's proposal. Parties A and C can easily find a policy package, say X, that they both prefer to B. Package X is closer to the preferred positions of both party A and party C than is package B; and parties A and C between them control a majority. But this is not the end of the story. Party A and party B can easily find a package, say package Y, that they both prefer to X (or, indeed, to any conceivable package that A and C can come up with that both prefer to B).

But then, of course, B and C can easily come up with a package that they prefer to Y or to any package like it (even B's preferred policy position does this).

If nothing intervenes to put the parties out of their misery, such 'voting cycles' can continue for ever. The infinite series of voting cycles that seems likely in such circumstances represents the chaos in what has become known as the chaos theorem, stated in its most elaborate form by McKelvey,[27] who proved that, if one actor could control the agenda of proposals voted on, he or she could construct a sequence of proposals that would take the outcome from any point in the policy space to almost any other point.

A useful way of looking at this potential for chaos in a legislature, and one that can be applied rather fruitfully in the European context, concerns the game-theoretic concept of the 'core'. The one-dimensional policy space described in the top part of Figure 5.2, as we have seen, leaves party B in a very strong position by virtue of the fact that it controls the median legislator. Since there is no policy proposal that can defeat a proposal to enact policy B, we say that point B is in the 'core' of the voting game. There is always a core point in a voting game defined in terms of a single dimension of policy; this is the policy position preferred by the median legislator. In the two-dimensional example in the lower half of Figure 5.2, there is no policy package that can defeat all others and therefore no core to the voting game. This is a general phenomenon and not just a special feature of a situation in which different parties control the median legislator on different dimensions. A long tradition of game-theoretic research has shown that, while majority voting always generates a core in a one-dimensional policy space, it generates a core in two dimensions only in unusual circumstances and it almost never generates a core in a policy space of more than two dimensions.[28] In simple terms, this work has proved that any policy space of more than one dimension is generically prone to voting cycles and chaos.

An important qualification should be made, however, about the degree of chaos that can occur. If we consider only proposals involving small changes in the policy packages offered by coalitions, then the only outcomes that are likely to prevail in the two-dimensional case are those within what is known as the 'Pareto set' of the parties. If, however, the proposals put forward by potential coalitions can swing outside this set then it is indeed the case that almost any outcome is possible.[29] (The Pareto set of the parties A, B, and C in Figure 5.2 is the area bounded by the triangle ABC. If a proposal is outside the Pareto set, then *all* parties would be made better off by agreeing to some proposal inside the set. Thus, in Figure 5.2, *any* policy position outside the triangle ABC is such that there is a position inside the triangle preferred by all parties. Take policy position Q, for example, outside the Pareto set. All parties prefer policy Q*, inside the set. But consider policy position P, inside the Pareto set. *Any* move from policy P will make at least one party worse off. Thus, there is *no* policy that is preferred by all parties to policy P. A similar argument can be constructed for every point inside the Pareto set.)

Assuming that proposals will not be made that make everyone worse off, then only proposals within the Pareto set need be considered. The set of policy proposals that can occur as a result of this sequence or 'cycle' of possible coalitions is known as the

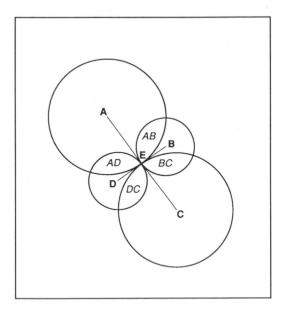

FIG. 5.3. A symmetric five-party system in a two-dimensional policy space

'cycle set'. This has been proposed as a solution to voting games when the core is empty. In Figure 5.2, for example, the cycle set is precisely the set of policy positions bounded by the triangle ABC. This simply reflects the fact that we have no reason to expect one coalition rather than another in this context. In more complex examples that we will consider below, the cycle set will be contained within the Pareto set and will reflect the bargaining strength of the parties.

In certain quite special circumstances, a two-dimensional policy space can have a core and thus allow a stable voting equilibrium, as can be seen from the hypothetical five-party system described in Figure 5.3. In this example, any three of the five parties A–E are needed to form a legislative majority and the preferred policy positions of each party are marked in bold type. The core point is the policy package preferred by party E, in the centre of the space. This arises because the other parties, A, B, C, and D are arranged 'symmetrically' around E. (Symmetry in this special sense means that E is simultaneously on the halfway points of lines drawn between A and C and between B and D). The set of policy packages that each party prefers to package E is contained within the circle of which that party is the centre; every policy package within this circle is preferred to package E by the party in question. Party E, of course, prefers no package to package E. Where two circles overlap, both of the parties in question prefer the packages inside the lens-shaped area of overlap to package E. These overlapping areas are marked in Figure 5.3 by the names of the pair of parties that prefer these packages to package E, shown in italic type. Where three circles overlap, all three of the parties in question prefer the packages in the overlapping area to package E. Since any three of the five parties can defeat any package between them, the area where three circles overlap defines a set of policy packages that can defeat package E. There is no such area in the configuration described in Figure 5.3. Hence no package can defeat package E. Hence package E is a core of the voting game. The 'cycle set' is empty. If package E is proposed, there will be no voting cycles, no chaos.

The problem, of course, is that the type of configuration described in Figure 5.3 is extremely unlikely to arise in practice. Worse, even if it does occur, it is very susceptible to any slight disturbance in the positions of the parties, as Figure 5.4 illustrates.

Figure 5.4 shows the same party system, except that Party A has changed its position slightly from position A to position a. Nothing else has changed. This small move has generated a set of policy packages, labelled *aDC* in Figure 5.4, which each of three parties prefers to package *E*. Since these parties between them control a legislative majority, they can combine to replace package *E* with a package in the area *aDC*. But this is just the start of a voting cycle. Once the symmetry conditions are no longer satisfied, the core disappears. There is no point in the space that cannot be beaten by another on the basis of a majority vote.

The equilibrium shown in Figure 5.3, therefore, is an 'unstable' equilibrium. Analogously, if you have a steady enough hand, you can balance a pencil on its point; but the very slightest disturbance of its environment brings the pencil tumbling down. What happens if the equilibrium is destroyed by such a perturbation? It can be shown that the cycle set must then be non-empty and must consist of a star-shaped figure constructed by joining the five points **A**, **B**, **C**, **D**, **E**. In practical terms, any policy point contained within this area can come into being as a viable option.

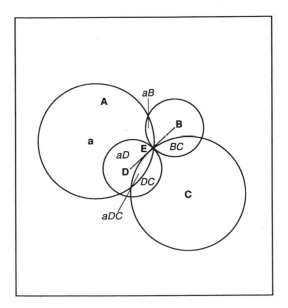

FIG. 5.4. An asymmetric five-party system in a two-dimensional policy space

And the worst is yet to come. If there are three dimensions of policy, then the cycle set comprises the entire policy space. The full force of the chaos theorem is that anything could occur. Of course, this is implausible and it is quite possible that various mechanisms will limit policy choices to those in the Pareto set.[30] Just as slight deviations from perfect symmetry seem rather plausible when we think of the real world of legislative politics, so do slight deviations from perfect unidimensionality. The instability and the possibility of voting cycles described in Figure 5.4 obtains even if the second dimension is almost insignificant. In other words, the potential for chaos exists in any policy space other than one with strictly one dimension.

To put the problem in a nutshell, if legislators value more than one dimension of policy (and it seems very likely that they will, even if only a little bit), if each legislator has one vote and casts it independently and if all decisions are made on the basis of majority voting (as the rules require in most legislatures) then the eventual outcome of their voting will be unstable, unpredictable, and susceptible to manipulation.

Most attempts to 'solve' the theoretical 'problem' of the apparent potential for legislative chaos have taken one of two general approaches. The first and most straightforward has been to incorporate into the analysis a consideration of particular legislative structures, such as the committee system,[31] or particular decision making rules, such as the amendment procedure.[32] The second and more abstract approach has been to reconsider and refine the basic assumptions upon which the chaos theorem is based, while retaining the general theory of legislative voting in a relatively 'institution free' environment. Such approaches have concentrated, for example, upon the role of uncertainty and imperfect information,[33] or upon that of party discipline.[34] Krehbiel's review[35] does such a good job of summarizing this work that we draw attention here only to the broad thrust of those results which may throw light on the politics of coalition in Europe.

Institutions and procedures can clearly make a vast contribution to imposing stability on potential legislative chaos. One of the most striking findings in this tradition was presented by Shepsle,[36] who showed that the operation of the Congressional committee system could easily impose a bargaining equilibrium upon an otherwise unstable situation. Shepsle's notion of the 'structure induced equilibrium' (SIE) has had a powerful influence on subsequent research. For Shepsle, the two key features of the role of congressional committees are their control of the legislative agenda and their specialization. Specialization means that each committee deals with only a single policy dimension. Each important policy question is first considered by a committee which considers only that question. The committee's control over the agenda means that it has the power to decide whether to recommend action on this matter to the legislature and, if so, what action to recommend. If the committee decides not to report to the legislature then the matter cannot be settled. If the committee does make a recommendation then this may be accepted or rejected but cannot be substantially modified. Any modifications to a bill can deal only with policy matters that are 'germane' to a particular committee. All of this has the effect that the key decisions are only taken on one dimension at a time and that it is not possible to trade off policy shifts on one dimension against policy shifts on another. The operation of the committee system, Shepsle argues, means that dimensions cannot be linked to each other by trade-offs; and the very important consequence of this is that the overall package of policies agreed by the legislature will be made up of the policy position of the median legislator on each dimension taken separately. In this way, the committee system can 'induce' an equilibrium where none would otherwise prevail.

This finding, and those which developed and expanded it, are clearly of great significance for the politics of coalition in Europe. As we shall see in Chapter 8, there are institutional constraints on coalition formation in all European systems. These range from investiture and dissolution procedures to electoral systems, committee systems, the need to place cabinet ministers at the head of government departments, and to many other things besides. Given the findings on the impact of the committee system in the US Congress, it is easy to see that any one of a number of constraints might have the same level of impact on a given European system, though there has not, to our knowledge, been much research on this matter.

Tackling the same general problem, others have seen the potential for chaos in policy spaces of two or more dimensions resulting from the use of the pure majority decision rule.[37] The key conclusion arising from this work is that the potential for stability depends crucially upon the particular decision rule in use and, specifically, upon the size of the 'blocking group' that can prevent the passage of a particular proposal. This has a direct bearing upon the role of committees and other institutions. Schofield sees institutions such as committees as modifying the decision rule that really operates in the system as a whole, making this rule a very much more complex one than simple majority voting by giving veto powers to quite small groups of legislators. On this view, a heavily institutionalized legislature does not really operate on the basis of simple majority decision making at all, something which is a considerable source of stability. Schofield's general argument is that 'actual political systems generally are not pure majority rule systems, but instead involve hierarchies of committees or constituencies'.[38] In this case, the number of dimensions in a policy space that can sustain a stable equilibrium in a real legislature may in practice be quite large. This is another theoretical result with profound practical consequences for the politics of coalition in Western Europe, though, once more, detailed research on the area has barely started. It is clearly the case, in Schofield's terms, that no European coalition system operates under the simple majority rule. This immediately suggests an entirely new way of looking at minority and surplus majority governments, by looking much more closely at the 'real' decision rule in operation in those systems in which such governments are endemic. More significantly, it sets the implications of Shepsle's work on structure induced equilibrium in a more general context. It suggests that the way forward in the European context is not to look at committees merely because in some general sense they might be stability inducing mechanisms, but rather to review the structural features of each political system to assess the extent to which these cause it to depart from 'pure' majority decision making. The easiest way to do this in the first instance is to look within institutions and structures for the existence of significant veto groups that comprise less than a majority of the legislature.

Overall, however, there can be no doubt that US legislative research in this tradition offers a very rich and exciting source of ideas about how best to improve our understanding of the politics of coalition in Europe. The issues raised by the possibility of applying these insights in Europe are the matters to which we now turn.

Legislative and Executive Coalitions A legislative 'coalition' is no more than a group of legislators who vote together on a particular issue. This concept of coalition here carries no connotation of permanence, of institutional status, or of any executive role whatsoever. A government coalition carries a very heavy connotation of stability, of agreement over a wide range of issues, of a formal institutional status that is only occasionally tested in the legislature, and of executive control, via cabinet portfolios, over all key policy areas. Yet, as we saw in Chapter 4, the system of parliamentary government in Europe means that executive coalitions must retain the confidence of the legislature, so legislative and executive coalitions are clearly related to each other here.

The operation of parliamentary democracy in Europe means that there is one particularly important legislative coalition: the legislative coalition that sustains an executive in office on the basis of a confidence vote. The European confidence vote might be described, in US legislative terms, as an extremely complicated omnibus proposal. If such a proposal is passed, certain legislative parties take over the executive. These parties consume all of the intrinsic benefits of office-holding, including control over a comprehensive set of patronage appointments. They control the cabinet portfolios that give sweeping *de facto* control over policy outputs, outputs that relate both to public goods and to distributive goods targeted at particular constituencies. Finally, the executive coalition of parties retains office on the basis of a policy programme. This comprises in part a programme of legislative action, in part a programme of executive action that can be reversed only by bringing down the government.

If the confidence vote passes, all of the consequences of the implicit omnibus proposal take effect. They are all, however, reversible, either as a whole (by bringing down the government) or in part (by passing specific legislation). The legislative coalition that passes the vote establishing the government is in no sense a binding agreement. A no-confidence motion may be proposed at any time. If this succeeds it has the effect, by destroying the executive coalition, of reversing the decision to establish the

government (although none of the payoffs that have been distributed in the meantime or the irreversible policy decisions that
have been implemented can, of course, be retrieved). The executive
coalition that forms as a result of the vote of confidence has a
formal constitutional status that is recognized by virtue of its
investiture by the head of state and by numerous references to
its duties and responsibilities in the constitution. Typically, not
only the Prime Minister but also the individual cabinet ministers
are appointed by the head of state, who must also accept their
resignation. Formally, therefore, the executive coalition is a
binding agreement between the parties, though there are relatively
few examples of heads of state refusing to accept resignations
when these are offered.

TABLE 5.8. Seat distribution in Denmark, 1957 and 1964

Party	No. of seats		Minimal winning coalitions	
	1957	1964	1957	1964
Communists (DKP)	6	–	SD, KF	SD, KF
Socialist People's Party (SF)	–	10	SD, V	SD, V
Social Democrats (SD)	70	76	SD, RV, DKP	SD, SF, RV
Radicals (RV)	14	10	SD, RV, KRF	V, KF, RV, SFP
Liberals (V)	45	38	V, KF, RV	
Conservatives (KF)	30	36	V, KF, DKP, DRF	
Justice Party (DRF)	9	–		
Others	1	5		
TOTAL	175	175		

Putting all of this together, we can sum up the broad differences
between the legislative coalitions studied by most formal theorists
and the executive coalitions that form the basis of most European
governments:

1. European executive coalitions are generated by a complicated
   legislative coalition formed to support the wide-ranging proposal
   that a particular government be sustained in office, with all that
   this entails.
2. Once a European executive coalition has formed, it develops
   something of a life of its own, given the constitutional requirements
   associated with its formation and dissolution, together with the fact
   that possibilities to defeat it present themselves only now and again.
3. Thus what goes on inside an executive coalition will to some extent
   be divorced from what goes on inside the legislature. Anticipations

of what goes on inside an executive coalition must clearly condition the government formation process, though research on this matter has barely begun.

The Theory of Government Coalition Formation in a Multi-dimensional Policy Space

We argued above that a legislature, operating under a system of simple majority rule in which each actor has precisely one vote, will in general exhibit no core, or stable equilibrium. In this event a form of chaos can occur, with never-ending cycles of policies being proposed and countered. If there is strong party discipline, however, chaotic voting cycles need not occur. For an illustration of this, consider Figure 5.5, which shows the location of the Danish parties in a two-dimensional policy space derived by Holmstedt and Schou from a content analysis of party manifestos.[39] The 'old left–right' dimension corresponds to the usual economic policy scale; the 'new left–right' dimension can be interpreted in terms of attitudes towards social policy and welfarism. (Table 5.8 gives the strengths of the parties in 1957 and 1964.) The position of the Justice Party (DRF) is not given in Figure 5.5, but we may estimate it to be near the positions of the KF or Venstre.

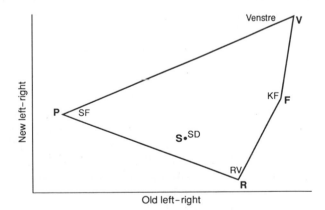

FIG. 5.5. A two-dimensional view of the Danish party system, 1964

Consider first the situation in 1964. On the first dimension, the three right-wing parties—the Radicals (RV), Liberals (Venstre),

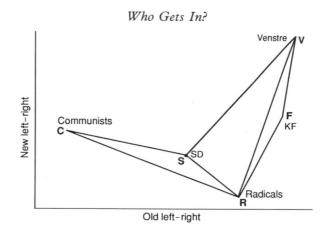

FIG. 5.6. A two-dimensional view of the Danish party system, 1957

and Conservatives (KF)—do not form a majority. Hence the Social Democrats are at a median position. On the second dimension, Venstre and the Conservatives were unable to form a majority coalition with the Socialist People's Party, which implies that the Social Democrats were at the median position on this dimension as well. Indeed, the Social Democrats are at the core of this two-dimensional voting game. To see this more vividly note that, if the three right-wing parties attempt to form a majority government excluding the Social Democrats, they need the left-wing Socialist People's Party. In their bargaining, the four parties must agree to a compromise policy within the set determined by their preferred policy positions, that is, within the area *PRVF*. This compromise set contains the preferred position of the Social Democrats (*S*). Consequently, whatever point in (*PRVF*) is chosen, the Social Democrats can persuade at least one of the prospective coalition partners that *S* is to be preferred. Thus the preferred policy position of the Social Democrats is likely to prevail. Indeed, since the Social Democrats are effectively in a position to dictate policy, they can form a policy viable minority government, which is precisely what happened in Denmark between 1964 and 1968. Note that this situation is stable, unlike the one described in Figure 5.3. Even if party policy positions and weights are perturbed slightly, the bargaining logic remains the same.

In 1957, however, the situation in Denmark was rather different, as Figure 5.6 shows. As we noted above, the Radicals were at the median position on the first dimension. The three right-wing parties between them have a majority. In bargaining among them over coalition formation, it seems reasonable to expect that a compromise policy within the set (RVF) will emerge. On the other hand, the Social Democrats can form a majority with the Communists and the Radicals and find a compromise within the set (SRC). Finally, the Social Democrats can form a majority government with Venstre and agree to a policy on the line SV. Consider any possible policy in the set (SRV). There must be a point on the line RV that is preferred by the Radical/Liberal/Conservative coalition. There must be a point on SR that is preferred by the Socialist/Social Democrat/Radical coalition and one on SV that is preferred by the Social Democrat/Liberal coalition. Thus we could predict that a coalition of Radicals, Social Democrats, and Liberals would be unstable, but that one of the three coalitions that bound the 'cycle set' (SRV) will form. In fact, a coalition of Social Democrats and Radicals with the Justice Party formed and lasted until 1960, when the Justice Party left the government. As we have seen, the Social Democrats then formed a minority government until 1968. In that year the Radical/Venstre/Conservative coalition won enough seats to form a majority government, thus unseating the Social Democrats from the core position. In general, Danish politics does indeed tend to follow a pattern of the kind outlined in these two examples, with single-party minority Social Democrat governments forming when that party is at the core of the voting game and Social Democrat/Radical coalitions alternating with Liberal/Conservative coalitions when the core of the game is empty but the cycle set is non-empty.

Extending the model of coalition formation to incorporate two policy dimensions raises some complex possibilities, however. In contrast to the one-dimensional case, there is no reason to expect that a small party at the median position will be able to dominate the political process. In fact, it has been shown by McKelvey and Schofield that, in two dimensions, only the largest party may occupy a stable core policy position;[40] when this happens, that party can be expected to control the government. The principal difference between the analyses generated by the one- and the two-dimensional models is that, in one dimension, a small party (such as the Radicals in Denmark) should be able to control policy, while with two dimensions a small party will be unable to do this and instead we will expect the process of political bargaining to be focused on the largest party when it is in the core position. When the core is empty, there are theoretical reasons to expect coalition politics to focus on the centrally located parties that bound the cycle set. But then, of course, the opportunity is opened up for the moderate-sized parties to engage in strategic behaviour or manipulation.[41] In later work, we plan to use the qualitative 'spatial' theory that we have outlined here, together with the clustering technique developed by Laver[42] and discussed below, to examine this in more detail. For the present, however, the qualitative theory provides us with additional insights into the nature of coalition bargaining and suggests some embellishments to the one-dimensional typology of bargaining systems that we proposed in the first half of this chapter.

Bipolar Systems   With only three parties in Germany and in Austria for most of the period under consideration, the core must be empty with two dimensions, except when a single party wins a majority of seats. The argument outlined above suggests that, if a second dimension becomes relevant, then coalitions excluding the 'median' party can form. Since the median party was excluded from government only once in Germany and only three times in Austria, this suggests that there is no important second policy dimension in either of these two countries.

Unipolar (Centre) Systems   As we have seen, the one-dimensional median model is satisfactory in Luxemburg, but it does not explain the exclusion of the median Fianna Fáil party from governments in Ireland. As with the hypothetical example in Figure 5.2, the cycle set in Ireland is bounded by the triangle defined by the preferred policy positions of the three main parties. This suggests that any two can form a government but, while coalitions of Fine Gael and Labour have indeed formed, coalitions of either of these parties with Fianna Fáil have never been observed. Possibly a still more complex spatial representation of the Irish case is needed. More plausibly, the refusal of Fianna Fáil to join coalitions can be seen as the product of a longer-term strategic calculation by the party: that its electoral prospects of forming single-party majority governments—a position to which it is always quite close—are enhanced by going into opposition rather than by doing deals with the other parties.

Unipolar (Off-Centre) Systems As we noted above, the one-dimensional median model works well in Norway and Sweden. In Denmark, as the examples in Figures 5.5 and 5.6 indicate, we suppose the Social Democrats to be at the core position in a two-dimensional policy space in the mid-1960s, coalition politics at other times being structured by the precise configuration of the cycle set. In Iceland, with three main parties in a two-dimensional policy space, the cycle set is the full triangle bounded by their preferred policy positions. Indeed, coalitions containing each combination of these parties have formed in the past.

Multipolar Systems The one-dimensional median model seems to work well in Finland. With highly fragmented party systems, however, it is likely that a large centre party would constitute the core of the voting game even when there are two policy dimensions. While many different types of coalition may form, the centre party may dominate these in the way that we have described. Belgium is an interesting case in point. From 1961 to 1981, as a result of increasing fragmentation of the party system and the increasing salience of the language issue, the Christian Social Party was probably at the core position.[43] Before and after that time, only three parties were significant. In the period before 1961, the formation of a Socialist/Liberal coalition highlights the importance of the second policy dimension. After 1981, with the decreasing salience of the language issue, the Christian Social Party was at the median position in what might be considered to be a one-dimensional policy domain.

Although we suggested previously that both Italy and The Netherlands were systems with only one key policy dimension, it is conceivable that a second dimension is relevant in each case.[44] In both countries, however, the largest party (the DC in Italy and the KVP/CDA in The Netherlands) holds a moderate position on both dimensions and is surrounded by a number of smaller parties. Just as with Denmark in the 1960s, we may infer that these large parties dominate the political process. In fact, as Table

5.7 shows, they have belonged to every government coalition. In a two-dimensional policy space there is no reason to expect coalitions that are minimal connected winning in the first dimension. This provides some explanation for the fact, noted in Table 5.4, that non-MCW coalitions tend to occur in these countries.

TABLE 5.9. *Typology of coalition systems in terms of multidimensional policy space*

Type of system	Unidimensional median	Multidimensional core
Bipolar	Austria (typically ÖVP median) Germany (typically FDP median)	
Unipolar (centre)	Luxemburg (typically CSV median)	Ireland (no core)
Unipolar (off-centre)	Norway (Labour or Liberal median) Sweden (SD or Centre median)	Denmark (1960s) (SD core) Denmark (else) (No core; cycle set generated by SD against right-wing parties) Iceland (No core; cycle set generated by three parties)
Multipolar	Finland (SD or Centre median) Belgium (1981 on) (PSC median)	Italy (DC core) Netherlands (KVP or CDA core) Belgium (1946–61) (No core; cycle set generated by PSC, PSB, PRL) Belgium (1961–81) (PSC core)

Table 5.9 summarizes the inferences that we have drawn about the effect of the number of dimensions in the policy space on the nature of coalition bargaining in each of the systems under consideration. This typology is quite speculative, and its main purpose is to suggest ways in which the entire structure of the

coalition game might be affected by broad qualitative features of the bargaining environment. While, as we have seen, the basic decision rule may be modified by changes in the distribution of party weights and policy positions, many legislative situations may in practice be sufficiently stable for individual election results to have little impact in reallocating bargaining power. All sorts of norms and rules governing the business of coalition building may become established in stable bargaining environments such as these. In multipolar systems, in contrast, the distribution of *de facto* bargaining power is very sensitive to things that change from election to election, such as the seat distribution in the legislature and the constellation of policy positions. In these systems, conventional norms of political behaviour will be much less likely to emerge. In multipolar systems that are uni-dimensional, there will be a core party that can dominate the bargaining process. It is only in systems in which more than one dimension of policy is salient that the instability predicted by a number of the traditional theories of coalition formation might emerge.

As we have seen, considerable sophistication can be gained by adding a second policy dimension to the account of government coalition formation, though even this simple model generates complex issues. The analysis of multiparty systems with several dimensions of policy thus presents some daunting theoretical challenges. One way to proceed is to move outside the tradition of purely deductive theory, using more inductive and empirical methods to estimate what is going on. It is to this type of account that we now turn.

Empirical Coalition Formation in Multidimensional Policy Spaces

One approach to modelling the process of coalition building is to assume that coalitions develop as a succession of protocoalitions, with actors being added progressively to these until one or other formation criterion is satisfied. For example, politicians may seek to enter coalitions that are ideologically compact, thereby increasing the probability that the final agreed coalition policy package will be as close as possible to their own party's policy package. On this account, the first protocoalitions to form are the result of fusions between those parties that are closest to each other in the policy space. The next fusions then take place between those that are closest to each other given these prior fusions, and so on. This process is assumed to continue progressively until the government formation criterion is satisfied. We might think of this as a bargaining approach to coalition formation, since it is driven by empirical assumptions about the bargaining process that leads up to the final government coalition. It is an approach that has been implemented empirically, using two-dimensional survey data on policy positions and twenty-dimensional policy data drawn from a content analysis of party platforms.[45]

Grofman develops an account based on two dimensions in which 'each actor looks to form a protocoalition of himself and the actor nearest to him in N-space'.[46] He develops a notion of 'closeness' that takes account of the relative weights of the parties, which is a controversial matter,[47] but his model does yield reasonable coalition predictions. Grofman's model assumes that coalitions form according to a hierarchical process by which parties, once added to a particular protocoalition, can never leave it. Protocoalitions subsequently behave as if they are single actors. Grofman also assumes that the most important formation criterion for a government coalition is that it must command a legislative majority.

Laver generalizes this approach, proposing alternative formation processes and relaxing the requirement for majority coalitions.[48] In addition to a hierarchical process of coalition building in which the protocoalitions which form along the way go on to behave as if they were single actors, he suggests a hierarchical process in which the parties bind themselves together, but none the less continue to evaluate as individuals the alternatives on offer. (This is accordingly a model that implicitly puts considerable emphasis upon hitherto unexplored features of decision making within protocoalitions.) A more radical departure from this approach, also suggested by Laver, is that coalition building may be a non-hierarchical process, whereby the protocoalitions that form at one stage in the process may easily break up later on. After a period of 'at large' bargaining and exploration of the options, a coalition will form that simultaneously satisfies the requirements of the members on policy payoffs and some formation criterion. Hypothetical examples of the differences between these approaches are illustrated in Figures 5.7 and 5.8. Figure 5.7 shows a five-party

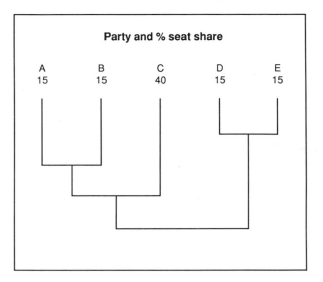

FIG. 5.7. Hierarchical coalition building in a five-party system

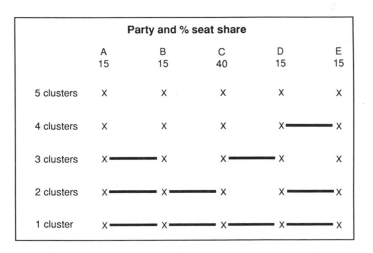

FIG. 5.8. Non-hierarchical coalition building in a five-party sytem

system in which the parties promote positions on up to twenty policy dimensions. Taking all of these into account, it is possible to calculate the 'policy distance' between each pair of parties. The closest pair of parties in the system is D and E. Thus the first stage of a hierarchical formation process is that D and E fuse together into the indissoluble protocoalition DE. The next closest pair of actors is A and B, which fuse to form AB. The next closest pair is the protocoalition AB and party C, which coalesce to form the protocoalition ABC. If for some reason, a majority coalition is required, then this will be the first majority coalition to emerge. Finally, the next fusion prediction will be that between the protocoalitions ABC and DE, to create the grand coalition ABCDE. Contrast this with the process described in Figure 5.8, which shows non-hierarchical 'at large' coalition building. The two closest parties are D and E, so these form the first protocoalition, as before. The next thing to happen, however, might involve the breaking up of DE, as protocoalitions AB and CD form. This could be because, while C and D are quite close to each other, C finds it much easier to join D alone than to join DE. If a majority government were required, CD might be the first to emerge, but these protocoalitions might later be broken up into the two groups ABC and DE, prior to the formation of the grand coalition ABCDE.

Choosing between the hierarchical and the non-hierarchical model of coalition building involves making fundamental assumptions about the bargaining process. Nobody would want to argue that coalition formation is a rigidly hierarchical process, with protocoalitions that form *en route* to the final outcome behaving as unitary actors and never being dissolved. It does, however, seem quite plausible to portray coalition building as a process in which actors with similar policy preferences first get together into some sort of provisional alliance and, only after this has been done (and possibly after commitments have been made among themselves), do they cast around for other coalition partners, adding these until the formation criterion is satisfied.[49] A simple real-world example of this approach can be found in Figure 5.9, which shows the situation in Luxemburg in 1964.

On the left-hand side of the figure is a matrix of policy distances between parties in a policy space defined by twenty issue dimensions and estimated using the content analysis of party manifestos. On the right-hand side of the figure are two diagrams that illustrate the formation process. The upper diagram illustrates what should happen if hierarchical coalition building is assumed;

the lower illustrates a process of non-hierarchical coalition building. As the distance matrix shows, the two parties that were
closest together were the Liberal Party (DP) and the Christian
Socials (CSV). Both models predict that these will form the first
protocoalition. After this, however, the two models diverge.
According to the hierarchical model, the LSAP will join the
DP/CSV protocoalition which will then, finally, be joined by the
Communists (KPL). According to the non-hierarchical model, if
the DP/CSV protocoalition does not satisfy the formation
criterion, it should break up and be followed by a protocoalition
between LSAP and CSV. After this, the DP will join the
LSAP/CSV protocoalition and, finally, the KPL will join. The
actual coalition that formed was one that included LSAP and
CSV, but not DP or KPL.

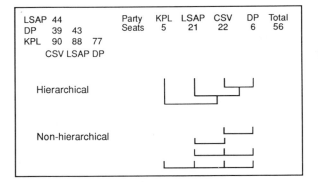

FIG. 5.9. Coalition building in Luxemburg, 1964

Without specifying precisely what the formation criterion is,
this approach none the less enables us to predict that the coalition
which actually forms will be found at some node in the formation
tree identified by the model. In the particular example of
Luxemburg in 1964, we see that the non-hierarchical model
succeeds in this, but the hierarchical model does not. This is
because the minimum winning coalition with the smallest ideological range, the CSV/DP protocoalition identified by both
models, clearly did not satisfy the *de facto* formation criterion,
despite having a legislative majority: the hierarchical coalition
building model fails by not allowing this protocoalition to be

broken up. What happened in practice was that another two-party protocoalition, the LSAP/CSV alliance, clearly did satisfy the *de facto* formation criterion.

In practice, it was quite often the case in the analyses reported by Laver and Budge that the distances between the parties were such that there was no substantial difference between the two models of coalition building.[50] When there was, notwithstanding this particular example, the hierarchical model seemed in general to work better and this was selected as the preferred model by most of Laver and Budge's contributing authors. While the studies reported by Laver and Budge cannot be taken to be the last word on the subject, their work quite clearly shows that there is considerable mileage in using empirical models of the process of policy based coalition building as aids to our understanding the composition of the coalition which actually forms.

SUMMARY AND CONCLUSIONS

That this chapter is by far the longest in this book does not by any means imply that the actual formation of coalitions is a more important process than the others that we discuss. Rather, it is a product of the fact that the formation of governments is the aspect of coalition politics that has attracted the lion's share of attention over the past twenty years or so, both from theorists and from empirical researchers. It is encouraging to note that real progress has been made over this period. The concept of coalition has been developed from Riker's elegant but simplistic model of 1963 into something much richer and more intriguing. On the theoretical front, most of the progress that has been made has had to do with legislative coalitions, though this work, appropriately modified, has clear applications to executive coalitions. The recent analyses of weighted voting have directly focused formal coalition theory on the problem of government coalition formation in Western Europe.

Most of the work that has been done on the politics of coalition in Europe has been essentially empirical in style. It has been driven fundamentally by the urge to account for the coalitions that actually form and has often sacrificed theoretical rigour in order to tell an interesting story about what actually happened.

There is nothing wrong with this. Indeed, many of the insights that have been added to coalition theory have been added by 'deductive' theorists who have kept a very close eye on the results of this practical inductive work. Overall, the interaction of the deductive theory and the empirical analysis of government coalition formation has been relatively productive. While there are certainly outstanding issues to be resolved, there can be no doubt that we know much more now about the formation of government coalitions than we did twenty years ago.

6

Will it Last?

The Stability of Coalition Cabinets

One of the most popular misconceptions about coalition government is that it is unstable. As with many popular misconceptions, this contention has an element of truth in it, but can only be sustained on the basis of carefully selected examples. Such examples are typically drawn from Italy or the French Fourth Republic—both coalition systems in which cabinet instability has, indeed, reached epic proportions. Rarely, however, do those who argue that coalition government is inevitably unstable talk much about Germany, Luxemburg, or Austria, each of which has been ruled more or less continually, over the post-war period, by stable coalition administrations.

There is no need to speculate about such matters, however, since a lot of research has been done on the duration of coalition cabinets. One tradition, which we might think of as the 'regime attributes' approach, has concentrated on the relationship between cabinet stability and a number of features of the political system in general, such as the 'size' or fragmentation of the party system. Another tradition, which we might think of as the 'coalition attributes' approach, looks at properties of particular coalitions that might contribute to their stability, the most obvious of which is majority status. A third possibility is to look at the structure of the bargaining system within which coalitions must exist. Finally, a more recent approach, the 'events' approach, attempts to take account of the fact the the actual downfall of a cabinet is typically the product of a particular 'critical' or 'terminal' event that is liable to occur at any time during its life. Before we consider these different views of coalition stability, however, we must take time to consider a matter that on the face of it looks quite straightforward, but which has posed a surprising number of problems for those involved in practical research on cabinet stability. This is the matter of how to decide when one government has ended and another has begun.

WHAT DO WE MEAN BY 'LAST'?

It may seem odd, given nearly twenty years of research on the general theme of government duration, that there is still much confusion about how, precisely, to measure the length of a government's life. But, as Warwick notes, defining what is meant by the duration of a cabinet is a 'surprisingly complicated issue'.[1] The key problem is how to decide when a government has ended; the most comprehensive review of the issues at stake was conducted by Lijphart, who came down in favour of taking a change in the party membership of the cabinet to be the sole definition of the end of a government.[2] This approach is close to that adopted by Dodd,[3] but most of the other authors who have written on cabinet durability adopt a quite different solution, permuting a selection of the following criteria in their definitions of the end of a government:

1. A change in the party membership of the cabinet;
2. A formal government resignation;
3. A change in the Prime Minister;
4. An election.

A change in the party membership of a coalition obviously changes its character fundamentally. No doubt for this reason it is the only criterion agreed upon without reservation by all who have written on cabinet stability and we can accept it without further discussion.

A formal government resignation—even if this is followed by the reconstitution of the same government under the same Prime Minister—is taken by many to signal a new government. However, this criterion is used neither by Dodd nor by Lijphart. One of the main problems here is that of cross-national comparability. In some systems, a particular type of government crisis or defeat in the legislature may require, according to the written or unwritten rules of the game, the formal resignation of the government, even when everyone knows that it will almost immediately be reconstituted in an effectively identical form. The Italian system, for example, seems to stimulate cabinet resignations that are followed by the reconstitution of a coalition of the same parties, even one under the same Prime Minister. In other systems this is not the case. There is certainly a strong argument to be made, for the sake of comparability between systems, for considering the same government to be continuing in office if it resigns and reconstitutes itself in an identical form; this is the convention that we follow in this chapter.

A change in Prime Minister is taken by many authors to signify the end of a government. The main exceptions, once more, are Dodd and Lijphart. The criterion is used without qualification by Browne *et al.* and by Strom.[4] It is used in a qualified form by Taylor and Laver and by Warwick, who do not regard a new government as having formed when a Prime Minister dies or resigns through 'ill health'.[5] One obvious problem here is that 'ill health' is very often cited by Prime Ministers who are really resigning for other, much more political, reasons. Indeed, when there is no convincing medical evidence, the 'ill health' of the outgoing Prime Minister can almost always be taken as code for 'I've been pushed out by my former party colleagues, but I've decided to go quietly.' For this reason, we do not take a simple change of Prime Minister to signal the end of a government.

The holding of an election is considered by all bar Dodd and Lijphart to define the end of a government. Very often, of course, an election will result in a change in the party membership of the government. However, if the same set of parties and the same Prime Minister form what might appear to be the same government after the election, should we not regard this as simply the continuation in office of the old government? This is the most critical point of difference between the approach used by Dodd and Lijphart and that used by all others in the field. If an election is assumed by definition to terminate a government, then the maximum duration of a government is fixed at the maximum possible time that the law allows between elections. If it is not fixed by definition in this way, then at least a few European governments can be seen to have lived to a ripe old age. To take possibly the best known example, the Swedish Social Democratic minority government led by Tage Erlander (Erlander III), formed in 1957, survived elections in 1959, 1961, and 1965 before being replaced by Palme I, a Social Democratic majority government, in 1969.

There is, however, at least one good reason not to adopt this aspect of the definition of duration proposed by Dodd and Lijphart. From the perspective of the account of coalition duration that we shall be considering in the next section, an election is an event that can cause key attributes of a bargaining system to change. One of the most important of such attributes is the constellation of party weights and policy positions, things that are almost invariably changed by an election. Thus, even if a cabinet does not resign, change its party composition, or change its Prime Minister as a result of an election, it will change some of its key attributes and in this sense might be seen as a different cabinet. For this reason we do regard the holding of an election to signal the end of a government. To sum up, we regard a new government as forming whenever there is an election or a change in the party composition of the cabinet, though we do of course accept that, for different purposes, a different definition of the end of a government might well be in order.

COALITION STABILITY AND REGIME ATTRIBUTES

Several attributes of the overall political system have been held to affect cabinet stability. First, there is the number of parties in the system, with multiparty systems assumed to make both coalition formation and coalition maintenance more difficult.[6] Second, there is the 'size' of the party system, most usefully represented, as we saw in the previous chapter, in terms of the 'effective number of parties' in a system; this is the index we use in the tables below.[7] Third, there is the presence of anti-system or other 'extreme' parties, assumed to have a destabilizing effect.[8] Fourth, there is the degree of ideological polarization or 'cleavage conflict', assumed to make it more difficult to form and maintain governments.[9] Fifth, there is the level of policy influence open to the opposition, based on the effectiveness of the legislative committee system.[10] Sixth, there is the salience of elections to the government formation process, with higher electoral salience assumed to make for more stable government since the consequences of a government defeat are more serious.[11] Finally, there is the presence of a formal investiture requirement, which will very quickly bring down a small number of the governments that form.[12]

TABLE 6.1. Government duration and the effective number of parties, by country, 1945–1987

Country	Average duration of government (months)			Effective number of parties	
	1945–87	1945–71	1971–87	1945–71	1971–87
Luxemburg	45	41	60	3.1	3.8
Ireland	39	43	34	2.8	2.5
Austria	38	37	40	2.2	2.2
Germany	37	40	34	3.2	2.5
Iceland	34	33	37	3.6	4.0
Norway	32	34	31	3.0	3.3
Sweden	28	30	24	3.1	3.4
Netherlands	27	27	30	4.8	4.5
Denmark	26	28	21	3.8	5.7
Belgium	22	28	16	2.9	5.8
Finland	15	13	20	5.0	5.4
Italy	13	13	15	3.4	3.4
TOTAL	26	27	26	3.4	3.9

Coalition stability varies very considerably from regime to regime, as Table 6.1 shows. The left-most column of figures in the table shows the average duration of cabinets, ranking each country in terms of stability over the entire post-war period. (The same ranking measure is used in all tables in this chapter.) The next two columns give average cabinet durations for each country during the periods 1945–71 and 1971–87. The two columns on the right-hand side of Table 6.1 give the effective number of parties in each system for these periods. These figures show that the evidence on the relationship between cabinet stability and the size of the party system, the most widely researched of the regime attributes mentioned above, is inconclusive. Several of the systems that tend to have shorter-lived cabinets do also have a higher effective number of parties—Belgium and Finland are obvious examples; several of the systems that tend to have longer-lived cabinets have an effectively smaller party system—Austria, Germany, and Ireland are the main examples. However, changes over time within these systems throw considerable doubt over the pattern of cause and effect in all of this. Taking all systems together, the average duration of a cabinet hardly changed between the two periods analysed. Looking at changes in stability on a country-by-country basis, however, we see that cabinet duration was more likely to rise than to fall when the size of the party system increased. Thus, while the size of the party systems in Finland, Luxemburg, and Iceland went up from the first period to the second, cabinet stability did not go down, as predicted, but actually went up instead. Similarly, while the size of the party systems in Germany and Ireland went down from the first period to the second, cabinet stability did not go up, as predicted, but actually went down instead. It is only in Belgium, Sweden, and Denmark that we can find clear evidence of the predicted relationship between cabinet stability and the size of the party system. Overall, Table 6.1 shows us very clear evidence that cabinet stability varies systematically from country to country and that countries with bigger party systems have less stable cabinets. However, looking at variations in cabinet stability within individual countries reveals little or no relationship between party system size and cabinet stability. This very strongly suggests the operation of other factors that change from country to country and are related both to cabinet stability and to the size of the party system.

In order to be able to assess the independent impact of various regime attributes upon cabinet stability, we must analyse the effect of each attribute, holding all others constant. This is the approach used by Strom, who investigated the independent relationship between most of the regime attributes that we listed above and cabinet duration, though he did not look at the level of cleavage conflict. His findings, summarized in a causal model,[13] suggest that only the salience of elections and, to a much lesser extent, an investiture requirement and the influence of the opposition, are independently related to cabinet stability. There is some question, however, as to whether the measure of electoral salience used by Strom is really independent of the duration of cabinets.[14] Correcting for this, King *et al.* reconstructed Strom's model and estimated results which strongly suggest that the fragmentation of the party system and the polarization of the opposition are the regime attributes most strongly associated with cabinet duration. The greater the fragmentation and the more polarized the opposition, the more short-lived the cabinet.

COALITION ATTRIBUTES AND CABINET STABILITY

The second set of attributes that are related to the duration of governments are properties of the cabinet that actually forms rather than of the regime in general. It does on the face of it seem logical to assume that the same factors which help a particular coalition to form should also help it to stay formed. On this view, the lifespan of a cabinet comprises a continuous stream of decisions about whether or not to keep it formed and the maintenance of a coalition is seen as an extension of the decision to form it in the first place. This view has characterized a number of studies of cabinet stability.[15]

Several attributes related directly to the coalition formation process have been analysed, the most basic of which is majority status. Most existing coalition theories, as we have seen, are based upon the fundamental assumption that cabinets must control a majority of legislative seats. There is thus a strong tendency to assume that minority governments will tend to be less stable than others. Another thread that runs through much of coalition theory is that coalitions will be minimal winning, in the sense of carrying no passengers. This leads to the prediction that coalitions which are not minimal winning will be less stable than those that are. The logic behind these arguments, though rarely explicit, is straightforward. Minority governments, at least in theory, can be defeated at the pleasure of the opposition. We have argued extensively above, of course, that there are many situations in which the opposition may find it very difficult to agree upon defeating the government. Existing research on cabinet stability does not explore this avenue systematically, however, though it appears promising given the finding that the durations of governments in general are related to the polarization of the opposition.[16] It would not be a difficult matter to test whether minority governments facing divided oppositions last longer than minority governments facing united oppositions. Most existing work on the subject, however, holds all other things very firmly equal. All minority governments are assumed to be more susceptible to defeat than all majority governments.

Arguing along the same basic lines, minimal winning majority governments should be less susceptible to change than surplus majority governments. Quite simply, surplus majority governments can lose surplus members without losing their majority. A surplus majority coalition should be more likely to fall because the group of pivotal parties within it can shed surplus members and return to power as a minimal winning coalition. Shorter-lived surplus majority coalitions should thus be followed by minimal winning coalitions that are subsets of the outgoing government. Once more, however, existing research has held everything else equal and predicted that, taking all cases together, surplus majority governments will be shorter-lived than minimal winning ones.

A third coalition formation criterion, the ideological compatibility of coalition members, has also been used to predict cabinet stability. Implicit in coalition formation theories based upon ideological diversity is an assumption that ideologically compact coalitions form both because the members find it easier to reach agreement in the first place and because they anticipate that they will be better able to withstand the strains imposed by the need to make unanticipated policy decisions during the lifetime of a government. Considering only one dimension of policy, this approach has been developed, as we have seen, into the prediction that minimal connected winning coalitions will form. It can be extended to predict that minimal winning coalitions will also be more likely to stay formed.

To sum up, the basic coalition attributes that have been argued to have a bearing on a cabinet's stability are its majority status, its minimal winning status, and its minimal connected winning status. While recently collected data enable the testing of the link between cabinet stability and far more elaborate conceptions of ideological compactness, this has yet to be attempted. The relationship between cabinet stability and majority or minimal winning status can be seen in Table 6.2, which shows the average duration of single-party majority cabinets, minimal winning

TABLE 6.2. Average duration (in months) of European cabinets, by type, 1945–1987

Country	Single-party majority	Minimal winning	Surplus majority	Minority	Total
Luxemburg	n/a	47	5	n/a	45
Ireland	49	42	n/a	30	39
Austria	46	40	24	20	38
Germany	n/a	33	49	n/a	37
Iceland	n/a	39	40	8	34
Norway	48	37	n/a	24	32
Sweden	24	24	n/a	30	28
Netherlands	n/a	31	34	4	27
Denmark	n/a	43	n/a	22	26
Belgium	46	25	12	7	22
Finland	n/a	19	15	10	15
Italy	n/a	17	17	9	13
TOTAL	45	33	21	19	26

cabinets, surplus majority cabinets, and minority cabinets in each country studied.

The evidence from this table is rather more impressive than that from Table 6.1. First, there can be no doubt that majority cabinets are more stable than minority cabinets, a finding that holds both for the set of countries taken as a whole and on a country-by-country basis. The only exception is Sweden, which has had ten minority governments during this period, four of which lasted longer than average. There can also be no doubt that single-party majority cabinets last the longest of all. Thus the received wisdom with which we began this chapter turns out, for a change, to be more or less backed up by a systematic review of the evidence. Of the various types of coalition cabinet, minimal winning cabinets tend to last longer than the others, including surplus majority cabinets. (Though surplus majority cabinets lasted longer in Germany and The Netherlands.)

Table 6.2 shows that different types of coalition have different average durations, even within the same country. This suggests strongly that there is an independent relationship between coalition

TABLE 6.3. Proportional duration of government by cabinet type,
1945–1987

Country	Single-party majority	Minimal winning	Surplus majority	Minority	Total
Luxemburg	0	99	1	0	100
Austria	37	48	10	5	100
Ireland	44	28	0	28	100
Germany	0	77	23	0	100
Iceland	0	73	24	3	100
Norway	40	19	0	41	100
Sweden	5	27	0	68	100
Netherlands	0	40	58	2	100
Denmark	0	18	0	82	100
Belgium	10	82	7	1	100
Finland	0	22	58	20	100
Italy	0	11	61	28	100
TOTAL	11	45	20	24	100

TABLE 6.4. Frequency of European cabinets, by type, 1945–1987

Country	A: Single-party majority plus minimal winning	B: Surplus majority plus minority	A as % of A + B	Average duration
Luxemburg	9	1	90	45
Ireland	7	5	58	39
Austria	10	3	77	38
Germany	10	2	83	37
Iceland	10	4	71	34
Norway	7	8	47	32
Sweden	6	10	38	28
Netherlands	6	11	35	27
Denmark	2	18	10	26
Belgium	16	6	73	22
Finland	5	27	16	15
Italy	3	32	9	13

attributes and cabinet duration. Tables 6.3 and 6.4 show us that many of the differences in cabinet stability between regimes could well be a product of differences in the frequencies of different coalition types. Table 6.3 gives the proportion of the post-war period during which each country has been governed by each type of coalition. This shows that those regimes in which coalitions tend to be more durable are far more likely to have been governed by single-party majority cabinets or by minimal winning coalitions. The regimes in which coalitions tend to be less durable are far more likely to have been governed by surplus majority or minority cabinets. The only exception to this pattern is Belgium, governed for much of the post-war period by short-lived minimal winning coalitions. As we saw in Table 6.1, Belgium is the major example of a country in which there is strong evidence of an independent impact of regime attributes on cabinet stability. The fragmentation of the Belgian party system as a result of the language problem, described in Appendix A, clearly made even minimal winning coalitions there much less stable.

The main thrust of these arguments is summarized in Table 6.4, which shows the relative frequency of the 'long-lived' coalition types in each system and relates this to average cabinet duration. The five systems with the most stable cabinets—Luxemburg, Austria, Ireland, Germany, and Iceland— all had a preponderance of the most stable cabinet types, majority governments or minimal winning coalitions. The six systems with the least stable cabinets, granted the Belgian exception that we have already noted, all had a preponderance of minority or surplus majority cabinets. The relationship between cabinet instability and the absence of minimal winning cabinets is particularly striking for the least stable systems—Denmark, Finland, and Italy.

Combining the evidence of Tables 6.2 and 6.4, we have a relatively clear picture of what is going on. Majority and minimal winning cabinets are more stable than others, even within particular countries (Table 6.2). Majority and minimal winning cabinets are much more common in systems with high average cabinet durations, with the exception of Belgium (Table 6.4). Quite a bit of the variation in cabinet durability between systems may thus be a product of variations between systems in the frequency of different cabinet types. However, it is also the case that most types of cabinet, and majority coalition cabinets in particular, are less stable in those systems where cabinet stability is lower generally (Table 6.2). Minimal winning coalitions last 47 months on average in Luxemburg, for example, but only 17 months in Italy. We thus observe a pattern of differences between systems in the incidence of stable cabinet types, but also a pattern of differences between systems in the apparent durability even of stable cabinet types. Thus we cannot explain everything in terms of the predominance of more durable cabinet types in those systems with more durable cabinets.

The evidence that deals with the relationship between a coalition's ideological compactness and its longevity can be dealt with much more quickly. Both Sanders and Herman and Warwick failed to identify a strong ideological effect on cabinet stability.[17] More compact coalitions do not appear, other things equal, to be more stable, a finding reproduced by Schofield.[18] Considering only minimal winning coalitions, ideologically connected cabinets were more stable in Belgium and The Netherlands, but less stable in Iceland, Luxemburg, and Finland.[19] Considering only surplus majority coalitions, ideologically connected cabinets were more stable in Iceland and less stable in The Netherlands. No other patterns emerged, so that none of the studies that has been conducted to date provides any sustained evidence of a systematic relationship between the ideological diversity of a coalition and its life expectancy, a result that on the face of it seems rather surprising.

All of this leaves us with two important loose ends that need to be tied up. The first is that there is considerable unexplained variation between systems in the average duration of cabinets. The second is that the duration of cabinets seems to be unrelated to policy matters, despite the fact that party policy greatly enhances our ability to explain the formation of governments in the first place. One way forward in an attempt to tie up those loose ends is to explore the qualitative differences that exist between bargaining situations, as opposed to those between regimes or cabinets. We have already shown that these differences are related to coalition formation; it may also be the case that there is something about the bargaining context in which a coalition is forced to survive that affects its stability.

THE IMPACT OF THE BARGAINING ENVIRONMENT ON
CABINET STABILITY

Before we can go further, we need a systematic account of why one bargaining environment might support more stable cabinets than another, a task attempted in an ambitious piece of work by Larry Dodd.[20] Dodd set out to explain both the type of coalition that formed and the duration of the government on the basis of several structural features of the bargaining system. His most important explanatory variables were the degree of 'cleavage conflict' or ideological diversity in the system as a whole (rather than just in the cabinet) and the level of fragmentation in the party system (which we have already seen to be related to cabinet stability). A number of detailed criticisms can be levelled at Dodd's approach, mainly concerning the distinctions that he makes between minority and surplus majority governments.[21] None the less, this analysis does establish at least a prima facie case for looking more closely at the relationship between cabinet stability and general features of the bargaining system, a task to which we now turn.

Returning to the qualitative distinctions between bargaining systems elaborated in the previous chapter, it will be remembered that the most important differences were those between bipolar systems, unipolar systems, and multipolar systems. In bipolar systems such as Austria and Germany the bargaining situation tends to be simple, clear-cut, and unchanging. Dramatic changes in the weights or policy positions of the parties are needed to disturb anything that is important about the bargaining logic of the coalition game. Changes in the anticipated results of the next election as a result of shifts in the opinion polls, for example, or changes in the policy platforms of the parties as a result of internal party politics, are almost certain not to produce changes in the bargaining logic, which remains dominated by the simple fact that any two-party coalition is viable. This raises the very important possibility that bargaining solutions, once settled upon, may well be more stable in these systems than in others. In unipolar systems such as Ireland and Luxemburg, a single party may be able effectively to call the shots from the centre of the system. Since no plausible election result or policy shift is likely to affect this, we may find a situation analogous to that in Austria and Germany, in which there are few incentives to break up one coalition and form another as a result of exogenous changes in the bargaining environment.

In unipolar systems such as Iceland and Norway, in which the strong party is some distance away from the centre of the policy space, we may find much more alternation in government membership. This need not produce less stable governments, since the 'two-bloc' party system that tends to emerge pits a government with one set of incentives against an opposition with another set of incentives, all of which are unlikely to change during an interelection period. Nevertheless, such bargaining systems clearly do have a greater potential for change and we might think of them as having an intermediate status, in terms of potential cabinet stability, between bipolar and multipolar systems.

In multipolar systems such as Belgium, Denmark, Italy, and Finland, the more complex pattern of party weights and policy positions generates a distribution of bargaining power that is far more susceptible to slight perturbations. For this reason, we expect coalitions in multipolar systems to be less stable than those in others, since there are many more small changes in the parameters of the system—changes in the opinion poll ratings of the parties, for example—that change its bargaining logic and thereby create incentives for politicians to unpick a particular deal even after a coalition has taken office.

Overall, the key distinction that emerges from this classification of different types of bargaining systems contrasts multipolar systems on the one hand with bipolar and unipolar (centre) systems on the other, with unipolar (off-centre) systems being in an intermediate category. In bargaining systems that are not multipolar, it takes a major change in the parameters of the system to create incentives to renegotiate the coalition. When we start to get down to real-world cases, we find several European bargaining systems in this relatively stable position, in which nothing of major significance for coalition bargaining is likely to change from election to election. Election results might change the allocation of seats but they don't change the balance of power; changes in the policy positions of the parties have the same limited effect. This means that anticipations of changes in the election result do not imply anticipations of changes in the balance of power, and hence such anticipations are unlikely to have a destabilizing effect on the system. Luxemburg, Austria, Ireland, Germany, Iceland, Norway, Sweden, and Denmark before 1971 all fall into this category, though a continuation of the rise of the Green Party in Germany might put its position in this group in question. In multipolar systems, small changes in the pattern of seats or policies, of the type that occur in any election, are likely to reallocate bargaining power. This should make parties much more sensitive to anticipated election results and to detailed changes in policy positions and thereby create continual incentives to renegotiate coalitions, making all coalitions less stable. Table 6.5 summarizes this argument, treating both Belgium and Denmark as each having had two quite distinct bargaining systems, one before and one after 1971. It provides powerful prima facie evidence for the case that what conditions the stability of coalition cabinets is the qualitative nature of the bargaining system. This case turns upon key parameters of the bargaining game, including the constellation of party weights and policy positions, and suggests that cabinets are more likely to be unstable in situations where small changes in these parameters generate significant changes in the set of possible coalitions. Table 6.5 provides a persuasive interpretation of this proposition rather than a formal test, though it could be tested more rigorously in a relatively straightforward manner, given an objective indicator of the 'multipolarity' of the bargaining system.

THE EVENTS APPROACH TO CABINET DURATION

A major common feature of all the above analyses of the durability of coalitions is that they are 'deterministic' in the sense that all of the information they use to predict how long a government will last is known when the government forms. Nothing which happens after a cabinet takes office is used to explain its duration. This appears to fly in the face of at least one of the things that we know about the lifecycle of governments, which is that unexpected events often bring them to a sudden and apparently untimely end. Criticizing the general approach of these 'attributes theorists', Browne, Frendreis, and Gleiber have proposed a model of cabinet stability that rests fundamentally upon the assumption

TABLE 6.5. Cabinet stability and types of bargaining system

Country	Bargaining system	Average duration
Luxemburg	Unipolar (centre)	45
Ireland	Unipolar (centre)	39
Austria	Bipolar	38
Germany	Bipolar	37
Iceland	Unipolar (off-centre)	34
Norway	Unipolar (off-centre)	32
Denmark 1945–71	Unipolar (off-centre)	31
Sweden	Unipolar (off-centre)	28
Belgium 1945–71	Multipolar	28
Netherlands	Multipolar	27
Denmark 1971–87	Multipolar	21
Belgium 1971–87	Multipolar	16
Finland	Multipolar	15
Italy	Multipolar	13

that the actual fall of governments is caused by random events: 'the dissolution of cabinets [the event that establishes a coalition's duration] is the result of a process that contains important elements, the timing of which [is] not predictable by actors'.[22] The basic model put forward by the Browne team assumes that each cabinet must exist within a flow of destabilizing events, some of which are lethal. Throughout the lifetime of a government, there is a continuing possibility that one of these 'critical' or 'terminal' events will occur and bring it to an end. Making the further assumption that the possibility of such a 'terminal' event is constant throughout the lifetime of a government, Browne *et al.* argue that the durations of cabinets in a particular system, taking all cabinets together, will conform to a particular mathematical distribution, the negative exponential distribution. The properties of this distribution are very well known and the research project of the Browne team is to observe whether the set of actual cabinet durations does indeed conform to the negative exponential distribution, for any given system. They find evidence of this in four countries: Belgium, Finland, Italy, and Israel.

It is particularly striking that these are the very countries that also tend to have the least stable governments (if Israel were to be added to the tables already presented it would be located very near the bottom of the stability scale). In these countries, Browne *et al.* conclude, there may be

little in the environment of their cabinets that impedes the impact of randomly generated critical events on the ability to govern. With respect to the remaining countries in the analysis (Austria, Denmark, Germany, Iceland, Ireland, Netherlands, Norway, and Sweden) [the results] indicate a possible deterrent, or stability-inducing, effect reflecting the durability of these cabinets.[23]

It is at this point that the 'events' approach and the 'bargaining system stability' approach outlined in the previous section prove to be remarkably compatible. In the previous section we identified, using an a priori theoretical argument, a set of systems in which the bargaining logic is most susceptible to small perturbations in the environment. Browne *et al.* identified, using an empirical analysis, a set of systems (and these were essentially the same systems) which are most susceptible to the impact of random events. What the Browne team failed to do, and this is the shortcoming complained of most strenuously in a stern critique by Strom,[24] is to identify in any convincing manner the factors that are related to the inherent stability of certain cabinets, and this is where the theoretical argument developed above can be of use.

The two approaches fit together quite neatly. The combined account suggests that coalition cabinets exist in a bargaining environment that is continually changing in unpredictable ways. These changes may be produced by the random events that are liable to occur in any social environment. Some bargaining systems (those we have called multipolar systems) are more likely to be disturbed by such changes than others; they are thus inherently more unstable. This is because coalition members in these systems are far more likely to find themselves, once they have taken office, in a situation in which they suddenly develop incentives to unscramble the deal that forms the fundamental basis of the coalition. This is because, in these systems, the balance of bargaining power is more susceptible to changes in system parameters. In inherently more stable bargaining systems there are, quite simply, far fewer changes in the parameters of the system that are likely to disturb the balance of bargaining power. These systems are thus less susceptible to random shocks.

A model that synthesizes the 'events' and the 'attributes' models of cabinet durability and thus bears directly upon this argument has been developed by King, Alt, Burns, and Laver.[25] In this model, the actual durations of cabinets are predicted to fit the negative exponential pattern suggested by the 'events' theorists. Within this general assumption, King *et al.* explored the impact of those regime and coalition attributes identified as important by earlier theorists, controlling for the incidence of scheduled elections (which obviously have an 'automatic' impact on cabinet duration) and for the incidence of short-lived caretaker cabinets. After testing for the impact of a wide range of variables, their most effective model homed in upon three regime attributes—the fragmentation and polarization of the party system, and the existence of an investiture requirement—and two coalition attributes—the majority status of the government and the number of failed attempts to put together a government at the formation stage. The higher the degree of fragmentation and polarization, the shorter-lived the governments; the existence of an investiture requirement tends to shorten the average length of governments; majority cabinets last longer; the more failed attempts to form a cabinet, the shorter time it lasts. The King *et al.* model can accommodate both the impact of random shocks and the influence of regime and cabinet attributes and therefore subsumes much of the work that has been done on the subject of cabinet stability. We note that this more comprehensive account of government stability reproduces the findings that majority governments last longer and that an investiture requirement tends to reduce average cabinet duration. Most significantly for the main thrust of the argument developed in this chapter, however, we note that the fragmentation and polarization of the party system appear as important variables in an analysis that controls for a wide range of matters and even takes account of the impact of random shocks. These, of course, are precisely the variables that we identified as being important parameters of the stability of the bargaining system and thereby liable to have an impact on cabinet stability.

The King *et al.* model can thus be interpreted as describing the lifecycle of a government in terms of the interaction of two processes. On the one hand, there is a set of factors that tend to make a particular cabinet more, or less, durable. The theoretical account in this chapter lays particular emphasis on the stability of the bargaining system. A measure of this stability might well be the number of alternative coalitions that appear to be viable at any given time and an indicator of this could be the number of failed attempts to put together a coalition at the government formation stage; the more failed attempts, the more possible alternatives. While some coalitions are more durable than others, all coalitions, even the most durable, are subject to the potential impact of random events. Those that are more durable, however, are better able than others to withstand the impact of such events and will therefore tend to last longer than those others. Even a very 'durable' government, however, can in practice have quite a short 'duration' if a particularly important event happens to bring down the government early in its potential life.

SUMMARY AND CONCLUSIONS

Many things have been found to bear on the duration of coalitions. Some of these are properties of the coalition that forms. Some identify more 'stable' bargaining systems. In addition, recent research has shown that the pattern of cabinet dissolutions conforms to a process in which governments are brought down as a result of random shocks. The model developed by King *et al.* shows that, even working within the assumption that random events are responsible for the demise of governments, some types of government are likely to last longer than others.

The key features of a bargaining system can in theory change from election to election. Indeed, it is the very essence of parliamentary democracy that these things are at least liable to change as a result of an election. However, the configuration of political parties in many political systems is such that, as a matter of actual political practice, the key features of the bargaining system do not often change. Patterns of electoral and political strength tend to be stable over long periods or to change only slowly. One of the most important ways in which party systems differ appears to be in the extent to which they are 'responsive', the extent to which changes in electoral politics generate changes in the politics of forming and maintaining a government.

Some changes, of course, occur in all systems. These appear to follow one of two general patterns in relation to cabinet stability. There is 'slow' change, of the type that has taken place in The Netherlands and Italy, systems in which a dominant central party or group has slowly lost support, resulting in eventual change in the qualitative structure of the bargaining game; and there is 'fast' change, of the type that we have seen in Belgium and Denmark, where change has been so rapid and so radical that what amounts to a completely new bargaining system has been created, one in which the inherent level of cabinet stability is quite different from that which prevailed beforehand. The dramatic changes in the stability of coalitions in Denmark and Belgium, furthermore, can only readily be explained in terms of the changes in the logic of the bargaining system brought about by electoral upheavals.

7

Who Gets What?

Coalition Payoffs in European Politics

Throughout the discussion so far, one central notion has pervaded our portrayal of the politics of coalition. This is that political actors are bargaining with one another—that the coalition outcome is the product of a process of wheeling and dealing between parties. In Chapter 3 we considered at some length the matter of what the actors might be bargaining about. Looking at the stakes in the coalition game, we considered two major motivations for playing: the desire to gain office and the desire to influence policy. We saw, furthermore, that office may be pursued instrumentally in order to enhance control over policy, and conversely that policy may be pursued instrumentally in order to improve the chance of getting into office. The time has now come for us to look at how successful the various actors are in all of this bargaining. In this chapter, therefore, we look at the payoffs of the coalition game in Europe.

Coalition payoffs are fundamental for all sorts of reasons. For those who are interested in West European party systems, payoffs represent the bottom line of the political process. There is party competition, there are elections, there is legislation, there are votes of confidence, and so on. But at the end of it all some politicians get control over key government positions and some get the chance to turn their policy packages into reality. The payoffs of the bargaining game, whether they are denominated in terms of office or of policy, are real and tangible expressions of the outcome of the political process. Coalition payoffs are also of fundamental importance for those who are interested more in theories of coalition bargaining than in what goes on in Western Europe. Each of these theories builds upon certain assumptions about the motivations of the actors an account of three basic things: the membership of the coalition which forms, its duration, and the distribution of payoffs among its members. Of the things that the theories set out to explain, it is only the distribution of payoffs among members that provides us with any information about the validity of the assumptions upon which the theories were built in the first place. If, when all is said and done, an office-seeking coalition theory makes predictions about the distribution of the rewards of office that bear no relation at all to reality, then we have considerable cause for concern. And we should be concerned, however good the theory might be at predicting coalition membership. If coalition members are consistently not paid off in the way that a theory predicts that they will be paid off, then a fundamental doubt must exist over what, precisely, the parties are bargaining about. Analyses of payoff distribution can thus go a long way towards validating the starting assumptions of the models with which we have been dealing.

Obviously, we must evaluate the distribution of coalition payoffs in the same basic currencies that we consider to motivate the actors. This means that we must look at both the office and the policy payoffs of coalition bargaining and consider both the intrinsic and the instrumental reasons for wanting these payoffs. We begin by discussing office payoffs, since these have received the lion's share of attention from political scientists.

OFFICE PAYOFFS

The Wide Range of Office Payoffs

As we saw in Chapter 3, the potential rewards of office are many and splendid. They range from a Prime Ministership and a place in the history books to a position as part-time dog catcher up a dead-end street. The set of cabinet portfolios, of course, represents a particularly glittering array of prizes which ambitious politicians may crave above all else, but many other patronage appointments can be very grand indeed. A European Commissionership, after all, or a position as governor of the central bank are not at all to be sneezed at. There is rarely a formal constitutional prohibition on giving cabinet posts to people outside the legislature (only Britain and Ireland have explicit provisions to this effect). However, it is overwhelmingly the political practice that cabinet portfolios go to senior legislators in the governing parties. Many of the non-cabinet patronage positions that government parties have at their disposal, however, may be given to people who are outside the legislature. They thus represent a way in which a party may reward those of the faithful who have, in one way or another, rendered it service. Ólafur Grímsson's account of the situation in Iceland illustrates this point rather nicely:

Patronage . . . is among the chief strands in the Icelandic coalition network, and consequently, a very valuable payoff. In many respects, patronage can benefit the parties more than the implementation of various policy items. It can produce gains on all levels of the system and constitute a significant political investment; today's patronage can be a future resource. A party which over time has controlled the recruitment to ministries and other government institutions, furthered the growth of various enterprises through state funds, or built up local strength by supporting public works in particular areas becomes in the future a much stronger coalition partner than a party which has been out of office for a long time.[1]

Furthermore, 'because public servants obtain life terms on appointment, the effects of prolonged single party control over a ministry can last for decades'.[2] Thus, while many of the other benefits of office can vanish in a puff of smoke once the government has fallen, patronage appointments cast a long shadow. This has long been recognized in Italy, where the Christian Democrats (DC) have set considerable store by their control over patronage. According to Marradi:

the technique used to preserve and further DC control is simple: new offices are created and old appointments are renewed when the DC is governing alone. In every legislature after this device was invented by Fanfani there have been one or two DC *monocolori* [single-party minority governments], skillfully timed to suit the need. The parties supporting the *monocolori* often protested, but left it at that. In the bargaining over the next coalition, they were silenced with a few important spoils and many *ad hoc* vice presidencies, totally devoid of power, but good sinecures for mounting *apparatchiki* or declining leaders'.[3]

To the best of our knowledge, there has been no systematic analysis of the distribution of patronage payoffs in European coalition systems, so the evidence on this matter is at best anecdotal. Thus, while all of Browne and Dreijmanis's authors were asked to comment on coalition payoffs, only Marradi and Grímsson, both mentioned above, dwelt at any length on patronage. Notwithstanding this, and given the very lucrative terms and conditions that attach to certain patronage appointments made by national governments, the role of these appointments as coalition payoffs doubtless merits further study. There will inevitably be very considerable variation in patterns of patronage from system to system, however, for reasons discussed in Chapter 3 above, so it is probably the case that evidence on this matter will always be anecdotal. At this stage in our understanding of the politics of coalition, therefore, we can do little more than remind ourselves of the vast array of potential patronage appointments that may be made outside the legislature, and move on. We should, however, make a mental note that if we come across peculiar patterns of coalition payoffs in relation either to policy or to cabinet portfolios, this might be because a shortfall or surplus in one payoff currency is being compensated by additional patronage appointments.

On purely pragmatic grounds, however, there can be no doubt that the payoff of office that is both the most clear-cut and the easiest to study is the ministerial portfolio. In particular, the cabinet portfolio is an especially attractive object of study for a number of reasons. The 'cabinet', after all, is probably the single most important decision making structure in most West European governments. This is why the most accurate formal signal that a party is a member of the executive coalition is that it controls at least one cabinet portfolio. Parties who vote for the government, even on a very regular basis, but who do not control at least one cabinet portfolio are typically thought of as giving the government 'outside' support rather than as being on the inside of the executive. For all sorts of reasons, therefore, cabinet membership is special. This means that it is of special importance to those who are concerned with the politics of coalition to be able to understand how cabinet portfolios are distributed, a matter that has received particular attention from political scientists.

Cabinet Portfolio Payoffs

After the November 1982 election in Ireland, Fine Gael and the Labour Party agreed to form a coalition government. As a result

TABLE 7.1. Portfolio payoffs in Ireland, November 1982

	Fine Gael	*Labour*
Portfolio (% of govt spending)[a]	Taoiseach (0.1)	Tanaiste/Environment[b] (12.4)
	Foreign Affairs (0.6)	Health[b]/Welfare (37.4)
	Finance (1.7)	Trade, Commerce, Tourism (2.5)
	Industry/Energy (2.7)	Labour (1.9)
	Agriculture (4.6)	
	Justice (4.9)	
	Education[b] (15.5)	
	Defence (4.2)	
	Gaeltacht, Forestry/ Fisheries (1.2)	
	Public Service (0.1)	
	Communications (8.6)	
No. of portfolios	11	4
Percentage of portfolios	81	19
Percentage of govt's seat total	73	27
Proportionate share of portfolios	12	3
Share of govt spending controlled by party portfolios	44	54

Sources: Portfolio distribution: Laver & Higgins (1986); Government spending allocations: Book of Estimates 1986, (Stationary Office, Dublin, 1986).

[a] 1.6% of all government spending could not be attributed to a single ministry—the expenses of running the Oireachtas, for example.

[b] 'Big spending' portfolios (see text).

of their negotiations, the coalition partners allocated themselves cabinet portfolios in the manner reported in Table 7.1. Garret FitzGerald, leader of Fine Gael (the larger coalition partner), took the office of Taoiseach (literally 'Chief', equivalent to 'Prime Minister'). Dick Spring, leader of Labour (the smaller coalition partner), took the office of Tanaiste (literally, 'Heir Apparent', equivalent to 'Deputy Prime Minister'). Senior Fine Gael figures Peter Barry and Alan Dukes took, respectively, the key portfolios of Foreign Affairs and Finance. The rest of the allocations can be seen from the table. What is striking is that the number of portfolios allocated to each party conformed closely, but not precisely, to a norm of 'fairness' or 'proportionality'. Each party got a share of portfolios corresponding quite closely to the share of legislative seats that it contributed to the government majority.

Another striking pattern to emerge from Table 7.1 is that, aside from the number of portfolios going to each of the two coalition partners, the nature of the Labour portfolios differs significantly from that of the Fine Gael portfolios. Specifically, Labour controlled three of the four 'big spending' portfolios, with Labour ministers in charge of Environment, Health, and Welfare. Fine Gael, in contrast, despite being by far the larger coalition partner, controlled only Education. ('Big spending' in these terms is defined as controlling over 10 per cent of all government spending. The Environment portfolio in Ireland deals with housing, as well as roads and other environmental expenditures.) Table 7.1 throws further light on this by listing the share of government expenditure that fell under the auspices of each portfolio for fiscal year 1983, the first full year after the coalition took office. From this we can see that the four Labour ministers between them actually controlled far more government expenditure than the eleven Fine Gael ministers. Indeed 50 per cent of government spending was controlled by just two Labour ministers, party leader Dick Spring and Health and Welfare minister Barry Desmond!

We can interpret this information in a number of ways. We might, for example, attempt to develop some ranking of the importance of the ministries in terms of their control over government spending. This would not be very sensible, however, given the widely held view that, at the very least, the 'non-spending' offices of Prime Minister, Foreign Affairs, and Finance are significantly more important than any other. A more productive way of looking at the spending power of the portfolios would be to take account of the greater concerns of the more left-wing Labour Party for policy areas, such as health and welfare, that involved public spending. Control over these ministries could be seen, not in office-seeking terms at all, but in terms of an instrumental desire to control government policy in these fields. In evaluating the worth of different portfolios, however, we should also take account of the near certainty that, in a time of drastic cutbacks in public spending, control over a big spending ministry can be more of a liability than an asset. It is the big spending ministers, after all, who must most often stand up and defend cutbacks in popular public services in times of financial stringency. In this specific instance, it was more often than not Labour ministers who had to stand up and defend cutbacks in health, welfare, and housing provisions, despite concrete promises made in each of these areas in the Labour manifesto. Labour ministers could, and did, assert that these spending cuts would have been far worse but for their presence in government but this counterfactual argument is difficult to sell to voters.

The spending cutbacks in Labour ministers' own departments, furthermore, were agreed by a coalition cabinet in which Labour was in a clear minority. Not only this, but the Fine Gael ministers who controlled the majority of cabinet votes were by and large in charge of non-spending ministries. In times of drastic spending cuts it is clearly more attractive to be a non-spending minister. Viewed in terms of exposure to public opprobrium during periods of fiscal restraint, this means that Foreign Affairs is pretty much the dream portfolio. It has a high profile and provides plenty of perks, but carries no obligation to defend nasty spending cuts. In the 1982–7 Fine Gael–Labour coalition in Ireland, Fine Gael ministers more or less monopolized portfolios, such as Foreign Affairs, Finance, and Industry, with a high profile and a low budget. Quite apart from their intrinsic or instrumental policy preferences, therefore, which might well have favoured spending cuts anyway, Fine Gael ministers had a strong tactical incentive to vote for cuts in health, welfare, and housing spending, since these were likely to damage Labour Ministers.

The only real power that the Labour ministers had over their Fine Gael colleagues derived from the threat to withdraw from the cabinet and bring down the government, a course of action that they finally did take in January 1987 in protest at further proposed cutbacks in health spending. Unlike voting in cabinet meetings, however, the threat to bring down a government can be enacted only once. In other words, while the power of the Fine Gael ministers over their own destiny was built into the structure of cabinet decision making by virtue of Fine Gael's position as a majority party in cabinet, the bargaining power of Labour ministers could only be exercised on the basis of adventures in brinkmanship. In such cases the attractiveness of spending ministries is further reduced, since the exposure of a Labour minister to the downside political costs of holding such a portfolio was much greater than any power he had to control these costs at the cabinet table.

All of this goes to show that the allocation of cabinet portfolios after a period of coalition bargaining—and the November 1982 Irish coalition cabinet is but a single example of this—comprises a rich and many-faceted coalition 'payoff'. There is, of course, the number of portfolios going to each party to be considered; but there is also their nature, viewed in terms of their public profile, the control that they offer over particular policy areas, the exposure that they offer to the costs of governing, and many other things besides.

The Numerical Distribution of Cabinet Portfolios   Of all these considerations, this is the one that has received most attention from political scientists. What is more, this attention has uncovered some of the strongest relationships to be found anywhere in the realm of the social sciences. In a seminal article, Browne and Franklin tested a proposition about the distribution of cabinet portfolios, derived from the earlier work of Gamson, that the 'percentage share of ministries received by a party participating in a governing coalition and the percentage share of that party's coalition seats will be proportional on a one-to-one basis'.[4] They tested this proposition on portfolio distributions for all post-war coalition cabinets in thirteen countries (Austria, Belgium, Denmark, Finland, Germany, Iceland, Ireland, Israel, Italy, Luxemburg, Netherlands, Norway, and Sweden). Browne and

Frendreis, following up this work, constructed a simple regression of the actual number of portfolios gained by a party Y against a prediction that this would be directly proportional to this party's share of the coalition's legislative seats X.[5] For a perfect relationship, the regression equation should be

$$Y = a + bX \qquad a = 0, b = 1.$$

In fact, analysing cabinets that formed between 1945 and 1978, Browne and Frendreis found a very strong relationship that corresponded closely to this:[6]

$$Y = 0.97 + 0.83\ X \qquad R^2 = 0.93.$$

The fit that they found between prediction and reality was quite remarkable, the type of regression coefficient that, as Browne and Franklin remarked in their original article, passes the 'inter-ocular trauma test . . . it hits you between the eyes'.[7] In other words, 93 per cent of all of the variation in the distribution of portfolio payoffs was explained by variations in the legislative seat shares of the government parties. Aside from the astonishing statistical strength of this relationship, another aspect of it is also striking. This is that smaller parties tend, on balance, to get slightly more than a proportionate share of portfolios, while larger parties tend to get slightly less. Browne and Franklin dubbed this the 'relative weakness' effect and interpreted it in two ways. First, they considered the possibility that a small party is more likely to be a pivotal party, the addition of which gives the coalition its majority (this depends on the assumption that the focus of most coalitions is a larger party, to which smaller parties are added until a coalition becomes viable). Second, they considered the possibility that a small party is more attractive as a coalition partner because of its very smallness, which makes it is less likely to cramp the style of a larger partner. Either way, the smaller party may be rewarded with a 'bonus' portfolio or two. They were not able to test these interpretations directly but indirect evidence can be gleaned from the fact that the relative weakness effect disappears in large coalitions, in which the bargaining impact of any particular small party may well be less. Overall, however, the key feature of the Browne and Franklin findings is that they suggest the operation of a very strong proportionality norm governing the distribution of portfolio payoffs. Schofield and Laver subsequently reproduced the Browne and Franklin results, also finding very strong evidence that portfolio payoffs are proportional to legislative weight.[8] A norm of 'fairness' quite definitely seems to be at work.

In many ways this result is rather surprising, since it seems to confound the idea that the bargaining which takes place during the process of coalition formation has to do with the division of the spoils of office. If this were indeed the case, then the spoils should be allocated according to the bargaining power of the parties, rather than their legislative weight. Given, as we have seen, that zero sum bargaining power often bears little relationship to the distribution of legislative seats, why do parties with a lot of bargaining power not flex their muscles and demand the lion's share of the cabinet portfolios, regardless of the seat distribution in the legislature? Going back to the Irish example in Table 7.1, the question can be put in a more specific way. Despite the differences in their seat totals, both Fine Gael and Labour had the same zero sum bargaining power. However you look at it, both were needed to form a government and neither could go it alone. In terms of bargaining power, therefore, the fact that Fine Gael had many more legislative seats than Labour was irrelevant. The question relating to coalition payoffs concerns why, given that Labour had as much bargaining power as Fine Gael, did it not demand the same number of cabinet portfolios?

Empirical attempts to answer this type of question can be used to give us additional insight into the process of party negotiation, though to do so we need to set out more fully what we mean by bargaining power. Consider again the situation in Denmark in 1957 and 1960, discussed in Chapter 5. A coalition of the Social Democrats, Radicals, and Justice Party formed in 1957. Under the proportionality norm, the Social Democrats, who had 78 per cent of the legislative seats controlled by the cabinet, should have had twelve of the sixteen portfolios. This is the 'Gamson prediction' listed in Table 7.2. Note that the other two parties received rather less than they should have under the proportionality norm, consistent with the relative weakness effect.

As a way of accounting for the discrepancy, Schofield and Laver proposed a version of a formal game-theoretic solution concept known as the bargaining set, the predictions of which are also listed in Table 7.2.[9] This approach assumes that each member

TABLE 7.2. Legislative seats and cabinet portfolios in Denmark, 1957–1960

	1957				1960			
	Seats	Portfolios	Bargaining set	Gamson	Seats	Portfolios	Bargaining set	Gamson
Communists (DKP)	6							
Socialist People's Party (SF)					11			
Social Democrats (SD)	70	9	8	12	76	10	10	13
Radicals (RV)	14	4	5	2	11	5	5	2
Liberals (V)	45				38			
Conservatives (KF)	30				32			
Justice Party (DRF)	9	3	3	2	–			
Others	1				7			
TOTAL	175	16	16	16	175	15	15	15

of the coalition attempts to form a new coalition excluding the previous coalition partners, and they in turn retaliate. For example, suppose the Social Democrats have eight portfolios and they approach the Liberals to offer them control of seven. The Radicals and the Justice Party, since together they originally controlled eight portfolios, could counter by offering the Liberals eight portfolios to form a government with them. Thus, the attempt by the Social Democrats to increase their payoff could leave them out of office. The 'bargaining set' predictions listed in Table 7.2 give the 'stable' distribution of portfolios that reflects the bargaining power of the three members of the coalition, formalized in this way. Notice that the bargaining set prediction closely matches the actual prediction, the main difference being that the Radicals were underpaid slightly. After the 1960 election, a coalition between the Social Democrats and the Radicals formed, allocating portfolios in the proportions predicted by the bargaining set approach.

This approach is very much tied to the theory of constant sum games and may thus, of course, not be entirely appropriate when different parties put a different value on the same portfolio, as they may when policy considerations are important. However, even in this case, portfolios may be seen as a fixed set of prized opportunities to have an impact on policy and, for this reason, the constant sum approach may retain some validity. In the Danish and Irish cases that we have just considered, bargaining power and seat shares differ considerably. Typically, however, as a party's seat share increases, so does its bargaining power. It might therefore be the case that the proportionality norm appears to work only because it is related in some way to bargaining power. Schofield and Laver set out to answer this question by looking at the independent predictive power of the proportionality norm and of bargaining power, holding the other constant. They found that, at least when all cases were considered together, the proportionality norm was by far the more effective method of predicting portfolio payoffs.[10]

A norm, however, is a culturally specific sort of a thing. It seems likely that different political systems will have different norms dealing with the allocation of seat distributions. Schofield and Laver thus set out to investigate the potential variation from system to system in the pattern of portfolio allocations and

the results they obtained were quite striking. Comparing the
proportionality norm and bargaining power as the basis for
allocating seat distributions, 'one model or the other fits very
well for most countries'.[11] It turns out, therefore, that coalition
systems can be classified into those in which the proportionality
norm appears to be used to allocate portfolios and those in
which there is evidence that bargaining power is brought into
play. These results are summarized in Table 7.3. The
'proportionality' systems, according to Schofield and Laver, are
Austria, Germany, Ireland, Luxemburg, and Norway. The
'bargaining' systems are Belgium, Denmark, Finland, Iceland,
Italy, and Sweden. (The empirical results from The Netherlands were ambiguous.) The question that must now be settled,
of course, concerns why some political systems appear to allocate portfolios in one way while others appear to do it in
another.

TABLE 7.3. Relative performance of 'proportionality' and 'bargaining'
norms in allocating portfolio payoffs

Country	Norm best predicting actual paryoffs	Bargaining system
Luxemburg	Proportionality	Unipolar (centre)
Ireland	Proportionality	Unipolar (centre)
Austria	Proportionality	Bipolar
Germany	Proportionality	Bipolar
Norway	Proportionality	Unipolar (off-centre)
Iceland	Bargaining	Unipolar (off-centre)
Sweden	Bargaining	Unipolar (off-centre)
Denmark	Bargaining	Multipolar
Belgium	Bargaining	Multipolar
Finland	Bargaining	Multipolar
Italy	Bargaining	Multipolar

Source: Adapted from Schofield and Laver, 'Bargaining Theory and
Portfolio Payoffs in European Coalition Governments', p. 161.

Schofield and Laver put forward two speculative answers to
this. In the first place they argued that it is possible that policy
competition is more intense and policy payoffs are more important

in some systems than in others. Perhaps, in these 'policy oriented' systems, most of the real bargaining takes place over policy, with portfolios being allocated according to some conventional rule of thumb. Evidence to test this notion is bound to be rather anecdotal but, on the face of it, the case is not promising. Among the systems in which policy bargaining is supposed to be especially important are Ireland, Germany, and Austria; among the systems in which policy is presumed to be less important are Denmark, Italy, Finland, and Sweden. This is rather the opposite of the received wisdom about the relative importance of policy in these systems. Certainly, in the extensive set of content analyses of party programmes recently reported by Budge, Robertson, and Hearl,[12] the conventional left–right policy dimension emerged much more readily in Denmark, Italy, and Sweden than it did in Ireland, Germany, or Austria. It does not look, therefore, as if it will be easy to sustain the case that policy is a more important element in coalition bargaining in those systems where portfolios are allocated according to a pro-portionality norm, though this case has not been systematically investigated.

The second interpretation of the distinction between systems that use a proportionality norm and those that use bargaining norms is more promising and relates directly back to the discussion of cabinet durations in the previous chapter. Indeed, the com-parison between Table 7.3 and Table 6.5 is quite striking. Those systems in which the proportionality norm is used are overwhelmingly those with the most stable cabinets—Luxemburg, Austria, Ireland, Germany, and Norway. Those in which the bargaining norm is used are overwhelmingly those with the least stable cabinets—Italy, Finland, Belgium, and Denmark. There is an almost perfect correlation between the norm used to allocate payoffs and the average duration of cabinets, two completely different outputs of the coalitional process. This strongly suggests that the same forces underlie both.

When we discussed the possible causes of variation in cabinet durability, we laid the heaviest emphasis on qualitative differences between different types of bargaining system. The most important single distinction that we drew between systems was between those that are multipolar and those that are not; and the key feature of multipolar systems that we were concerned with was that the distribution of bargaining power was much more liable to change from election to election. In other, more stable, bargaining systems, the distribution of bargaining power was liable to remain the same from election to election. This distinction can be seen to have a direct bearing on the allocation of cabinet portfolios.

When the distribution of bargaining power does not change from election to election, despite changes in seat distributions, this might appear to be an ideal environment for the 'emergence' of a norm that governs payoff distribution. In such cases, furthermore, it might be felt by the political elite that election results should have at least some impact on the political system. If political rewards are allocated according to bargaining power in systems such as these, elections will have no effect, since bargaining power remains the same despite election results. If rewards are allocated according to seat distributions, of course, then elections do make a difference. (Note that this interpretation does not deal with the process that might lead such a distributional norm to emerge; rather it deals with an implicit consequence of it, should it emerge.) This distinction between stable bargaining systems that sustain a norm of proportional payoff distribution and more competitive and unstable bargaining systems that sustain bargaining norms allows us to indulge in some further speculation about the negotiation process operating in the various countries that we have considered.

It is quite clear from the Schofield and Laver analysis[13] that the proportionality norm is a much better payoff predictor than the bargaining norm in bipolar systems. In Germany, for example, each of the three main parties has the same bargaining power as the other two, despite the fact that the Free Democrats win far fewer seats than the other two parties. Yet the distribution of payoffs almost perfectly matches the proportionality norm each time a coalition forms. This suggests that there is little attempt to renegotiate coalition payoffs, and is a finding consistent with the classification of Germany as a stable bargaining system. The same phenomenon can be observed in 1983 in Austria, when the Socialists, with ninety seats, and the Freedom Party, with twelve seats, formed a cabinet in which they controlled twelve and three portfolios respectively, even though their formal bargaining power was identical.

Among unipolar (centre) systems, the bargaining norm is again less accurate than the proportional norm, albeit for slightly different reasons. In Ireland, the dominant position of Fianna Fáil allows it to refuse to deal with any other party and enables it to form a single-party government for much of the time. When there is a coalition between Fine Gael and Labour, therefore, neither can exercise bargaining power against the other, and a proportionality norm appears to have emerged as a reasonable procedure for allocating portfolios. In Luxemburg, the pivotal central position of the Christian Social Party (CSV), if pushed to the limit, would give it an almost dictatorial position and virtually all of the portfolios. In 1954, for example, the CSV won exactly half of the seats and formed a coalition with the Socialists (LSAP). According to the bargaining theory, the CSV should have taken all of the portfolios; in fact, the parties shared the portfolios equally between them. Thus the very powerful position of the centre party in a unipolar (centre) system also seems to encourage the development of a norm of proportionality.

In the unipolar (off-centre) systems some differences emerge between Norway and the other three countries, Sweden, Denmark, and Iceland. In Norway after 1961, as we have seen, cabinets have alternated between coalitions of three or four bourgeois parties and single-party minority Labour administrations. Each bourgeois party could in theory have formed a coalition with Labour, but in practice, given the longer-term incentives facing both Labour and the bourgeois parties, such coalitions were not realistically available. The proportionality norm governed portfolio allocations within the bourgeois coalitions since these parties, in effect, had decided not to use their bargaining power against each other. On the other hand, the Agrarian or Centre Party in Sweden and the Radicals in Denmark have been in a position to form a governing coalition with both left- and right-wing parties. This is precisely the situation in which we might expect bargaining power to be exercised as one side is played off against the other and, indeed, we do find that the small centre parties have typically done better than was warranted by a purely proportional allocation of payoffs. Finally, coalition possibilities in Iceland seem to be quite unrestricted in what appears to be a two-dimensional policy space, evidence for which is that most possible combinations of parties have gone into government together. Coalition bargaining seems to be given full play, and the bargaining norm works very well indeed as a payoff predictor.

Bargaining in the multipolar countries—Belgium, The Netherlands, Denmark, Finland, and Italy—will depend, as we argued above, upon whether or not the largest party occupies the core position in what we have assumed to be mainly two-dimensional policy spaces. In such systems, precise election results and policy positions can be crucial and slight changes in these can transform the bargaining logic of the system. It is precisely in such situations that we would expect to find bargaining power to be exploited to the full. Certainly in Belgium, Denmark, and Finland we found that the bargaining norm predicted payoffs far better than the proportionality norm. In Italy, the distinction between the two was less clear, though small parties do tend to get more portfolios than their size alone would warrant and for this reason the bargaining norm seems the best predictor. In The Netherlands, the predictions of the proportionality and the bargaining norms were very close to each other and, for this reason, could not be distinguished statistically.

Overall, however, there is a strong empirical relationship between the stability of the bargaining environment in which the parties operate and the norm that they employ to allocate cabinet portfolios. In more stable systems, the proportionality norm is overwhelmingly dominant. A proportionality norm is clearly also in use in the very stable unipolar (centre) systems. In less stable multipolar systems, the bargaining norm is by far the best predictor. The more ambiguous bargaining logic of the unipolar (off-centre) systems means that we must look at each system in this class individually in order to see which payoff norm is the more likely to emerge. This pattern is consistent with the general model of bargaining stability proposed by Dodd, in which uncertainty pays a key role.[14] What remains much more obscure, however, is the process that might allow particular norms to emerge and to be maintained. It is clear that in many, if not all, political systems, parties will differ over which norm they would prefer, and none of these accounts offers any clue about the processes that might lead one norm to prevail over another.

There is more to the allocation of political payoffs than the counting of a small number of cabinet seats, however. We argued above, for example, that different parties may well value different policy areas in different ways. We can use analyses of the particular portfolios that appear to be especially prized by particular parties to attempt to gain some insight into this. Indeed, Browne and Franklin suggest that it is this, qualitative, allocation of portfolios that lies at the heart of coalition bargaining, and that 'parties in governing coalitions restrict their bargaining over the distribution of ministries to the question of which ministries each partner is to receive'.[15] In other words, they suggest that bargaining concerns qualitative rather than quantitative aspects of cabinet portfolio payoffs, the matter to which we now turn.

The Qualitative Basis of Portfolio Allocations   The business of deciding who gets which particular portfolio has also attracted the attention of political scientists. We have already considered the possibility that politicians may wish to control cabinet portfolios either because they value these offices in and for themselves or because they value them instrumentally for the control that they give over policy. These two motivations provide quite distinct justifications for politicians to treat different portfolios in different ways.

Those who are concerned only with the benefits of office may well rate each portfolio as having a particular status and/or desirability. It would certainly be conventional, for example, to regard the premiership as the most glittering prize of them all, followed by a limited collection of senior portfolios that almost always include foreign affairs, internal affairs, and finance and which may include others, such as defence or agriculture, depending on specific local circumstances. Further on down the pecking order we find other ministries, such as health, education, welfare, industry, and so on, that rate as cabinet portfolios in almost every West European system, however small the cabinet. Further down again we find portfolios that are less important still, possibly tourism, fisheries or sport. These will not be cabinet portfolios in most European systems, and may tend to be filled by unimportant politicians, or by important politicians who are being punished for some reason or another by party hierarchs.

It is also the case that different politicians may take a different view of the same portfolio. One may dream of being Foreign

Secretary, for example, shying away in horror from the prospect of being Prime Minister. Another may value the public works portfolio for the patronage possibilities that it offers. By and large, however, there is usually some reasonable consensus in a given system on the pecking order of portfolios, so that most of those who are in tune with the politics of the day will be able to make a judgement, when a minister is moved from one portfolio to another, as to whether the change was a promotion, a demotion, or a sideways move. If there is reasonable agreement among the participants on the pecking order of portfolios, even though one trophy may be worth much more than another, then the set of portfolios taken together represents a sack of trophies with a fixed total value.

An attempt to investigate the pecking order of portfolios was made by Browne and Feste.[16] They did this indirectly, looking at the control of particular portfolios by the more powerful parties in a coalition, on the assumption that the most powerful parties will get the richest pickings. They found that the office of Prime Minister was almost always controlled by the largest party in the coalition. After this, defence, finance, economics, education, and foreign affairs, in that order, that were likely to be controlled by the largest party. The Browne and Feste analysis suggests that there is an overall global ranking of portfolios, taking all systems together, which runs from Prime Minister through defence, finance, economics, education, and foreign affairs to a cluster of other portfolios for which no clear pattern emerges. The surprises in this ranking are the presence of education and the absence of internal affairs, though the regularity of conflicts over educational policy in post-war Europe offers a clear interpretation of the first of these puzzles.

Obviously, the conclusions that we can draw from such broad-brush cross-national research are rather tenuous. Each European system, without any doubt, operates on the basis of a quite different set of evaluations of the worth of specific cabinet portfolios. Operating on this crude level, however, we can confirm, on the basis of more than mere gut feeling, the higher evaluation of the premiership, defence, finance, economics, and foreign affairs. On the basis of the same analysis, our attention is drawn to the higher than expected evaluation of the education portfolio and to the fact that, in practice, the internal affairs portfolio seems to be less sought after by the big parties than we might otherwise have been tempted to assume.

A more fundamental set of issues arises when different parties within the same system consistently put different values on the same cabinet portfolio. This may happen when each party has a particular set of policy concerns, seeing control over a specific portfolio as an instrumental means of advancing these. As a result of this, within a given coalition of parties, a ministry can remain for a considerable period under the control of a single party that has a special interest in the particular policy area involved. The most extreme example of this can be found in Austria, during the period (1955–66) that was dominated by the Red–Black grand coalition between the People's Party (ÖVP) and the Socialist Party (SPÖ). For the lifetime of these governments, 'the ÖVP dominated the Chancellorship, Finance, Agriculture and Forestry, Defence, Education, Commerce and Reconstruction, and the Power and Economic Planning Ministries. The SPÖ's domain consisted of the Vice Chancellorship, Interior, Social Administration, Transportation and Electricity, Transportation and Nationalised Industries, and the Public Nourishment Ministries. The Foreign Affairs Ministry was equally divided between the two parties.'[17] In other words, certain portfolios were the clear bailiwick of certain parties.

We should also note that the particular allocation of portfolios in Austria echoes that of the Irish case described in Table 7.1. The conservative party took the PM's job together with finance, industry, agriculture, education, and defence. The social democratic party took the deputy PM's job, together with the health, welfare, housing, and public works portfolios. The stronger position of the Austrian SPÖ means that it did better than the Irish Labour Party, getting foreign affairs some of the time and internal affairs all of the time. But otherwise the pattern is quite striking. The question that obviously arises, therefore, is one of whether these qualitative patterns in portfolio allocations are part of a systematic tendency for certain parties to take certain ministries, or are merely coincidences.

This matter was addressed by Browne and Feste, who investigated the proposition that 'certain ministerial types will be disproportionately received by parties of specific ideological orientations'.[18] As it happens, Browne and Feste tested this proposition, not because they viewed parties as intrinsic policy-seekers who instrumentally wanted to control certain ministries, but because they believed that 'some portfolios will be viewed by parties as being especially important for the purpose of reinforcing the loyalty of certain extra-parliamentary clientele groups on which they depend'.[19] The fact that Browne and Feste viewed the concern of particular parties for particular ministries exclusively in instrumental electoral terms, however, does not detract from the relevance of their findings for our argument, since they were simply looking for an association between a party's ideological type and the ministries that it tends to control. They classified parties (in the same set of thirteen countries as the Browne and Franklin study[20]) into eight ideological types: communist, socialist, radical/liberal, religious, agrarian, conservative, nonparty, and residual. On the face of it, there did appear to be a relationship between certain ministries and certain party types, but most of this vanished once account was taken of the size of the parties. In particular, while socialist and religious parties seemed to be associated with certain ministries, this turned out to be because socialist and Christian Democratic parties also tended to be large and thus to get these higher-ranked ministries more frequently by virtue of their size. Controlling from the effect of party size significantly reduced the impact of party ideology on qualitative patterns of portfolio allocation.[21] Only the agriculture portfolio appeared to be truly linked to party ideology, typically being controlled by agrarian or religious parties in the cabinet regardless of their size. Viewed on a systematic cross-national basis, therefore, the rather plausible assumption that certain types of party will get certain types of portfolio was not borne out. This suggests either that our earlier examples taken from Austria and Ireland were indeed isolated instances rather than part of a pattern, or that the pattern must be specified in a more sophisticated manner.

One of the problems with an aggregate cross-national analysis such as that performed by Browne and Feste is that it cannot take account of the fact that particular combinations of party types may result in particular qualitative portfolio allocations. Our original examples of Ireland and Austria, after all, both dealt with coalitions between social democratic and centre–right parties. Perhaps if a right-wing liberal party were to be substituted for the centre–right party, for example, the pattern of portfolio distribution would be quite different. In other words, it might be the case that particular qualitative allocations of portfolios are associated with particular ideological configurations of coalition, rather than merely with particular parties. This is an almost impossible proposition to test, since there are so many different ideological configurations of coalition. Ian Budge attempted to go at least some of the way down this route, basing his research on a model of party competition that is derived from the assumption that parties are policy-seekers.[22] Rather than making blanket predictions that certain types of party will always get certain types of portfolio, Budge makes a set of conditional statements about the general circumstances in which particular parties will get particular portfolios. He first confirms the Browne and Feste finding that the big parties tend to carve up the 'important' ministries. (Budge assumes the important offices in this context to be those of PM, Deputy PM, and the ministries of foreign affairs, economics, and interior. Note the potential empirical qualifications, discussed above, to this plausible a priori assumption). Budge then moves on to develop the findings of Browne and Feste about the destination of the agriculture ministry. He tests the proposition that 'Agrarian Parties take the Ministry of Agriculture/Fisheries out of all cases of coalition government where (i) Agrarian Parties participated in the coalition and (ii) there was a Ministry of Agriculture'.[23] This is confirmed for forty-seven out of forty-nine relevant cases. Budge then adapts the other Browne and Feste finding, that religious parties also tend to get the agriculture portfolio, into the proposition that 'Christian parties take Agriculture in coalitions where (a) no Agrarian party exists, (b) a Christian party participated in the coalition, (c) there is a Ministry of Agriculture'. This is confirmed in 94 per cent of all cases.[24] We may combine these findings with those of Browne and Feste to conclude that the agriculture portfolio goes to agrarian parties, regardless of size and, failing an agrarian party, to a Christian Democratic party.

Budge was unable to establish an equivalent pattern for the education portfolio. When clerical and anti-clerical parties were in government together, 'control of the Education ministry obviously passed in a relatively unpredictable fashion between [them]'.[25] The education portfolio, as befits the 'important' status we might infer for it from the Browne and Feste study, is clearly in dispute between the parties. Finally, Budge attempted a very general prediction about the social welfare ministry. Unfortunately, the proposition here is so general as to tell us very little. 'Socialist *or* Christian Parties take the Ministry of Labour or Social Affairs or Welfare or Health where a) Socialist or Christian Parties participate in the coalition and b) there is a Ministry of Labour or Social Affairs or Health.'[26] This proposition is confirmed in 147 of 148 cases. But quite a few coalitions contain only Socialist and Christian parties, and for these the proposition is true only tautologically. In most other coalitions, either a Socialist or a Christian party will be the dominant actor. To predict that the dominant actor will control at least one out of four secondary ministries almost certainly has far more to do with size than with ideology, especially when the two parties concerned are ideologically distinct. Indeed, this interpretation is specifically implied in the Browne and Feste findings, which show the ideological significance of the social affairs ministry vanishing once the effects of size are controlled for.

We may conclude by noting that, although the assumption that certain parties will particularly value certain ministries in order to further certain policy goals is supported by the impressionistic accounts of portfolio distribution in a range of coalition systems that were collected by Browne and Dreijmanis,[27] systematic documentation of this phenomenon has proved troublesome. In stark contrast to the very clear-cut findings relating to the quantitative allocation of portfolios, a full understanding of qualitative portfolio allocations has thus far eluded researchers.

POLICY PAYOFFS

The other main objective that may motivate parties in coalition bargaining is the desire to influence policy. As we have seen, this may be because of an intrinsic concern with policy on the part of politicians or it may be because of an instrumental desire to maximize long-term chances of gaining office. In the latter case, parties bargain over policy because of a sequence of events in which they make policy promises to the electorate at one election, then may or may not go into government, then must fight another election, and so on. In the subsequent election, parties may lose votes if they appear to exert no influence over policy, either by failing to get into government at all or by going into a government that enacts policies that differ from those that they promised at election time. Either way, every party has an 'ideal' policy point. This may represent a policy package that is intrinsically preferred or it may simply be one that is instrumentally valued because it is the best long-term vote-maximizing policy package. For parties that are intrinsically concerned with government policy in and for itself, any deviation of government policy from their preferred policy will impose relative costs, whether the party concerned is in or out of office. For parties that are instrumentally concerned with policy as a vote-maximizing device, a deviation of government policy from party policy only imposes a direct cost if the party is in government. If it is out of office, then such a party does not care at all what government policy is, save for the indirect impact of this on future elections. (Other long-term electoral costs may fall on an office-seeking party that fails to get into office, of course, but we may safely assume that an office-seeking opposition is not blamed if its policies differ from those of the government.) The crucial distinction to bear in mind is that policy payoffs go to all policy-seeking parties, in or out of office, but go to office-seeking parties only when they are in office.

It has become common, as we saw in Chapter 3, to conceive of each party's view of government policy outputs in terms of the distance between the policy position of the party and the policy position of the government; the further apart the two are, the less the party likes it. Policy bargaining, as we also saw in Chapter 3, can then be conceived of as a matter of attempting to minimize the policy distance between a party's ideal policy point and the policy point of the government. This implies that each party's 'policy payoff' is inversely related to the distance between party and coalition policy—the bigger the policy distance, the lower the policy payoff. We saw in the previous section that policy payoffs might also come in the form of control over particular portfolios, but that patterns in this process were difficult to discern.

When policy payoffs are denominated in terms of the distance between party and coalition policy, they can also be difficult to pin down in practice, despite the apparently unambiguous way in which they can be defined in theory. In part the problem arises because of a lack of systematic data on the policy positions adopted by coalition cabinets. There is more to the problem than this, however. Even when data become available, it is clear that 'the policy position' of 'the coalition' may mean many things and, worse, may mean quite different things in different systems. Until recently, such operational problems were of little practical significance, since systematic data on government policy positions did not exist. This has meant that most accounts of coalition policy payoffs have been rather impressionistic. The authors in the Browne and Dreijmanis volume all address themselves to the matter of whether parties are paid off in policy terms, and all conclude that policy payoffs are important while providing little hard information on them.[28] A valiant attempt to discuss policy payoffs in Israel, for example, is made by Ofira Seliktar:

We may obtain a notion of the parties' relative degree of satisfaction by assessing the degree to which the coalition agreement deviates from the stated electoral policy positions of the parties. Judgements of this kind are quite subjective . . . It is possible, however, to rank cabinet coalition parties by the degree to which their policy preferences are satisfied by the coalition agreement. In general, the party that has least compromised on policy position in Israeli coalitions is the Labour Party. *Mapai*'s success was due not only to its dominant position in Israeli cabinets, but also to its gradual shift to the center. As a result, Labour's issue preferences often represented the ideological center of the various coalitions . . . Those to compromise their policy positions most were the more Marxist and religious parties. Regarding the former, *Mapam* had to compromise markedly on economic issues . . . The NRP, which has strived to promote some theocratic goals, has been rather compromised by its membership of cabinets controlled by secular parties.[29]

Beyond commenting in such general terms upon the 'obvious' importance of policy in coalition bargaining, however, more precise information on policy payoffs has been hard to come by. This has meant that a key element in policy-driven models of coalition bargaining has remained beyond empirical investigation. However, the ECPR research group on party manifestos, in the project discussed in Appendix B, has also completed a full-scale content analysis of the policy programmes of coalition governments in most West European systems.[30] This work has generated quantitative data which allow estimates to be made in the same terms not only of the 'stated electoral policy positions' of parties but also of the 'coalition agreements' referred to by Seliktar. By measuring the distance between these two positions we can make an empirical estimate of the policy payoff of a party.

Now that we no longer have the excuse of having no data, we are forced to clarify a number of ideas that have hitherto been rather vague. The most notable of these concerns what we really mean by 'the' policy position of the government, the position that determines the 'policy payoff' going to all parties. Any real-world government, of course, can be thought of as having a number of different policy positions. In the first place there is the position agreed as a result of bargaining between the parties. This is often encapsulated in a policy declaration, issued at the end of coalition negotiations, which details the policy compromises that have been reached. While such a document is unambiguously the immediate output of coalition bargaining over policy, we must none the less be wary about its real political significance. It might, after all, be little more than window dressing. As Marradi says of Italy,

bargaining is by no means limited to the coalition formation stage, but continues throughout the coalition's life. In particular, the DC is aware that it can accede to many of its partners' requests in the program drafting stage, since it retains an almost absolute control upon which policy measures to take, which to block, and which to subvert. Considering the official program of any government, one is astonished at the number of important reforms it lists. However, considering the program of the next government, one finds almost exactly the same items.[31]

Any document issued as a result of coalition negotiations, therefore, may not mean very much if the parties have no intention of implementing it. Yet the main alternative method of conceiving of coalition policy, which is to attempt to look at what 'really' happens in the form of policy outputs, is even more problematic. Actual government policy outputs are notoriously hard to monitor. The ECPR manifesto research group has also taken on this task, however, looking both at the enactment of specific manifesto pledges,[32] and at the relationship between the party composition of the cabinet and public expenditure flows.[33] The analysis of real expenditure flows, in particular, can tell us something about the payoffs of actors in policy areas involving the distribution of public monies, though only certain policy areas, of course, fall into this category. Thus, Hofferbert and Klingemann conclude that the FPD in Germany has done quite well out of both the

SPD and the CDU/CSU as coalition partners, but this conclusion cannot be documented for social policy, for foreign policy or, indeed, for any other policy area in which there is either little expenditure or in which the main crux of the policy debate does not concern whether there should be more, or less, expenditure on particular items. None the less, the systematic extension to other European systems of analyses that link party policy to flows of government expenditure may well add greatly to our understanding of at least one aspect of coalition policy payoffs.

TABLE 7.4. Party and coalition policy on selected issues, Luxemburg, 1974

| Policy area | % of party policy programme devoted to each area | | | | |
	Communist (KPL)	Socialist (LSAP)	Liberal (DP)	Christian (CSV)	LSAP/DP coalition
State intervention in economy	16	16	4	10	6
Social conservatism and traditional morality	0	3	3	6	7
Agriculture and farmers	1	2	5	4	5

For the time being, however, the most detailed information that is available on the policy positions of governments can be found in the content analyses of coalition policy declarations by the ECPR group. An example of how such data can be used to throw light on the relationship between party and coalition policy can be found in Table 7.4 which shows the situation in Luxemburg in 1974. Luxemburg has been selected as a relatively 'simple' coalition system, with a Communist Party (KPL), a Socialist Party (LSAP), a Christian Social Party (CSV), and a Liberal Party (DP). In 1974, breaking with a long tradition of CSV leadership of coalition governments formed with either the LSAP or the DP, a coalition led by Gaston Thorn was formed between the LSAP and the DP, excluding the CSV. The observed 'policy payoffs' in this coalition throw considerable light on this situation. As we can see from Table 7.4, most of the parties had something to say in the previous election about the benefits of state intervention in the economy. The KPL and the LSAP each devoted 16 per cent of their entire manifesto to this theme, the

CSV 10 per cent and the DP 4 per cent. The LSAP/DP coalition policy document reported a compromise between the LSAP's 16 per cent and the DP's 4 per cent, devoting 6 per cent of its text to the matter of state intervention. The government policy statement is clearly closest to the DP manifesto on this dimension. To take another policy dimension, only the CSV dwelt long on the need to protect traditional values and morality. The final agreed coalition policy document, however, devoted more space to this theme (7 per cent of the total) than even the CSV, which was not a coalition member. The CSV manifesto was closest to the government policy statement on this particular dimension, even though the CSV was out of office. Turning to agricultural policy, there was quite a difference between the coalition partners. However, the eventual emphasis of the government policy declaration was identical to that of the DP, and quite different from that of the LSAP. Indeed, government emphasis on agriculture was closer to that of the opposition CSV than it was to that of the LSAP, a government party. These policy 'payoffs' illustrate quite clearly the argument made in Chapter 5 about the role of policy in coalition bargaining. The CSV was the core party in a unipolar system, excluded very untypically from office by the other main parties in 1974. Despite this exclusion, the core position of the CSV appears to have meant that the policies of the government could not stray far from those of the CSV.

Notwithstanding the relatively clear-cut situation in Luxemburg, with its entrenched core party, the general results of the ECPR study suggest that the policy payoffs of coalition bargaining will not be easy to analyse. Just as patterns in the qualitative allocation of cabinet portfolios have proved difficult to uncover, so the precise role of the published coalition policy document appears to be ambiguous at best in complex bargaining systems.[34] Indeed, there are indications that it is downright obscure. There are several reasons why it is very difficult to read a meaning into what appears on the face of it to be a fairly straightforward document, the policy statement issued by the coalition partners at the conclusion of their negotiations. For example, parties with fundamental policy disagreements that none the less decide to go into government together will not want to draw attention to what divides them. Conversely, when there is clear agreement between parties on policy, they are likely to publicize this, however trivial the issue. Much more complex strategic calculations may also come into play. One party may want to minute a particular agreement while another may not, for example. Thus the parties may agree upon the deal that they have done but disagree upon whether to publicize it. No agreements made in the run-up to the formation of a government are binding, but putting a deal into a published coalition policy statement at least puts the credibility of the signatories on the line, and may for this reason alone be worth more than the paper that it is written upon. But the coalition partners may not want to stake their credibility on all of the deals that they have made. Thus the published policy statement is a highly strategic document, the meaning of which may be obscure to all but the most sophisticated of insiders.

One way around this would be to concentrate upon 'real' policy outputs—legislation and audited government expenditure flows, for example—rather than upon the 'cheap talk' of published policy declarations. In fact, research on these matters is only just beginning. The ECPR research group on party policy has extended its purview to include the fulfilment of campaign pledges (whether these have to do with legislation or otherwise) and the allocation of government expenditure to particular programme areas. Neither task is at all straightforward, however. There is remarkably little legislation in any political system, while the matter of whether less specific campaign pledges have been honoured can be difficult to determine in any 'objective' manner. Even if it can be demonstrated that campaign pledges have not been honoured, it can be difficult to determine whether this failure was the result of self-conscious decisions by the politicians involved, or was the result of circumstances beyond their control, as they would so often like to have us believe!

Meanwhile, public expenditure flows are quite 'sticky' over rather long periods of time, and it is very difficult to filter out the effect on government expenditure of self-conscious government decisions. We have yet to establish an order of magnitude for the type of change in particular government expenditure flows that we might reasonably expect an effective government party to be able to bring about, though it seems likely that even very small changes in many spending areas involve very big political efforts from those concerned.

Putting all of these results together, what is clear is that empirical researchers have not yet got on top of the problem of measuring the 'real' policy positions of governments, something which unfortunately leaves in limbo the assessment of real-world coalition policy payoffs.

SUMMARY AND CONCLUSIONS

Given all of this, what conclusions can be drawn from the empirical evidence on coalition payoffs? The striking findings on portfolio payoffs, combined with the difficulty of pinning down hard evidence on policy payoffs, can be synthesized as follows:

1. Office *is* important. There can be no other explanation for the very close relationship between a party's legislative weight and the number of portfolios that it receives from its coalition partners. This underlines the importance of portfolios as things that should be shared out carefully, but does not suggest bargaining over them. This remains one of the most striking non-trivial empirical relationships in political science.[35]

2. Policy payoffs may take two forms:
   a. *Control over particular ministries.* This is the type of policy payoff emphasized by Browne and Franklin. 'Government ministries are the most tangible manifestations of policy payoffs to governing parties.'[36] While it can be shown that some ministries are more highly valued than others, it has not been conclusively demonstrated that particular parties value particular ministries to any systematic degree.[37] The agriculture ministry is an exception and there may be other as yet unrevealed patterns here. Certainly, there is as yet no evidence of strong patterning in policy payoffs that are denominated in terms of the qualitative allocation of specific portfolios.
   b. *Influence over the coalition policy package.* Parties do bargain over policy when they are negotiating a coalition deal and they do issue an agreed policy statement at the end of these negotiations. The links between party policy and coalition policy declarations, however, are obscure,

given the complex strategic status of the published coalition policy package.[38]

There can be no doubt, given the hitherto disappointing empirical results on coalition policy payoffs, that the development of a much more comprehensive research programme designed to assess the relationship between the policies of a coalition and the preferences of its members remains one of the most important pieces of unfinished business in the political science of government coalitions.

Coalitions in a Constrained Real World

It is an interesting fact of academic life that those who specialize in the politics of a particular country tend, when the chips are really down, to be deeply suspicious of general theories. There is an understandable reluctance to accept that any theory which can be applied to many different political systems could possibly capture the richness, the detail, and the splendid complexity of any one of them. Theories of coalitional behaviour have thus fallen victim to vigorous attacks from country specialists who almost invariably argue that it is just not possible to understand the politics of coalition in Italy, Germany, The Netherlands, or wherever, without a detailed knowledge of the special features of the system in question.

Klaus von Beyme is one of the most outspoken European critics of 'formal' coalition theories:

Research on coalitions on the basis of game theory has not come to terms with the peculiarities of European party systems, since it has started out from American assumptions of a system where all the relevant groups are seen to have 'allgemeine Koalitionsfähigkeit' and to calculate in a rational way the advantages of forming coalitions.[1]

Most of the specific propositions of coalition theories do not work under the conditions of a European multi-party system . . . The zero sum assumptions underlying most formal coalition theories overlook the heterogeneity within parties . . . intervening variables such as the electoral system and the role of the head of state in cabinet formation are neglected since they are not open to quantification.[2]

It is not surprising, therefore, that von Beyme finds no room for general theories of coalitional behaviour in his analyses of the politics of coalition in Germany. He is by no means alone in these views. Pridham argues that 'while formal theories have had the merit of focusing on certain obviously key components of coalition politics . . . it is evident that they fail to take account of a range of variables or determinants of coalitional behaviour'.[3] Not surprisingly, Pridham concludes that 'formal coalition theories are that much less applicable to Italy than most other West European countries because of the "complexity" of Italian co-alitional situations'.[4] As for The Netherlands, 'to explain the particular coalitions that have been built one has to take a look inside the parties. And it is questionable whether formal theory is of any use in this respect.'[5] In Belgium 'traditional coalition theory . . . rests upon two basic assumptions: (a) that parties are monolithic actors; and (b) that payoffs are discernible prior to coalition negotiations. Both these assumptions . . . are violated in the case of Belgium.'[6] In Scandinavia, 'traditional theory is too one-dimensional . . . the understanding of coalitional behaviour in Scandinavia must be in the party systems viewed more broadly rather than merely in relation to formalistic concerns.'[7] In the same way, 'most coalition theories have found little support in the Austrian case . . . the maximization of a coalition partner's power is not always necessarily the main goal, nor is coalition formation an isolated single event.'[8] Finally, we note that 'the normal processes of coalition bargaining are severely constrained in Ireland'.[9] From all of this we might be tempted to conclude that coalition theories cannot be used in an unmodified form in Germany, Italy, The Netherlands, Belgium, Denmark, Finland, Iceland, Norway, Sweden, Austria, or Ireland—in other words in eleven of the twelve European systems to which they have typically been applied. (And we can take it that the fact that we have found no proscription on the use of coalition theory in Luxemburg is because nobody has yet got around to writing one down.)

The essential thrust behind each of these objections to the use of 'coalition theory' in any specified political system is that each country has special features which must be taken into account before a meaningful interpretation of the politics of coalition there can be developed. This is a problem for comparative theories in general, of course, but it seems to be particularly acute for theories that deal with coalition. This, presumably, is because some of the real-world local constraints upon coalition bargaining are so strong that it seems particularly wanton to ignore them. Thus it is senseless to ignore the role of the constructive vote of no confidence, for example, when developing an account of government formation in Germany. The constitutional provision that the Federal Chancellor can only be defeated in office by a no confidence motion that specifies his successor quite clearly makes it much more difficult to defeat an incumbent government. Furthermore, this provision was explicitly included in the German constitution, in reaction to the instability of the Weimar Republic, in order to make governments more difficult to defeat. It has most certainly contributed to the durability of coalition cabinets in the Federal Republic of Germany.

Nobody who works within the general field of coalition theory has, to our knowledge, suggested that such obviously important facts of political life be ignored. On the contrary, much of the work that has been done in the 1980s to develop and expand the spatial model of party competition was actually driven by a desire to explore the role of some of the institutional and procedural features of the bargaining system under consideration. This work has already been referred to in Chapter 5, and the 'structure induced equilibrium' approach introduced by Shepsle is a good example of the crucial role attributed by many formal theorists to particular institutions.[10] This is thus often referred to as the 'new institutionalism'.

Most of the models of coalitional behaviour that have been applied in Western Europe, it must be said, have tended to assume a bargaining environment more or less free from constraints. The models tend to assume, for example, that parties can shop around freely for potential coalition partners. They tend to assume, other things being equal, that every arithmetically possible combination of parties has at least some finite chance of forming, that none can absolutely be ruled out. When such models are applied to empirical data on a cross-national basis, furthermore, it is undeniable that all other things are implicitly assumed to be decidedly equal. Little or no attempt is made to tailor particular theories to specific local circumstances, thereby ignoring the strong possibility that very many theoretically feasible coalitions have no realistic chance whatsoever of forming. The real world of coalition politics is a world of constraints, and empirical coalition theories have in practice tended to ignore this.

This should not be taken to imply that those who have conducted this research are uninterested in the impact of the institutional features of particular systems. And it should certainly not be taken to imply that the impact of such features cannot be explored by general models in a systematic manner. Rather, the ignoring of local bargaining constraints has stemmed from a desire to concentrate upon one feature of coalitional behaviour at a time. Thus, models that have homed in upon the minimal winning status of the coalitions which form, for example, or their ideological diversity, have been concerned to isolate the general importance of these particular factors, rather than to provide an all-embracing account of coalitional behaviour in any conceivable system. There *is*, when all is said and done, a strong tendency for the coalitions which form to be minimal winning, despite the fact that many of those which actually do form are not. The attempt to isolate the impact of this particular force was clearly not a worthless exercise.

As the writings of the new institutionalists have shown us, however, it is also possible to develop intriguing and powerful models that are driven by assumptions about the structural features constraining coalition bargaining. Critics of 'coalition theory' are obviously right when they complain that not enough account has been taken of institutional matters in accounts of the politics of coalition in Europe. But the new institutionalists have shown that this is not an impossible task. The way forward is to get going with the business of specifying the type of institutional factor that it seems plausible to assume conditions coalition bargaining. This is the task to which we now turn.

GENERAL OR *AD HOC* CONSTRAINTS?

The general analysis of structural constraints on coalition bargaining is a delicate task. On the one hand we do want to end up saying more than that the world of coalitional politics is a fascinating and complex place and that it is difficult to draw any conclusions about it without taking into account every minute detail of each local system. On the other hand we do not want to ride roughshod over local realities for no better reason than to be able to apply a particular general theory. There is, however, a middle way. This involves recognizing the existence of real-world bargaining constraints and classifying them into those that will always be *ad hoc* and unique to a particular system and those that can be generalized.

Some constraints, however potent they might be, are the product of very specific local circumstances and can only be added to theoretical accounts of coalition bargaining in an *ad hoc* manner. Take personality clashes, for example. It is probably a fact of Irish political life that Charles Haughey of Fianna Fáil and Desmond O'Malley of the Progressive Democrats (PDs) disliked each other so deeply in 1987 that no coalition between Fianna Fáil and the PDs had the slightest chance of forming, despite the ideological closeness of the two parties. This personality clash was a powerful constraint on Irish politics, but it is difficult to generalize anything about it. We can do little more than to note the power of personality clashes and to consider them in an *ad hoc* manner when the need arises.

The fact that a bargaining constraint is *ad hoc* certainly does not mean that it is uninteresting, 'even' to theorists. We should note, for example, that even one little personality clash that prevents two parties going into government together can vastly reduce the range of theoretically viable coalitions. It is quite possible to explore the impact of a local *ad hoc* constraint such as this in a systematic manner, by applying it to a more general theoretical model. In other words, general models are useful precisely because they help us to isolate the impact of local factors, even when these are *ad hoc* and cannot, therefore, be built back into a more complex model of the process under consideration.

To take an extreme example that highlights this point, imagine a three-party system in which two parties, the Reds and the Blues, each control 48 per cent of the seats while another party, the Whites, controls the remaining 4 per cent. Arithmetically, any two of the three parties, or all three together, can form a winning coalition. If Red Leader and Blue Leader loathe each other so comprehensively that they will *never* sit at a cabinet table together, then both the grand coalition and the Red/Blue coalition must be excluded from consideration. The two coalitions that remain viable—Red/White and Blue/White—both contain the Whites, which cannot be kept away from the cabinet table given the bargaining constraint imposed by this personality clash. This constraint, therefore, turns the Whites into dictators who can demand, if they care to do so, almost all of the payoff from the other two parties. The personality constraint dramatically reallocates bargaining power and we can explore the impact of this, in a non-trivial way, using a simple model of the bargaining process.

Thus it is important not to relegate *ad hoc* constraints to the realm of the theoretically uninteresting. On the contrary, a good model will be able to tell us a lot about their impact and, indeed, this is one of the main reasons why it is important to have a good model in the first place. However, it will be difficult to build such constraints into a more general model and, for this reason, their analysis does not have a significant cumulative effect upon our understanding of the processes at work. This, indeed, is why we must do more than explore the *ad hoc* constraints on any given situation if we wish to push forward our understanding of the coalitional process in general.

Many of the constraints upon bargaining that we are liable to come up against, however, are generalizable in the sense that they can be specified without reference to a particular individual politician, party, or election—or even without reference to a particular political system. Some of these constraints concern real and rigid features of the institutional setting of politics. Others may concern more informal behavioural matters, though they are no less potent or generalizable for that.

For example, in most political systems in Western Europe, certain parties have what almost amounts to a 'pariah' status, being excluded from the bargaining process by all other parties. Many Communist parties, the neo-Fascist MSI in Italy, the fundamentalist Protestant parties in The Netherlands, and the radical right-wing Progress Parties in Scandinavia might all be considered to have been pariahs at some stage or another. This status involves more than mere policy. Many pariah parties do have extreme ideologies, to be sure, but others do not and yet are none the less treated as being out in the wilderness by the others. Thus it is difficult, for example, to detect a significant difference in the policies promoted by the Italian Communist Party and those promoted by sections of the Italian Socialist Party. The ECPR manifesto analysis often places the Communists to the right of the Socialists,[11] yet there is no doubt that the Communists were treated as unacceptable coalition partners by the other Italian parties for much of the post-war period while the Socialists were not, and indeed went into government on several occasions.

Notwithstanding the appeal of presenting strong behavioural regularities such as the ostracism of pariah parties as constraints upon bargaining and building them into models of coalitional behaviour, there is a serious danger in doing this. It implies that certain social features of the bargaining process should be treated as 'laws', over which the actors themselves have no control whatsoever. But such patterns, however inflexible they may appear to be, are not really laws at all, but are rather the consequences of purposeful decision making by the actors themselves. In short, behavioural 'constraints' such as these should be treated as outputs of the bargaining process rather than as inputs to it. They are things to be explained rather than things to be used, like magic wands, to do the explaining. Return to the example of 'pariah' parties. One of the strongest behavioural regularities that we observe in the politics of coalition in Europe is that certain parties are designated by the others as 'non-coalitionable'. A general account of coalitional behaviour should be able to tell us why this is the case. Simply to assume that such-and-such a party can never go into the government in Denmark, for example, because this is one of the 'rules of the game', does not get us very far. It is assuming what we should be setting out to explain. In the discussions that follow, therefore, we shall confine ourselves to considering only formal institutional factors to be structural constraints and influences on bargaining. Behavioural regularities, however strong, will be treated as part of the question, not as part of the answer.

INSTITUTIONAL CONSTRAINTS ON COALITION BARGAINING IN EUROPE

Even if we confine ourselves to the effects of formal institutional factors on coalition bargaining, there is plenty to be going on with. Some of these factors operate as rigid side constraints upon bargaining, in the sense that they rule out particular coalitions.

Such side constraints range from the absolute banning of a specific political party, as with the Communist Party of Germany in 1956, to rules specifying the inclusion of certain parties or types of parties, as in Belgium. More frequently, however, institutional factors exert an influence rather than a side constraint upon bargaining, by imposing additional incentives that change the calculus of the decision makers rather than by actually forcing their hands. Examples include the rules governing the investiture and removal of governments, such as the *formateur* system in The Netherlands or the constructive vote of no confidence in Germany.

Given the role of all European constitutions in guaranteeing equality before the law, rigid institutional side constraints on the formation of particular coalitions are not very common. The main exceptions can be found in ethnically divided systems in which formal 'consociational' arrangements have been institutionalized. The most obvious example of this is in Belgium and deals with the representation in government of the two language communities, the Flemings and the Walloons. Article 86B of the Belgian constitution states that 'with the possible exception of the Prime Minister, the cabinet comprises an equal number of French speaking and Dutch speaking members'.[12] Article 59B states that, on issues related to the language question, legislation 'must be passed with a majority vote within each linguistic group of both Houses, providing the majority of the members of each group are present and on condition that the total votes in favour of the two linguistic groups attain two thirds of the votes cast'.[13] These are very strong side constraints on the coalition formation process, ruling out absolutely many of the coalitions that would otherwise be possible after a given election result. As Rudd notes:

These constitutional conditions established certain parameters for the formation of governments throughout the 1970s . . . The problem facing the political leaders . . . was how to bring together a coalition with a two thirds overall majority and a majority in each linguistic group. Two broad alternatives were available: a three-party (or 'grand') coalition of the traditional parties or a coalition of two traditional parties and one or more of the [language] community parties. As any coalition without the Christian-Social parties would not have obtained . . . a two thirds majority, there were only two options within this second alternative: Christian-Social and Liberal and Community party(ies) or Christian-Social and Socialist and Community party(ies).[14]

In other words, the constraints imposed by the formal institutions of consociational democracy in Belgium not only reduce the range of possible coalitions that can form very considerably, but also made it impossible, for a time, to form a government without the Christian Socials. We might thus speculate that this constraint gave the Christian Socials a lion's share of the bargaining power. In such circumstances, it is obviously difficult to justify the application of theories that assume the feasibility of all arithmetically possible coalitions. In the Belgian case, many of these coalitions are not merely unlikely, they are unconstitutional, and any theoretical account that ignores this is doomed to failure.

Similar constraints were imposed by the British Government on the Northern Ireland 'power sharing' executive, formed in the coalition system generated during the brief and ill-fated life of the Northern Ireland Assembly. In this case the requirement, written into an Act of Parliament, was that at least one party representing each 'community' (a codeword for religious group) be represented in any executive that formed. This imposed particular types of coalitional arrangement on the Northern Ireland Assembly, in this case even if the election result had yielded a single-party legislative majority.

Rigid institutional side constraints on coalition formation such as these are rare, however, and tend only to arise in circumstances in which attempts have been made to institutionalize particular solutions to problems of bitter communal strife. Much more frequent are institutional features of the bargaining situation that exert a powerful influence on the formation probabilities of the range of possible coalitions, rather than constraining this absolutely by eliminating certain possibilities altogether.

OTHER INSTITUTIONAL FACTORS

The number of institutional factors that might influence the politics of coalition in Europe is immense. It is obviously impossible to provide an exhaustive list of these. In order to give an idea of how such factors can affect the bargaining process, therefore, we shall concentrate upon two institutional matters that have obvious and radical impact upon coalitional behaviour. These are the electoral system and the rules governing the investiture and defeat of governments.

Electoral Systems and Electoral Coalitions

The electoral system can obviously have a major impact on coalition bargaining. In the first place, the proportionality of the electoral process affects the 'size' of the legislative party system. Less proportional electoral processes reduce the size of the legislative party system, for a given pattern of votes cast by the electorate, by boosting the size of large parties and reducing the size of small parties or even eliminating them. It is well known that 'most single party parliamentary majorities are "manufactured" by electoral systems'.[15] Thus one of the most radical outcomes of the politics of coalition, the single-party majority government, is often an artefact of electoral law. Very few single-party majority governments in Europe won over 50 per cent of the popular vote at the preceding election. One of the most obvious effects of electoral law is to create incentives for politicians to form electoral coalitions. These can be attractive, even essential, to certain parties in systems in which electoral law distorts representation in the legislature in favour of large parties (so that a party with 40 per cent of the vote wins far more than twice as many seats as a party with 20 per cent of the vote, for example). Electoral coalitions can also be very attractive in systems that involve the transferring of support from one party to another, an explicit feature of the Irish single transferable vote (STV) or the Australian alternative vote (AV) systems, and an implicit feature of the French second ballot or the Anglo-American first-past-the-post systems.

The electoral coalitions that formed in 1983 and 1987 between the Liberal Party and the Social Democratic Party (SDP) in Britain offer good examples of the impact of the first-past-the-post electoral system in this regard. The Liberals had won 14 per cent of the vote in the 1979 election; this gave them eleven (less than 2 per cent) of the 635 seats. The Conservatives on the other hand, in a typical first-past-the-post result, won 53 percent of the seats with 44 percent of the vote. When the politicians who set up the SDP broke away from Labour, it was clear that neither the Liberals nor the SDP would stand much of a chance under the

British electoral system if they fought each other for the middle ground. Their only hope of success was to join forces and to attempt to develop the 'critical mass' of about 30 per cent of the popular vote which was felt sufficient to overcome the distorting effects of the electoral system.

The 'Liberal/SDP Alliance' (or the 'SDP/Liberal Alliance', depending on your point of view) was therefore formed. A deal was done whereby Liberal and SDP candidates would not contest the same seats and a joint electoral programme was issued. While the parties retained entirely separate legal identities, no separate policy positions were maintained during the 1983 election campaign. In the event the alliance was to no avail and the distorting effects of the British electoral system were merely exaggerated. The Conservatives' vote share decreased from 44 to 42 per cent but their seat share increased from 53 to 61 per cent. Labour won 32 per cent of the seats with 28 per cent of the vote. The Alliance won less than four per cent of the seats with over 25 per cent of the vote. Notwithstanding this, the two parties feared an even greater electoral disaster if they abandoned their alliance and fought the 1987 election once more as an electoral coalition with a single policy package. The election results were equally disastrous for them and, largely as a consequence, a process was set in motion which led in 1988 to the combining of the two parties into one.

There is no doubt that the British electoral system provided overwhelming incentives for an electoral alliance between the SDP and the Liberals and that, as a consequence, the two parties functioned for many purposes as a single entity during the 1983 and 1987 election campaigns. It is not difficult to envisage circumstances that would have led to the splitting of this alliance; indeed, parts of the SDP did split away after the acrimonious discussions that subsequently led to the formal fusing of the two parties. It is clear, however, that the two parties were more usefully seen as a more or less stable protocoalition during this period than as two quite independent actors. It is very likely, had the Alliance held the balance of power in the legislature, that it would have functioned as a single component in any bargaining that might have ensued, making a single set of demands and deciding as a bloc whether to go into or stay out of a particular set of arrangements.

The STV electoral system offers precisely the same incentives, providing a major inducement for parties to form pre-electoral coalitions. This happened in Ireland in 1973, when Fine Gael and Labour got together and hastily agreed a fourteen-point electoral programme. They announced that they would form a government together if they won sufficient seats and each party encouraged its supporters to give lower preference votes to the other. The consequence was that the two parties, despite losing votes in aggregate, gained seats and took power. The outgoing Fine Gael–Labour government fought the 1977 election on a joint programme and a promise to resume their coalition if they were re-elected; they were not. In 1981 and 1982 the two parties campaigned on the basis of separate policy packages but continued to encourage supporters to engage in mutual vote transfers and continued to announce that, provided a policy package could be agreed, they would form a government together if they were able to do so. The electoral arrangement between Fine Gael and Labour ended in 1987 when Labour brought down the government by withdrawing its ministers from the cabinet. Vote transfers no longer flowed between the former coalition partners. As a consequence their rival, Fianna Fáil, lost first preference votes but won seats and formed a government.

In each of these cases the electoral system gives the parties strong incentives to form electoral coalitions. In each case the electoral coalition which did form subsequently had a legislative impact. This is because, in order to make an effective appeal to voters, members of an electoral coalition typically announce their intention to go into government together if they are able to do so. As a matter of fact, furthermore, such parties do indeed tend to go into government together when this is possible. This means, in short, that particular electoral systems set up a coalition formation phase before elections rather than after them, a matter that has an absolutely fundamental impact upon the politics of coalition. Certain electoral systems in effect place protocoalitions rather than single parties before the electorate. In this way, the politics of coalition and the politics of electoral competition become inextricably intertwined.

The Government Formation Process and the Identification of Coalition Nuclei

A second set of major institutional constraints on bargaining has to do with the provisions that regulate the formation of governments. We outlined the government formation process in Chapter 4, summarizing it in Figure 4.1 and Table 4.1. It can be seen from this summary that, even if we consider only a very simple set of institutional factors circumscribing the lifecycle of a government, every European government formation process employs a different set of rules. For example, a number of West European constitutions require that an incoming government survives an investiture vote, and even when this is not a formal written requirement it may be an informal constitutional convention. Alternatively, it may be the case, as it is in Denmark and The Netherlands, that a cabinet can hold office so long as it is not defeated and has no obligation to survive a positive vote of confidence before it can take office. Whether an incoming cabinet needs a positive vote of confidence or merely must be able to avoid a vote of no confidence can make a big difference to the politics of coalition in a given system. The lack of a requirement for a formal investiture vote in Denmark, for example, is held by Pesonen and Thomas to make minority governments more likely, since it 'allows governments to seek their support from different quarters on different issues'.[16]

More generally, an investiture requirement forces an incoming government to survive on the basis of its programme and cabinet taken as a whole, rather than on the basis of a package of proposals that can be considered one at a time. The investiture requirement thus provides a much sterner test and quite possibly makes it more difficult for minority governments to form, a factor that, as we saw in Chapter 6, also has an effect on the duration of cabinets.[17] In the absence of an investiture requirement, more minority governments may be viable in the sense that they cannot be defeated, since the entire government package does not need to get the agreement of a majority of the legislature.

Whatever the rules of the government formation process in a particular political system, there must always be a government, even throughout the coalition formation phase. This typically leaves either the outgoing government or a part of it in office as a 'caretaker', pending its replacement. The caretaker government obviously has a special bargaining status since it is the status quo which will continue in office until it is replaced. It might well be the case, therefore, that the party or parties in the caretaker government are prepared to be tougher in coalition negotiations;

they have less to lose than the other parties should these negotiations fail.

Perhaps the most crucial institutional feature of the government formation process, however, concerns the role played by the head of state. This role can be that of active participant or mere figurehead, a matter that is largely determined by the formal rules and informal conventions that between them comprise the working constitution in any given system. Four broad types of arrangement can be identified. In some states, such as Ireland, the President is nothing more than a figurehead, who has no real role in the appointment, let alone the selection, of the government. While the Irish constitution provides for the appointment of a new Prime Minister (Taoiseach) by the President on the nomination of the parliament (Dáil), this role is utterly formal. Thus, when the prospect arose in 1987 of there being no agreed nomination from the Dáil, the President felt that he would have had no alternative but to call another immediate election, having no discretion whatsoever in the matter. Under such arrangements, coalition formation is a matter of 'freestyle' bargaining and negotiation between the legislative parties, along the lines assumed by most coalition theories. Coalition formation protocols can have no particular effect on bargaining. Such a situation, however, is rather rare.

Another possibility, the practice in Israel and West Germany, is that the President makes the nomination to the parliament, which approves the appointment. Obviously, in such circumstances the head of state will, for reasons of prestige, be careful only to make nominations that are likely to win parliamentary approval. In such cases, the balance of power in parliament clearly remains the dominant factor, but the intervention of the head of state may break a bargaining deadlock by nominating a particular nucleus for the coalition formation process. In such cases, to say that the legislature may reject any nomination by the head of state is not to say that the head of state has no power. Often it may be the case that any one of a number of potential coalitions might be able to win parliamentary approval. In such circumstances, the role of the head of state in taking the initiative by nominating a particular coalition is clearly critical. In bargaining situations in which there are multiple equilibria, the preferences of a head of state who has an 'agenda setting' role in the government formation process may well prevail.

A much more common situation is one in which the head of state actually appoints the Prime Minister, subject to parliamentary approval. This may be a formal requirement of the constitution, as in Italy, Belgium, or Greece, or an informal constitutional convention, as in Denmark, Luxemburg, The Netherlands, Norway, or Sweden. Once more, the head of state, wishing to avoid humiliating legislative defeats, typically engages in extensive consultations with the parties. In this situation, however, the head of state does have a veto on the selection of Prime Minister. Whether or not this veto is ever actually exercised, the preferences of the head of state cannot be ignored entirely.

While the appointment rather than the mere nomination of the Prime Minister may seem on the face of it to give the head of state a more powerful formal role in government formation, the practical political impact of both arrangements is the same. The head of state makes a move, the legislature must accept or reject it, and in each case it is the agenda setting role of the head of state, backed up by a veto, that is crucial. Differences between systems with this type of arrangement, therefore, will turn on differences in the willingness of the head of state to risk the parliamentary defeat of a proposal, a variable governed more by informal conventions than by formal provisions. It is this variable, however, that will condition the extent to which the head of state actively participates in the government formation process. In certain circumstances, the head of state may effectively wait, if at all possible, for an agreement between the parliamentary parties before making a nomination; this is the situation in Britain. In other circumstances the head of state plays a much more active role in the process of government formation; this is the case, for example, in The Netherlands:

The role of the Queen in the formation process is the most discussed topic in the unwritten part of the constitution and probably the main contribution to the great prestige of Queen Juliana (1948–81) and her daughter Beatrix. Both women are said to be well-informed (Juliana by the end of her reign had experienced sixteen formations, Beatrix holds a degree in political science) and very much aware of the political facts of life. Dutch political and public opinion expects the monarch to play an active role rather than being only a figurehead.[18]

The manner of the Dutch monarch's involvement in government formation is quite intricate since 'the Queen has to take the first step in the formation process . . . [this] has been to consult separately the Speaker of the Second Chamber, a member of the largest party in Parliament, and the Vice President of the Council of State, and together the leaders of all the parliamentary parties in the Second Chamber.'[19] Her intention is to find a *formateur*, a person charged with putting together a cabinet and, effectively, the putative Prime Minister designate. Unless the majority of parliament can agree on who the *formateur* should be, then the Queen appoints an *informateur*, typically an elder statesman whose job is to open negotiations between parties on who the *formateur* should be and report back to the Queen.[20] This system of *formateurs* and *informateurs* is the typical manner in which heads of state who are active in government formation interact with the legislature (see Table 4.1).

As Grofman, Noviello, and Straffin and Austen-Smith and Banks have pointed out, the process of coalition formation can be quite different when one party leader is asked to form a government.[21] If we envisage coalition formation as an incremental process in which parties are added in sequence to a 'nucleus' until some viability criterion or other is satisfied, then having the head of state specify the coalition nucleus obviously makes a big difference to the outcome. This is the typical sequence of events under a *formateur* system with an active head of state. Even when the head of state is not active, however, a norm may emerge under which one particular party leader, perhaps the leader of the outgoing government or the leader of the largest party, is automatically designated as the first *formateur*.

Above all else, it is clear that a government formation process that allows only one coalition nucleus to be specified at any particular stage in the bargaining process, the typical pattern under the *informateur–formateur* system that develops when the head of state takes an active role, produces quite a different bargaining environment to the 'freestyle' bargaining that is encouraged when the matter is entirely in the hands of parliament. As the brief analyses by Grofman *et al.* and by Austen-Smith and Banks show, it is quite possible to explore the process of coalition formation around a specified nucleus in a systematic manner.[22] The nature of the participation of the head of state in the formation process is thus not only an important constraint on the bargaining system but it is one that can form the basis of a generalizable theoretical analysis. Indeed, given the actual role that this factor can play, we may even generate quite different accounts of coalition bargaining, depending upon whether or not a particular actor can be designated in some sense as the nucleus of the coalition formation process.

The Death of Governments

The politics of coalition is constrained by the rules circumscribing the death of governments as well as by those dealing with their birth. Figure 4.1 and Table 4.1 indicate that two matters are of prime importance here. The first deals with the role of votes of no confidence; the second concerns the extent to which the defeat of a government heralds a new election.

In general terms, as we saw in Chapter 4, the operation of parliamentary democracy in Europe implies that governments must lie down and die when they are beaten in the legislature. Typically, such a defeat can be definitively established only if the government loses a confidence vote. Legislative defeats on 'important' issues may well also cause the death of a government, but here the situation is much less clear-cut. It is never the case that any legislative defeat is fatal for a government, regardless of the significance of the issue. Thus, in the absence of a subsequent vote of confidence, the government itself may decide whether a defeat on any particular legislative proposal is a resignation matter. Governments may make the tactical decision to raise the stakes on a particular vote by announcing in advance that they will resign if defeated, but whether they in fact go on to do so remains a tactical rather than a constitutional question. When all is said and done, however, European coalition executives cannot survive legislative defeats on motions of no confidence. This is the keystone of European parliamentary democracy and the only exception to this rule can be found in Switzerland.

Every system has different procedural rules affecting the operation of the confidence vote. These govern the ease with which opposition parties can get business onto the legislative agenda that might embarrass the government and with which they can propose votes of no confidence (although the impact of these matters on coalitional behaviour has not, to the best of our knowledge, been subjected to systematic empirical research). A common feature of all systems, of course, is that it is much easier for the government to place items on the legislative agenda— raising the stakes by proposing a motion of confidence, for example—than it is for the opposition. Precisely how often, how quickly, and how easily the opposition can initiate business in general and a motion of no confidence in particular obviously has a considerable bearing on the security of tenure of a cabinet and thereby has a significant impact, in any given system, on the politics of coalition in general.

A second structural factor associated with the death of a government has an impact on coalitional behaviour. This concerns whether or not the defeat of a government necessarily entails the dissolution of the legislature and the holding of an election. As Table 4.1 shows, most European legislatures cannot dissolve themselves, but most can be dissolved at the initiative of the government. European systems differ considerably in their precise provisions on the dissolution of the legislature, though differences are more matters of convention than of rigid clauses in the constitution. Few constitutions *require* the dissolution of the legislature following any defeat of the executive. None the less, it is certainly the convention in a number of systems that more or less any government defeat does indeed presage an election. In Iceland and Ireland, for example, this is almost invariably the case. In Austria, Luxemburg, and Sweden, while it is not invariably true that the fall of a government triggers an election, it is usually the case that this happens, so that only one government forms between each election. In other European systems, it is quite common for one government to fall and another to form without there being an intervening election. In Italy, perhaps the most extreme case, six governments formed after each of the 1968, the 1972, and the 1979 elections. In Belgium, Israel, and The Netherlands, it is not uncommon for up to three governments, often with quite different party compositions, to form without an intervening election. The situation in Norway is particularly distinctive. The constitution makes it very difficult to hold an election except at the scheduled four-year intervals. If, in exceptional circumstances, an additional election is held, then the scheduled election is not postponed to take account of this but must take place as planned. The fall of governments in Norway certainly does not automatically invoke a new election, therefore, and in some periods socialist and bourgeois blocs have alternated in office without placing the matter before the voters.

Whether the dissolution of the legislature is likely to follow the defeat of a government is obviously a key factor in the politics of coalition. If an election is likely to result from a government defeat, either because this is the norm or because a particular legislature is approaching the end of its life anyway, then it is obviously the case that politicians will anticipate the likely result of the election when calculating whether to bring down the government. In an age of widespread public opinion polling, politicians have good information about the likely electoral consequences of their actions. This information has a vital impact upon the politics of coalition, since it can affect the ebb and flow of bargaining power among coalition parties during the life of a cabinet. Effective power inside the government can thus be affected by changes in the opinion poll ratings of the parties. Those riding high in the polls may be eager for an election—with greater incentives to defect when they are in government, and to force an election if possible when they are in opposition. This means that the threats at their disposal, typically threats to bring down the government, are more credible. Other politicians will recognize this and be more inclined to give in to them rather than face the electorate. In this way, the bargaining power of those who are doing well in the opinion polls is enhanced.

If a particular group of politicians regard elections as costly things, as ordeals that force them to spend scarce time and money pandering to their supporters, for example, then they can use opinion poll findings to avoid the election that follows the defeat of a government by reallocating power within the cabinet rather than by bringing it down. Knowing that they will lose, parties who are doing badly in the polls can concede more in cabinet. Knowing that they will win, parties that are doing well in the polls can ask for more. In other words, if politicians use opinion polls to foresee changes in the pattern of electoral support, the distribution of power in the legislature can reflect anticipated election results. This argument has been made by an opinion pollster, John Clemens, though it has not to our knowledge been much considered by political scientists. Clemens's case is that 'public opinion [polling] has led to the creation of a new form of power in society, not just at elections . . . but also on a continuing, almost day-to-day basis'.[22] He applies his arguments only to Britain and the USA but the possibility that opinion polls can affect the balance of power in a coalition clearly merits investigation.

We have concentrated on only two types of structural constraint upon coalition bargaining, the electoral system and the set of links between legislature and executive. But we have seen, even in these two limited areas, that a single major institutional feature can make two otherwise similar coalition systems as different as chalk and cheese. Particular constitutional constraints, the German constructive vote of no confidence for example, were even designed with the specific intention of having an impact upon the politics of government formation. To ignore such matters would clearly be sticking our heads very deeply into the sand.

SUMMARY AND CONCLUSIONS: CONSTRAINED COALITION THEORY?

The assumption that bargaining between parties over government formation takes place in a relatively unconstrained way is fundamental to most existing coalition theories. As we have seen, structural factors have a major impact on the range of possibilities but this does not mean that general theories of coalition bargaining have no practical use. Rather, it means that they form a base-line against which the impact of structural factors can and should be tracked in a systematic and rigorous manner.

The development of the 'new institutionalism' by students of US legislative politics has shown us that institutional factors can be incorporated into general theories in a very productive way. Almost by definition, of course, powerful structural constraints will operate in different systems in different ways; the only way to avoid an entirely *ad hoc* approach to this is to specify in advance the constraints to be considered together with their likely effects. Pulling a new assumed constraint out of a hat every time the going gets rough is the sort of thing that gives theorists a bad name.

Structural constraints on bargaining are likely to change only slowly. The continual operation of the same constraints may imply the continual formation and reformation of the same coalition. This may have the effect that government membership may be determined, not by bargaining at all, but by some government 'formula' derived from the constraints of the situation. This does not mean that bargaining is not taking place. Rather, it means that the arena of bargaining has moved away from the government formation phase in which one coalition is selected out of a large universe of possibilities, towards the government maintenance phase, in which bargaining and negotiation take place within a single 'given' coalition.

What goes on inside a given coalition is a matter that has yet to attract the serious attention of mainstream coalition theorists, yet this is clearly a vital matter. In the specific context of this chapter, constraints on bargaining may dictate the formation of a particular cabinet, thereby transferring the real bargaining action to internal cabinet politics. In the more general context of this book as a whole, the anticipation of life inside a given cabinet obviously affects the entire business of forming a government. The actual experience of life inside a cabinet—not to mention anticipations of life inside the cabinets that might conceivably succeed it—obviously conditions the stability of any government. We cannot, therefore, consider ourselves to have a full understanding of the politics of forming and maintaining a government without having at least some impressions of life inside a coalition cabinet. Getting to grips with this particular matter is one of the most exciting intellectual challenges that confronts coalition theorists.

APPENDIX A

The Unitary Actor Status of Political Parties in European Coalition Systems

The various sections in this Appendix are in no sense intended as potted introductions to the party systems of the countries discussed; this would be a massive and daunting task. They do, of course, serve to introduce some of the huge cast of characters involved in the politics of coalition in Europe, but their main purpose is to review, on a country-by-country basis, the usefulness of the assumption that parties behave as if they were unitary actors as far as coalition bargaining is concerned. Thus the coverage of each system does not provide a balanced discussion of each party, but rather concentrates upon those parties which are particularly interesting from the point of view of the unitary actor assumption.

AUSTRIA

In a recent and comprehensive survey of the Austrian party system Gerlich concludes that

even if the parties are organised internally according to democratic principles, the national leadership holds a very strong position in internal decision-making . . . The one means of control, the normally biannual party convention, is . . . anything but effective. While different wings or, especially, the leagues of the ÖVP may compete openly on these rare occasions, as a rule the cohesion of both parties is very high.[1]

Gerlich does, however, go on to accept that, of the two main parties in Austria, the Socialists (SPÖ) are more homogeneous than the People's Party (ÖVP).[2] Dreijmanis further highlights this point, arguing that 'the ÖVP is coalitional in structure being an association of five federations'.[3] He claims that this does have an impact on the coalitional process in that

no federation controls the party. The party leaders thus must be brokers who can command the respect of the various federations without being dependent on any one of them. During the coalition period, the party leaders were Figl (ÖBB) [Austrian Farmers' Federation], Raab (ÖWB) [Austrian Business Federation], Gorbach (ÖABB) [Austrian Workers' and Employees' Federation] and Klaus

(ÖWB). Whenever the party leadership changed hands from one federation to another, that federation became the key one. The major party quarrels were over economic policy and the distribution of the various cabinet posts.[4]

We are thus painted a picture, for the ÖVP in particular, of a party within which there is considerable competition to control the leadership but over which the leadership of the day, once the issue has been settled, wields considerable control.

As far as the impact of this on the politics of coalition is concerned, Müller points to the difference between the ÖVP in opposition, when the factions create more dissension within the the party, and the ÖVP in government.[5] When the ÖVP is in power, the accumulation of a wide range of offices and mandates throughout the country by the party leadership ensures the rigid control of the leadership faction down through the party hierarchy. When the ÖVP is in opposition these offices get dissipated and it is easier for dissident groups to build power bases. This difference in the unitary actor status of the party, brought about by the difference between office and opposition, is one that can be found in a number of other systems. It is particularly significant in those systems, such as in Austria, in which an accumulation of mandates and offices by the party leadership is possible.

The impact of intraparty politics on party policy is discussed by Franz Horner, who considers the role fulfilled by the Basic Programmes (*Grundsatzprogramme*) of the main parties. These

are only changed after substantial theoretical debate and a special party convention, and may remain in force for decades. They are not keyed to a particular party leadership, nor to a particular election. Examples are the ÖVP Salzburg Programm which was unanimously accepted at the party conference in Salzburg in November 1972, the Neue Programm adopted by the SPÖ at a party conference in May 1978 in Vienna; and the FPÖ Bad Ischler Programm adopted in 1968.[6]

While the Basic Programmes, which lay down the philosophy of the party in quite an elaborate fashion, require very extensive discussion at all levels of the party, election manifestos (which should essentially be compatible with these) are produced much more centrally. The role of particular issues in campaigns has declined, however, as 'ideologies have been more or less replaced with sophisticated campaigning techniques'.[7] As a consequence, the centralized use of costly campaign tools such as media consultants and public opinion polling has put more power in the hands of the party hierarchy.

Taken together, these various features of the Austrian political scene suggest that, for coalitional purposes at least, the main parties can be treated as unitary actors without doing too much violence to reality. The ÖVP, a party that does have pronounced internal factions, tends to have one faction firmly in control at any one time. Party policy positions are derived within the general scope of broadly agreed and wideranging

Basic Programmes, while campaigning is increasingly a matter for party professionals.

BELGIUM

It need hardly be said that, for most purposes, the Belgian parties quite positively cannot be treated as unitary actors; this does, however, depend on precisely what we mean by a political party in the Belgian context, a matter that is highlighted by the current use of the term 'family' rather than 'party' to describe each of the main political groupings.

It is well known, of course, that political upheavals generated by the language cleavage resulted in the splitting of each of the main Belgian parties between 1968 and 1978. Before this, each of the three main families had reorganized so as to present two linguistic 'wings' to voters; in effect, two different store fronts to appeal to the respective language groups. The Catholic Party had become the Christian People's Party (CVP–PSC, *Christelijke Volkspartij–Parti Social Chrétien*) in 1949, the same year that the Belgian Workers' Party had become the Belgian Socialist Party (BSP–PSB, *Belgische Socialistische Partij–Parti Socialiste Belge*). The Liberal Party had become the Party for Liberty and Progress (PVV–PLP, *Partij voor Vrijheid en Vooruitang–Parti de la Liberté et du Progres*) in 1961.[8] Organizational niceties such as these, however, did not go to the heart of the language problem. A major row in 1968 over the location of the (francophone) Catholic University of Louvain split the Christian family into two quite distinct parts, the CVP and the PSC. The Liberals took a strongly unitarist stand but did badly with it at the polls. As a consequence, they split into the PLP and the PVV in 1972 and then again into the PL, the PLP, and the PVV in 1973. The PL and the PLP recombined into the PRL, *Parti Réformateur Libéral*, in 1979. The Socialists split in 1978, over a proposal for a common front on the language issue that would include each of the main French-speaking parties. They broke into the PS and the VS, after which the two factions co-ordinated their actions only loosely.[9]

The unitary actor status of the Belgian parties is made considerably more complex by the fact that each side of the CVP–PSC family is made up of a series of well organized 'estates', or *standen*, in a manner analogous to the Austrian ÖVP. The CVP, for example, has *standen* of workers (ACW), farmers (BB), and business people (NCMV). The position of these estates within the party is highly institutionalized and individual estates effectively control the nominations of the party's candidates at election time. (In 1985, 47 per cent of CVP representatives belonged to the ACW, 12 per cent to the BB and 27 per cent to the NCMV[10].) The

CVP's *standen* are discussed in more detail by Rudd, but his key conclusion is that they are relevant actors in the coalition game.[11] For example, CVP–PSC domination of most post-war Belgian coalition cabinets led to a situation in which, according to Rudd, 'the Agriculture Minister, is nearly always a Boerenbond [BB] "appointee" '.[12] Rudd also argues that the actual composition of coalition cabinets has been affected by factions within the CVP: 'There is little doubt that the ACW constitutes a major source of support for the CVP . . . with the main affiliated organisation of the ACW being the Flemish Christian Trade Union Movement (ACV) and with the majority of CVP voters identifying with the working class . . . the ACW has had some success in orienting the CVP towards centre–left coalitions with the socialists.'[13] Even the choice of Prime Minister has been affected: 'After the 1981 election, the possibility of a Christian-Social + Liberal coalition arose once more and, although the ACW was unable to prevent the formation of such a coalition, it did succeed in ensuring that Martens rather than Tindemans became Prime Minister.'[14]

On the Walloon side of the Christian family, the PSC contains two major factions, representing manual and non-manual workers respectively as well as the Alliance Agricole Belge, representing French-speaking farmers without being officially recognized by the party. The politics of competition between these factions has not only been more complex and bitter than that within the CVP,[15] but has involved the formation of movements, such as *Démocratie Chrétienne* (DC), that linked one PSC faction with members of other parties and pitted these against the other PSC faction. Thus we find a situation in which members of one party are acting against party colleagues in concert with members of other parties. This is surely a circumstance that must raise fundamental doubts about the wisdom of regarding the parties in Belgium as unitary actors, even for the relatively modest purpose of analysing coalitional behaviour. For the most part, however, interaction between factions within the Belgian parties has been relatively amicable in comparative European terms. At the same time the party leaders have been increasingly able, in Dewachter's view, to control events within their own parties, largely because of an erosion of internal party democracy over the postwar period.[16]

The existence in Belgium of 'language parties' that stress one dimension of policy far more than the others provides another interesting example of the way in which the coalitional process interacts with internal party politics. This can be seen most clearly in the case of the Rassemblement Wallon (RW). The cluster of 'ethnic' federalist parties that arose out of the language problem in Belgium have obviously brought this one issue to the fore and have tended to sublimate internal divisions on matters of socio-economic policy. Such a solution is of course possible when a party is in opposition but becomes impossible to maintain when it goes into government. The first of the federalist parties to go into a coalition cabinet was the RW, in 1974. Almost as soon as the party went into office, internal disputes over the appropriate social and economic policies began to rage and, facing mounting losses in the opinion polls, the party eventually split in 1976 with the leadership leaving and merging with the Walloon Liberals.[17] This party, effectively, was pulled apart by the politics of coalition.

One final and striking question that we must answer before settling on a cast of actors for the coalition game in Belgium concerns the extent of co-ordination between the Flemish and Walloon parties within the same political family. Dewachter and Clijsters argue that 'the former linguistic wings operate as autonomous parties, maintaining only loose ties on the national level, *but strong enough to prevent the other wing from joining a coalition without its linguistic counterpart*'.[18] Dewachter repeats this argument, adding, however, that even though members of the same family have thus far gone into and come out of government together, 'the manner in which [they] can be brought into the cabinet has been made considerably more difficult'.[19] Most authors, while noting that members of the same family have thus far always acted in concert over coalition formation, do not rule out the possibility of independent action.

In concluding this discussion of what is almost certainly the most difficult case that we will be considering we may note that, if we insist upon retaining a very hard-nosed operational definition of a party, then we may regard even the Belgian parties as unitary actors. If we treat the 'families' as if they were parties it remains the case that these families have thus far gone into and come out of coalitions together, while none has yet been in the position of being half in and half out of government. Links between language wings of the same family may be loose in some cases, but they are not yet loose enough for one wing to go into office without the other. Given the immense upheavals that have been seen in recent Belgian politics, however, even this possibility clearly cannot be ruled out.

DENMARK

Mogens Pederson, in a recent authoritative review of the Danish party system, describes the four 'old' parties which dominated the system up until 1973—the Social Democrats (SD), Radical Liberals (RV), Agrarian Liberals (V) and Conservatives (KF)—as 'highly cohesive and disciplined'.[20] What appears to be a typically Scandinavian model of tight party discipline fits the Danish case rather well in this period, though there was a significant split on the left in 1958 as a result of the expulsion from the Danish Communist Party (DKP) of Aksel Larsen, the party's long-time leader. This was the consequence of a doctrinaire dispute over de-Stalinization and unilateral Soviet disarmament and resulted in Larsen setting up the Socialist People's Party (SFP), which became one of Denmark's main political parties in the 1960s.[21] It supported the 1966–8 Social Democratic minority government at a time when the socialist parties between them controlled a majority. Indeed, Fitzmaurice argues that the offer of a formal coalition that had been made to the SFP by the Social Democrats in 1966 was an attempt to outmanoeuvre the SFP and thereby stem the electoral losses of the Social Democrats.[22] Bitter disputes within the SFP over the best parliamentary strategy in general, and over proposals for devaluation in particular, led the parliamentary party to 'split right down the middle' in 1967,[23] bringing down the government in the process and leading to the breakaway of a small left-wing group who went on to form the Left Socialists (VS).[24] The further splintering of the left produced by this breakdown in co-operation put a block on further co-operation between Social Democrats and the smaller socialist parties; thus it also paved the way for a change in party strategies among the other parties, most notably the Radical Liberals. 'The turbulence and shifting pattern of inter-party cooperation that characterise the parliamentary system during the years before 1973 can to a large extent be traced back to the conflict between the executive and the parliamentary party of the Socialist People's Party between 1966 and 1968.'[25]

A major explosion of new parties on to the Danish political scene occurred with the 'unfreezing' of the party system at the 1973 election, though only one of the five parties gaining representation for the first time at this election can be seen as the direct result of a split. Just before the election the Centre Democrats (CD) had split away in a rightward direction from the Social Democrats in a dispute over property taxation. The Communist Party and the Justice Party each regained parliamentary representation that they had lost in 1960. The other two new parties were Mogens Glistrup's Justice Party and the Christian People's Party. Both of these have since been subject to damaging internal party divisions and both have declined, in part as a result of these splits.[26] The 'new' parties are not as rigidly organized as the 'old' parties and have shown a much greater tendency to divide. None the less, the situation as regards legislative party discipline in Denmark has not been greatly changed by these developments. In his recent review of the position Fitzmaurice can still talk of 'the iron party discipline in parliament'.[27] Pederson concurs, arguing that 'coalition formation in parliament is still facilitated by the considerable cohesion of party groups . . . the traditional norms of parliamentary conduct have been preserved and upheld with only minor infringements'.

The threshold for electoral representation in Denmark presents few major penalties for formation of new parties in general and for party splits in particular. Thus, while each of the parties functions relatively coherently as a unitary actor at any point in time, the possibility of splits and new parties is ever-present in Denmark, a strategic environment that is clearly likely to have a major impact on the politics of coalition.

FINLAND

Finland provides another example of a Scandinavian system in which factional disputes within parties have taken place in an environment of tight party discipline in the legislature. Arter points out that 'at plenary votes . . . members tend to toe the party line . . . despite Article 11 of the Parliament Act, which states that "an Eduskunta member is obliged in his actions to observe the dictates of justice and truth; he is bound by the constitution but no other instructions" '.[29] This rigid party discipline tends to encourage intraparty divisions to be transformed into formal divisions and most of the main coalitional actors in Finland have split at one stage or another in the country's post-war political history.

The first to split was the Finnish Social Democratic party (*Suomen Sosialidemokraatinen Puolue*). A splinter from this, the Social Democratic League of Workers and Smallholders (*Työvaen ja Pienviljelijäin Socialidemoktraatinen Liitto*), formed in the late 1950s.[30] There then followed an era in which one or the other of the two parties, but never both, was in the government coalition until they reunited ten years later.

Another important split in a key coalition actor occurred within the Centre Party (*Keskustapuolue*) in the run-up to the 1970 election. This centred on the issue of relations with the Soviet Union, the successful management of which had always been a strong policy suit for the Centre Party, formerly the Agrarians. The breakaway faction, led by Vennamo, formed the Finnish Rural Party (*Suomen Maaseudun Puole*) and did well in the 1970 election.[31] However, the Rural Party was itself the subject of a split when the Finnish People's Unity Party broke away from it in 1973.

Finally, any discussion of party splits in Finland must include the formation in 1973 of the Finnish Constitutional People's Party (*Suomen Perustuslaillinen Kansanpuolue*). This was created from factions of the Swedish People's Party and the Conservatives and formed 'in protest against the alliance of all of the established parties which the same year passed exceptional legislation enabling Parliament to elect the President, Urho Kekkonen, for a further four year term of office without recourse to the popular elections prescribed by the Constitution'.[32]

We see in Finland, therefore, a situation in which party splits are not only common, but form an integral part of the coalitional process, with factions that have split from one another going into and out of coalitions at different times, and with splits arising in the first place because of the various coalitional possibilities on offer. The rigid party discipline typical of the Scandinavian system encourages this process. A consequence is that we may treat each party as a unitary actor at any single point in time, though it is particularly important in the Finnish case to take party splits into account in any dynamic account of the system.

FRANCE

The French Fourth Republic, as we have already mentioned, is typically cited as the classic case of a party system in which the parties are not unitary actors. Even confining ourselves to the parliamentary level, we find several cases where parties were not united in their support for coalition governments. As Grünberg points out, most of this instability was on the right.[33] Lauber describes a process of polarization around, on the one hand, a Gaullist nexus based on the Rassemblement du Peuple Française (RPF) and, on the other, a more traditional conservative nexus based on the Centre National Independent et Paysan (CNIP).[34] De Gaulle did not clarify matters by founding, in the RPF, a mass movement rather than a political party in the strict sense, and inviting members of other parties to join the RPF while also remaining within their own party.[35] McCrea provides a well known account of this period of instability[36] (possibly exaggerating the extent of the chaos as a result of his concentration on legislative roll calls) but what is clear is that there is no obvious set of well disciplined actors. In particular the Gaullists, who changed their name to the Union Republicaine d'Action Sociale (URAS) after de Gaulle had disowned them for their dealings with the Fourth Republic, were involved, in bits and pieces, in several governments: the Gaullist 'party' was half in and half out of the Pinay government in 1952 and the Mendès-France government in 1954. Any analysis of the politics of coalition in the French Fourth Republic, therefore, clearly cannot regard parties as unitary actors in any sense at all, even on the minimalist definition of actors that go into and come out of governments as single entities.

While the party system of the French Fifth Republic has been far more stable than that of the Fourth, France has continued to be a problem case for coalition analysts. Probably as a consequence, the French Fifth Republic is not discussed in any of the three recent collections of case studies of the politics of coalition.[37] It has also been excluded from most cross-national 'tests' of coalition theories.[38] The main problem in this instance is the power wielded by the President under the constitution of the Fifth Republic. This situation was established by de Gaulle but has been exploited by his successors, for example Mitterrand, to exercise very firm control over the parliamentary parties. Indeed, as a consequence of the accession of a Socialist President, 'the Socialist Party structure has been altered to eliminate the famous *courants*—formal internal factions—in an attempt to unite the party behind government policy'.[39] Prior to the period of 'cohabitation' between Prime Minister Chirac and President Mitterrand that ended with Chirac's defeat by Mitterrand in the Presidential elections of 1988, the Presidency and the legislative majority always tended to go to the same party. This, combined with the President's absolute constitutional power both to dissolve the legislature and to appoint the Prime Minister and other ministers, meant that it was very difficult to assess the independent impact of legislative politics on the behaviour of the executive. This dependence of the legislative party system on events at presidential level was further highlighted by the events that followed Chirac's resignation after his 1988 defeat. Mitterrand immediately appointed Rochard, a Socialist, as the new Prime Minister and called a new legislative election in the confident expectation of winning a comfortable majority for the Socialists. Thus the legislative game was transformed by events at executive level, a strong piece of evidence that legislative parties in France may not be independent (let alone unitary) actors in the coalition game. The party of the President, in particular, has always appeared to be very much under Presidential control. For this reason, analyses of the politics of coalition in France must inevitably proceed under special 'local' assumptions about the bargaining status of the various actors.

GREECE

The strong trend towards two-party politics in Greece in the period since 1974 has been helped by the electoral system, which gives a major bonus to the larger parties, New Democracy (ND) on the right and the Panhellenic Socialist Movement (PASOK) on the centre-left. This has meant that members of the main parties have had a strong incentive to remain within these large units rather than to split away from them. Of the two, New Democracy has been the more torn by internal conflict. Originally formed in 1974 by Karamanlis, one of the key politicians in the transition from the military junta, New Democracy became a 'party of notables which relied upon clientelistic networks'.[40] It formed the basis of the first Greek single-party government but, after Karamanlis was elected to the Greek Presidency in 1980, it lost its main unifying force and the subsequent leadership election 'brought to the surface significant differences of opinion'.[41] The party was thus split and disorganized when it fought and lost the 1981 general election. Since then, it has remained 'demoralised, faction-ridden and out of power'.[42] Its organization remains based upon personalities and patronage. While the party is out of office, this leads to a lack of discipline and constant leadership changes.

PASOK has grown fastest of the Greek parties and become very much a catch-all undertaking, leading some to suggest that it has at least the potential to fall apart.[43] For the time being, however, PASOK remains 'a movement structured around an undisputed charismatic leader, who has always been able to silence intra-party dissent either through recurrent expulsion or by balancing one tendency against another'.[44] Featherstone agrees that 'its leadership structure [is] hierarchical and dominated by Papendreou'.[45]

In the period since the restoration of parliamentary democracy, the other parties have come to be more like PASOK in their internal organization, with the higher levels of party discipline characteristic of Westminster-style two partism. Greece, in short, has a system in which the formal rules of the political game heavily discourage party splits, which makes it much easier for strong leaders to control dissidence within parties. As there have only been single-party majority governments since 1974, it is not really possible to say what the effect of a minority situation would be on the politics of coalition, though very tentative indications suggest that party splits might then become more likely.

ICELAND

The Icelandic party system remained stable for some time after the Second World War. Since 1968–70, however, it has become much more volatile, a situation attributed by Hardarson and Kristensen to the steady depoliticization of the civil service, which reduced the volume of patronage appointments available to the established parties, to decreasing party control over the mass media, and to the introduction of a primary system for selecting candidates, significantly weakening the power of party leaders.[46] This process culminated in some dramatic changes in the party system, which manifested themselves in the 1987 election, with the electoral success of two new parties, the Citizens' Party and the

Women's Alliance.[47] Each of the existing parties, too, was affected by internal change and conflict.

The Social Democratic Party (*Althyduflokkur*), has been one of the major coalition actors in Icelandic politics since the war, despite its small size. According to Tomasson, 'a high level of internal conflict has always characterised the Social Democrats'.[48] The party split in 1956 and one of the factions, together with the United Socialist Party (*Sameiningarflokkur athydu-Socialistaflokkurinn*) combined to form Iceland's major left-wing actor, the People's Alliance (*Althydubandalag*). The People's Alliance was joined in 1963 by the National Preservation Party (*Thjodvarnarflokkur Islands*), formed to oppose Icelandic NATO membership and the US air force base at Keflavik. This produced an alliance comprising ex-Communists, social democrats and radical nationalists, an unstable grouping that came apart in 1968. The result was the formation of the Union of Liberals and Leftists (*Samtokfrjalslyndra og Vinstri manna*) and the reorganization of the People's Alliance along the lines of a full-scale political party. The latter party still contains a wide range of different ideological components, something which 'in recent years has helped the PA to occupy most of the left-wing spectrum in Icelandic politics'.[49] What is significant from the perspective of the unitary actor status of the parties, however, is that the People's Alliance remains a party with the clear potential to split.

The Union of Liberals and Leftists, as we have seen, was the result of a split in the People's Alliance. It joined the coalition government after its success in the 1971 elections, 'but internal disputes, partly caused by the loose amalgamation of different groups, led to splits in the party *and contributed to the dissolution of the coalition*'.[50]

The other main parties, the Independence Party (*Sjalfstaedisflokkur*) and the Progressive Party (*Framsoknarflokkar*) had until recently seemed less prone to splitting than their rivals. In 1980, however, the Independence Party suddenly went into turmoil to provide one of the very few examples in modern Europe of a party being half in and half out of a coalition. This happened after 'a series of schisms emerged in the party . . . when the deputy leader, Gunnar Thoroddsen, supported by a few IP members of the *Althingi*, formed a coalition government with the PP and the PA, *leaving the bulk of the party, including party leader Hallgrimsson, in opposition*'.[51] Thoroddsen managed to remain within the party and, while he himself eventually left politics, his supporters were all re-elected, using the primary system, as representatives of the IP.[52] Indeed, one of these dissidents won first place in the Reykjavik primary, while the IP leader, Hallgrimsson, finished seventh and went on to lose his seat in the general election.[53] Since then, splinter groups have presented lists in a number of constituencies, while ideological rifts generated as a result of a move to the right by the main party provoked a breakaway when the Citizens' Party was founded in 1987.

The immediate cause of the formation of the Citizens' Party was a scandal embroiling Albert Gudmundsson, a former IP Minister of Finance who was accused of tax evasion. Claiming that he had made an honest mistake, he rallied considerable support around himself and established the Citizens' Party, which has subsequently taken a more pragmatic line than the increasingly doctrinaire and monetarist IP.[54] The party won 11 per cent of the vote and seven of the sixty seats in 1987.

Another victor in 1987 was the Women's Alliance, which was not formed as a result of particular party splits but which succeeded, rather, as a result of the failure of the left-wing parties to integrate the women's movement. The Women's Alliance took votes mainly from the left[55] and the party emerged from relative obscurity in 1983 to a position where it won 10 per cent of the vote and six of the sixty seats in 1987.

After a long period as a model of stability, therefore, party politics in Iceland has demonstrated in a quite spectacular manner the dangers of adhering slavishly to the unitary actor assumption.

IRELAND

By and large, the main Irish parties tend to be run on personalist lines, which has meant that internal disputes have focused largely on personalities rather than on policies. Divisions exist within each of the four main Irish parties, though these have rarely impaired their ability to act as unitary actors when it comes to coalition bargaining.[56] The two main parties, Fianna Fáil and Fine Gael, are both tightly organized structures dominated by their leaders. While pro- and anti-leader factions are quite usual, and while the STV electoral system is almost unique in the extent to which it allows voters to express meaningful intraparty preferences and thereby express a view on such divisions, the party leaders can effectively take their parties into and out of government in the knowledge that dissension in the ranks can be easily dealt with.[57] Charles Haughey, the leader of Fianna Fáil for much of the recent period, has demonstrated a remarkable ability to withstand challenges — to his position from within the party. During the various 'heaves' against the Fianna Fáil leadership that have taken place, feelers have been put out to other parties by members of anti-Haughey factions within Fianna Fáil, but nothing has ever come of them. The most spectacular example of the refusal to tolerate dissent in the ranks was the summary expulsion from the party of a pretender to the Fianna Fáil leadership, Desmond

O'Malley, for his disagreement with the party leadership over Northern Ireland policy. After his expulsion, O'Malley went on to form a new party, the Progressive Democrats, which attracted parliamentary defectors mostly from Fianna Fáil, voters mostly from Fine Gael, and did surprisingly well to get about 14 per cent of the vote in its first electoral contest in February 1987.[58] Though Fine Gael has been less affected by internal wrangles over the recent period, the party has the same authoritarian structure as Fianna Fáil, which makes it easy for leaders to enforce rigid party discipline.

The emergence of the Progressive Democrats transformed the politics of coalition in Ireland. It offered a new coalition partner to Fine Gael, while denying Fianna Fáil an overall majority after the 1987 election. The fact that the party organization, and the set of newly elected members of the parliamentary party, are drawn from the ranks of both Fianna Fáil and Fine Gael is a potential source of intraparty conflict. The prospect of coalition with either Fine Gael or Fianna Fáil could re-open wounds caused by the defections, since 'jumpers' have never been popular in Irish politics. In the same way, if the party were to slump at the polls, the potential is clearly there for lower-level activists to defect back to their original party; such re-defections, indeed, have already taken place in a number of instances.

The Labour Party was divided, during the 1973–87 period, precisely on the issue of coalition. A more left-wing faction, often identified with the then party chairman Michael D. Higgins, opposed coalition with Fine Gael. A more right-wing faction, typically centred on the leader of the parliamentary party, favoured coalition. Since the organizational structure of Labour gives considerable authority to the party conference and the national executive, neither of which is dominated by the parliamentary party, 'getting a coalition package accepted in the party has never been impossible for any leader, but it has always been difficult'.[59] Reacting to disastrous opinion poll performances during the 1982–7 coalition with Fine Gael, Labour set up a 'Commission on Electoral Strategy' explicitly to consider its options. The commission recommended that Labour enter no coalitions for the foreseeable future, a decision that was accepted first by the party conference and subsequently by the parliamentary leadership.[60]

Overall, while internal party politics is at least as lively in Ireland as anywhere else, the parties as constituted tend to function as unitary actors. Major divisions have resulted in party splits, on the Scandinavian model, but the legislative voting discipline of the parliamentary parties is very tight, allowing Irish governments to operate successfully with what, in European terms, have been wafer-thin majorities. Discipline is particularly strong in Fine Gael and Fianna Fáil, parties which clearly can be committed to coalition strategies by their leaders alone.[61] It is, therefore, reasonable to view the Irish parties as unitary actors at the point of entry to the coalition. If we take a more dynamic perspective, however, intraparty politics and coalitional behaviour quite definitely interact, with a clear potential to transform the party system.

ISRAEL

The Israeli party system is enough to bring tears to the eyes of the most stalwart coalition analyst, not so much because of the very large number of parties but precisely because so many of these have split or changed their names (and usually both) several times during the period since the creation of the modern state of Israel in 1948. Some of the main tendencies are summarized by Bara, and two examples serve to illustrate quite clearly the complexity of the Israeli coalition and party system:

> The main force within the religious tendency is MAFDAL (National Religious Party), which represents a merger between the Mizrahi and the Poalei Mizrahi groups . . . In addition there are two 'Agudah' (Association of Israel) parties, the Agudat Israel and the Poalei Agudat Israel . . . In 1949 all four groups contested the election under one banner but split immediately afterwards. Mizrahi and Poalei Mizrahi retained their close relationship and in 1956 formally entered a permanent electoral alliance, which has been maintained.[62]

> The nucleus of the right is the Herut . . . In 1965 a pact was forged between Herut and the General Zionist faction of the Liberal Party, which led to the formation of GAHAL . . . GAHAL formed the basis of the [Likud] which also encompassed other elements at different times; the State List (The RAFI faction that did not re-enter the Ma'arach in 1968); the Free Centre, a dissident Herut faction; Ariel Sharon's Shlomzion (Realisation of Zion) faction; the ultra-nationalist list in the 1981 election; and the extremist organization, Kach, which failed to win any Knesset representation.

One very simple conclusion that can be drawn from this is that Israel's ultra-proportional electoral laws make it possible for the significant constellations in the party system frequently to change their character in a way that depends very closely upon detailed doctrinal disputes between factions, personal animosity between politicians, and, of course, upon the politics of coalition. Particular examples are the shifting electoral protocoalitions of Ma'arach on the left and Likud on the right. Such protocoalitions clearly cannot be treated as unitary actors for any practical purpose, including analyses of coalition formation, despite the relative stability that they impose upon such a potentially chaotic party system. The Israeli case is thus one in which the unitary actor assumption does considerable violence to reality, however it is operationalized. This is one reason, no doubt, why Israel is often ignored by empirical coalition analysts.

ITALY

Italian parties span the full range from highly factionalized coalitions of *correnti* to rather well organised unitary actors. At the latter end of the spectrum stands the PCI, Italy's Communist Party, practising a watered-down version of democratic centralism:

a ban on true factionalism exists in the PCI, and it is in no danger whatsoever of being removed. Italian communists point with horror at the DC and PSI, both of which have been plagued by organized, and highly personalistic, factional politics for years. Sharp, personalized conflict is usually avoided in the PCI . . . there is a strong sense that decisions, once made, have to become operative.[64]

The lack of autonomy of individual PCI parliamentarians is accepted by all concerned and reinforced by very tight control over candidate selection, the very high proportions of incumbents who are not renominated by party selectors, and the refusal of the PCI to allow candidates to campaign for individual preference votes, otherwise a possibility under the Italian version of the PR list electoral system.[65] Thus the PCI can, for many purposes, be treated as a unitary actor, a view that is shared even by Pridham,[66] who is one of the main proponents of the argument that politics within parties is the key to coalitional behaviour in Italy.

Outside the PCI, however,

each of [the parties], down to the smallest, is continually plagued by a compulsive formation of internal factions . . . the number of factions, their adherents and their political lines are in a really constant state of flux . . . the differences are so open and so organised that they are openly acknowledged by the parties.[67]

This obviously has a major impact on the politics of coalition, not least because

all factions must be accommodated in the government. When a new governing coalition is formed, the twenty six or more cabinet seats and the sixty or more subcabinet posts are distributed not only by party but by party factions . . . Moreover, because factions extend their power out of the party and into the governing institutions, disagreements among them are carried into the government itself. As a result governments have been completely paralysed and on occasion have fallen because of factional disputes.[68]

From the perspective of coalitional politics, of course, the most significant factionalism is that which can be found within the Christian Democrats (DC), permanent members of all post-war Italian coalition cabinets. The DC have been colourfully described by Irving as 'not so much a party as a coalition of factions . . . the DC must be seen as a uniquely Italian phenomenon—a coalition of mini-parties run by an oligarchy of factional leaders . . . a ship whose crew is in a permanent state of mutiny'.[69] Pridham claims that this has had a profound impact on the politics of coalition in Italy, especially since the DC is above all a party of government:

the internal balance of the *correnti*, what form of intra-party coalition or of divisions exist between them, is crucial to the translation of the DC's strategy into coalitional choices. There has even been evidence of cross-party inter-factional links, such as between DC *correnti* and individual leaders of other parties . . . certain DC leaders, and behind them their *correnti*, have preferred coalition with the PSI, while others have leaned more towards an arrangement with the PCI.[70]

This is, indeed, a universally held view of the Italian DC; and its 'chaotic and disordered' methods of candidate selection[71] leave little power in the hands of the party hierarchy to reinforce discipline or to influence the factional character of its legislative representation.

Factionalism within the DC has restricted its ability to respond to the changing configuration of the Italian party system brought about by secularization and by the move of the PSI towards the centre. According to Pasquino,

the process of revitalisation of the party [was] largely distorted and in the end blocked by the historical leaders of the DC. Closely identified with their factions, they had enough power to prevent any major change in the structure of the party; no one by himself was capable of launching a process of renewal; stalemate in the internal power relationships was the outcome.[72]

This stalemate restricted the ability of the DC to consider and implement new coalitional strategies to match the new bargaining situations in which the party found itself. Paradoxically, 'the power of the DC factions and their competition has always had positive effects on the electoral strength of the party'.[73] The end product has been a large and powerful party that has almost always had a veto on the formation of governments in Italy. But it is a party, because of the internal stalemate often produced by internal factionalism, that has rarely developed a coherent coalitional strategy.

The Socialist Party (PSI) was once as riddled with factions as the DC but has become much less so under the leadership of Bettino Craxi.[74] Before this the PSI, as the main coalition actor on the non-Communist left in Italy, 'was never capable of producing a unified, coherent strategy at national level'.[75] It had split and recombined several times, primarily over the issue of fusion, or at least very close collaboration, with the Communists.[76] Craxi, however, set out to take full control of the party; and he succeeded, 'reducing the left-wing faction to no more than a fifth of the total and practically destroying the others. This process was accompanied by an unprecedented concentration of power in the hands of the Secretary and a few collaborators as well as by a sharp curtailment of party democracy.'[77] While Craxi may have succeeded in bringing some order to the PSI in the 1980s, however, 'significant internal conflict over personal ambitions and intense battles over preference votes remain much the same'.[78] Thus the potential remains for major splits within the party.

To add to the arcane complexities of Italian intraparty politics, the 1987 election saw the emergence of a new legislative party, the Greens.[79] While this was not the result of a split in any other party, it does illustrate the potential volatility of the overall configuration of parties. It is, however, what goes on inside parties that makes the Italian case such an interesting one from the perspective of the unitary actor assumption. Within the same political culture we see the democratic centralist PCI confronting a coalition of mini-parties in the DC; we see the PSI, a party that seems to have enhanced its bargaining position significantly as intraparty factionalism has declined; and, above all, we see a party system in which party factions have been elevated to having virtually an official status in national politics. In this environment, disputes between factions within parties can be more significant, in terms of the rise and fall of governments, than disputes between parties, the normal bread-and-butter of coalition theory.

LUXEMBURG

Luxemburg is one of Europe's more straightforward coalition systems, dominated by the *Chrestlech Sozial Vollekspartei* (Christian Socialists, CSV). The most significant party split in Luxemburg has taken place within the Socialist Party, the *Letzeburger Socialistesch Arbechter Partei* (LSAP). Decision making in the LSAP is dominated by the Party Congress, which has final power over the manifesto.[80] Reacting to a leftward shift in the 1960s, and in particular to proposals for co-operation with the Communists,[81] a group of right-wing deputies split away from the LSAP to form the Social Democratic Party in 1970. This enjoyed some success in the 1970s but then declined, and was assimilated into the CSV in 1984.[82] The Luxemburg Communist Party (KPL) is a highly centralized pro-Soviet party that votes as a solid bloc. It has not been prepared to make compromises in order to enter office and has thus been little affected by the politics of coalition.

Overall, this limited view suggests that the Luxemburg parties, with the exception of the LSAP split, can probably be treated as unitary actors for coalition purposes. Party discipline is strong and certainly the rather orderly nature of the politics of coalition in Luxemburg suggests little ambiguity about who the important actors really are.

THE NETHERLANDS

Given the very highly developed state of Dutch political science, it is not surprising that the bargaining status of the actors in The Netherlands' coalition game is rather well documented. It is a matter, furthermore, that has often been considered quite explicitly in the context of coalition theory.[83] In the first place it is quite clear that the ultra-proportional electoral system and the lack of a significant threshold on the parliamentary representation of small parties means that there is no obstacle to the formation either of new parties or of splinters from old parties. The very large number of actors in the Dutch coalition game is a testimony to this; for example, in 1972 there were fourteen parties in the legislature. In the second place, the individual Dutch parties, though liable to split on occasion, tend to operate coherent parliamentary strategies at any given time. Daalder attributes parliamentary cohesiveness not to the parties' disciplinary procedures, which are not taken particularly seriously by members of the parliamentary party, but rather to general norms accepted by most Dutch MPs, who

> know that they owe their mandate to a vote for their party rather than for themselves individually . . . parliamentary groups are relatively small, which makes for close personal contacts rather than formally organised groups or wings . . . Dutch governments have not fallen over individual defections in parliament, therefore, but only through conflicts in the Cabinet or by the refusal of support by a coalition party voting as a whole.[84]

Dutch parties thus go into and come out of cabinets as unitary actors.

In the third place, as well as the party splits that have been facilitated by the PR electoral system, there has been one highly significant party fusion in The Netherlands. This involved the three main Christian parties—the Anti Revolutionary Party (ARP), the Christian Historical Union (CHU), and the Catholic People's Party (KVP)—who formed what was at first an electoral alliance and then a fully integrated new political party, the Christian Democratic Alliance (CDA).

The process by which the CDA came to be formed is analysed from the perspective of coalition theory by de Jong and Pijnenburg and there is little point in attempting to reproduce their excellent account here.[85] In essence, three quite separate religious strands are reflected in the three component parts of the CDA: the Catholic KVP, the Dutch Reformed Protestant CHU, and the Calvinist ARP. Of the two Protestant parties, the ARP had by far the tightest organization, which helped it to maintain a strong position during the merger process. The turning points in the process were August 1975, with the first combined party convention, and October 1980, when the three elements formally fused into one party. Before 1975 there had been some informal co-operation; in the 1975–80 period there was a firm electoral alliance and a declaration that the parties would go into and come out of government together, while each party retained a separate identity and organization. After 1980 the CDA became a single party with a single formal organization, containing clearly identifiable currents. The internal strains remain considerable and have led to breakaways (as in the case of the defection in 1982 of two prominent CDA politicians, Scholten and Dijkuan, in protest at the rightward drift of the CDA in coalition with the VVD). Another major example of party indiscipline, when six CDA representatives voted against allowing US cruise missiles on to Dutch soil in 1986, was punished by placing those concerned well down the list of candidates at the next election.[86] Thus CDA central control has shown itself capable of using the potential of the PR list system to discipline dissident members. The net result is a situation that leads de Jong and Pijnenburg to describe the party as 'merely an odd mixture of anti-PvdA and anti-VVD elements'.[87] Given the recent steady polarization of VVD and PvdA, this suggests that the CDA has the potential to be pulled apart again. The conflict between progressive and conservative elements is certainly one of the main cleavages in the party, though the slim parliamentary basis of some recent CDA/VVD coalitions has led to the adoption of tougher internal party rules.[88]

As to the rest of the right, the VVD seems to have been a reasonably (though not completely) cohesive force, with the selection of candidates for winnable seats quite firmly in the control of the party executive,[89] so that any deviations from the party line can be punished by demotion to a lower place on the party list. Debates over details of confessional politics are elaborated by a galaxy of small Protestant parties, such as the SGP and the GPV.[90]

The role of the PvdA on the left provides another example of the dilemmas that face us when we are forced to identify the real actors in coalition bargaining. The formation in 1966 of *Democraten '66* (D66), as a rival to the PvdA on the left was followed by the formation in 1968 of *Politieki Partij Radilalen* (PPR) by a breakaway group of four left-wing KVP deputies. *Democratisch Socialisten '70* (DS70), was formed as a breakaway from the PvdA in 1970. The PvdA thus came to lead a cluster of left-wing parties rather than being the left's sole representative; and its candidate selection procedures are very decentralized, offering less scope for maintaining party discipline than is available to the other Dutch parties.[91] In 1971, the PvdA and D66 combined to announce that they intended to go into and stay out of any coalition as a unit and that, if the KVP would not agree before the election to join them, then they would not deal with the party in coalition negotiations afterwards. The KVP declined and subsequently went into government with the other religious parties, as well as DS70 and the VVD. In 1972 the PvdA, D66 and the PPR once more made the same pre-electoral offer to the KVP and this led ultimately to an informal coalition between the four parties, together with the ARP. The PvdA has thus acted as a focus for pre-electoral protocoalition formation, a position that reflects its role as the largest among a number of centre-left parties. During this period, the PvdA has responded by attempting to consolidate its position as a unitary actor by enacting rules which, for example, tie elected representatives more explicitly to the party platform.

Above all, therefore, the Dutch case highlights very clearly the role of *electoral* protocoalitions between parties. Since all Dutch parties fall a long way short of attaining a parliamentary majority, and since the ultra-proportional electoral system does not manufacture extra seats for the larger parties, coalition building is an utterly intrinsic part of the party system. This means that the main thrust of coalition bargaining gets under way well before elections are held, rather than after they are over, and that electoral protocoalitions make it easier for the Dutch electorate to evaluate post-electoral coalition options. In the CDA, we have the example of an electoral coalition that became a political party, a clear case both of the interaction between the politics of coalition and electoral competition and of the ambiguities about the precise bargaining status of the actors that can arise as a consequence.

NORWAY

Discussing the general processes of coalition government in Denmark, Norway, and Sweden, Sarlvik lays much stress on the impact of what he calls 'two-block' politics.[92] This creates a situation analogous in some ways to two-party politics and provides a considerable inducement for the parties not to split. Strom talks of the 'high degree of control' that leaders exercise over their parties, while Fitzmaurice lays stress on the 'iron party discipline in Parliament'.[93] It is worth noting, however, that Valen, in an analysis of the decentralized control of candidate selection in Norway, finds that 'if a representative opposes the leaders regarding some important matter, the leaders are not in a position to enforce their will by threatening to have the representative removed at the next election'.[94] He concludes, in effect, that the coherence of the Norwegian parties arises because legislators accept the norm of party discipline rather than because they respond to explicit threats and punishments.

The European Community referendum in 1972 'caused a major upheaval and significant party system change'.[95] These changes opened the way for a surge of support for the small left-wing Socialist People's Party, which opposed Norway's accession to the EC. Even this issue, however, has since died away. While the Labour Party was weakened as a result, the EC issue does not seem to have produced any serious splits within the established parties.

While the potential for splitting must always exist, of course, and at the risk of gross oversimplification, it seems to be the case that political parties in Norway function more as unitary actors than do those in most of the other West European systems. This is a product more of the general consensual norms accepted by Norwegian legislators than of any specific set of constraints on their freedom of action. Strom and Leipart put the point even more forcefully, concluding that it is 'eminently reasonable to model Norwegian parties as unitary actors with considerable capacity for strategic behaviour'.[96]

PORTUGAL

From the 1974 revolution until 1987, the Portuguese political system had four or five parties, none of which enjoyed a dominant position. The 1987 election marked a dramatic departure from this situation as the Social Democrats (PSD) gained an overall majority of the seats, something that no other party had achieved since the revolution. At least one author attributes the success of the PSD to the ability of its leader, Anibal Cavaco e Silva, to unite this 'faction-ridden' party after he 'seized the helm' in 1985.[97]

On the left of the party system, the Portuguese Communist Party (PCP) has always maintained a firmly centralized decision making structure. Its electoral alliances on the left, however, have been far more complex than those of most other European Communist parties. Relations with the Portuguese Democratic Movement (MDP) are particularly close. In an electoral alliance between the PCP and the MDP known as the APA, the two parties have won seats separately but have clearly acted in such a closely co-ordinated fashion that they might be seen as either one actor or two, depending on circumstance. The MDP has negotiated with other actors in the system, independently of the PCP, for example discussing policy with Socialist Prime Minister Mario Soares in the face of PCP opposition. It returned to an electoral coalition with the PCP in 1985 but unambiguously fought as a separate party in 1987.[98] In the 1987 election, the PCP fought under a new label, the United Democratic Alliance (CDU), which incorporated a new electoral partner, the small Green Party.[99] The Socialist Party (PS) led by Soares, has factions (*sensibilidades*) analogous to the Italian *correnti*, based more around personalities than policies. Considerable fighting between factions took place at party congresses and, for a time between 1980 and 1983, this threatened the party's ability to function as a unitary actor. The situation was ultimately resolved, however, in favour of Soares.

On the right, the two main parties are the Social Democratic Centre Party (CDS) and the Social Democratic Party (PPD, then PSD). These have co-operated in an electoral and legislative alliance rather similar to that of the PCP/MDP and have even formed a government together under the single banner of the Democratic Alliance (AD). The intention behind the formation of the AD was to present Portuguese voters with a clear choice between right and left in an explicit strategy of 'bipolarization'. 'The AD assumed the form of a coalition of electoral, parliamentary and governmental scope which applied to the elections for the Assembly on the Continent, but not on the islands of Azores, or Madeira, nor did it apply to local elections.'[100] For the period of the AD, from July 1979 to January 1983, it is not clear whether we should think in terms of one actor or two. Of the two main components of the AD, the PSD has been the most riven by conflict. Held together for a time by a charismatic leader, Francisco Sa Carneiro, the party started to fall to pieces after his death in December 1980. Sa Carneiro's successor, Francisco Pinto Balsemao, became Prime Minister of an AD coalition cabinet; after he was forced out in 1982, internal divisions within the PSD led to the fall of the AD government amd the subsequent break-up of the AD. The PSD went into government with the Socialists and the CDS went into opposition. The PS/PSD coalition that ensued was brought down after faction-fighting within the PSD forced the resignation of Prime Minister Soares. This resulted in an election and, as we have seen, the emergence in 1985 of a strong PSD leader, Cavaco, who enabled the party to present a far more united front and subsequently to win an overall majority.

In the 1985 election, the Renewal Party (PRD), formed only ten months previously, did unexpectedly well, winning 18 per cent of the vote and forty-five seats. It was formed around the personality of the popular ex-President Ramalho Eanes, who was ineligible to stand for a third term of office.[101]

Overall, the ease with which new parties can break into the system, and with which electoral alliances between existing parties are formed and re-formed, reflects the fluid party politics that operate during a transition from dictatorship to democracy. In that sense the situation in Portugal is quite similar to that in Spain, especially for the parties of the right. Tainted with an authoritarian past and permeated with a penchant for *caudillismo* (a cult of traditional authoritarian leadership), parties of the Iberian right have tended until recently to operate as coalitions of factions based around leaders, coalitions that are likely to group and regroup in step with the development of particular personal animosities and the search for short-term electoral advantage.

SPAIN

Spain, like Portugal, is rarely considered in analyses of coalition systems. Initially this was because it was a dictatorship for the period up to 1975, when most of the main cross-national data sets were first assembled. Latterly it has been because of the trend towards two-party politics and one-party majority government.[102] But the periods of minority government in the early days of the democratic system and again after June 1986, together with the very clear propensity of the Spanish parties to split, illustrate that Spain is essentially a coalition system. Each of the main parties has been riven with internal dissent. On the right, both the *Unión de Centro Democrático* (UCD), which formed single-party minority governments in the 1977–82 period, and the *Alianza Popular* (AP) which effectively replaced the UCD on the right after the 1982 election, were forged as coalitions of smaller parties. The UCD was formed in 1977, initially as an electoral alliance, then as a party, uniting at least three quite distinct traditions: a Christian democratic tradition, a liberal tradition and a social democratic tradition, together with some nationally famous independent candidates.[103] One of the independent group, Adolfo Suarez, headed the party as Prime Minister from 1976 to 1981 and the UCD developed as a presidential party with a strong hierarchy. Resistance to this development from other factions within the party eventually surfaced, however. The Liberal faction split off in 1981 to form the *Partido de Acción Democrática* (PAD). Also in 1981 Suarez resigned, in the face of demands from the remaining factions that his power within the party be curtailed. The UCD, however, continued to fall apart. A right-wing group left to join the AP in coalition, under the banner of the *Partido Democrática Popular* (PDP). A left-wing group split off to form its own party. Finally, in July 1982, Suarez himself left to form the *Centro Democrático y Social* (CDS).[104] In the October 1982 elections, the UCD suffered one of the most spectacular collapses in the history of party politics, its vote falling to 7 per cent of the electorate from 35 per cent in 1979, with the Prime Minister and twelve other ministers all losing their seats.[105]

The *Alianza Popular* began life in October 1976, also as an electoral coalition of ex-Francoist ministers; members were often prominent in organizations such as Opus Dei and Catholic Action. From 1978, however, the AP became a much more centralized institution as a result of a series of reforms that put increasing power in the hands of its prominent leader, Manuel Fraga.[106] The AP has been involved in a series of electoral coalitions with other parties, the first of which was the *Coalición Democrática*, formed in 1979 with some small right-wing parties and independents, and located to the right of the UCD. During the break-up of the UCD in 1982, however, the AP moved towards the centre to cash in on the vacated ideological territory. The electoral alliance strategy was attempted again for the 1982 and 1986 elections in the form of the *Coalición Popular*, a union of the AP with the PDP, a small Liberal Party, and some small regionalist parties. Electoral failure in 1986, however, despite denying the Socialist government an overall majority, led to serious splits in the AP. The Liberals and the PDP split away again to contest the centre with the Socialists, and the *Coalición Popular* collapsed.

The Spanish right, therefore, has been highly volatile, prone to splits and fusions. In part this is due to the uneasy position occupied by the right in post-Franco Spain: 'Even today the term "right" is never used on its own, except in the political discourse of what we would call the "extreme right". In conservative circles, the term is always accompanied by that of "Centre" ';[107] in part it is due to the intense regionalism which pervades Spanish politics and which succours both small right-wing regionalist parties and regional factions within national parties.

The Spanish Communist Party (PCE) is a democratic centralist party with, in theory, very tight party discipline. None the less, in the period running up to the 1981 party congress, deep divisions opened up. These arose both over the leadership of Santiago Carrillo and as a result of the ideological strains generated by the desire to appear 'moderate' during the transition to democracy and thereby to deprive former Franco supporters of the excuse to stage a coup. These divisions, which had led the party to be 'riven by expulsions and defection',[108] had hampered the PCE's strategic freedom of action but were largely resolved by Carrillo's victories over his opponents at the 1981 party congress.[109] Carrillo, however, resigned the party leadership after the PCE's disastrous electoral performance in 1982, and since then the party has been in decline, though its ability to function as a unitary actor has increased as the position of the leadership has strengthened.

The Socialist Party (PSOE) took office as a single-party majority government in 1982 largely because its opponents of both the right and the left were hopelessly divided allowing the party a virtual electoral walkover. The party had long been divided itself, however, and there had been a showdown between right and left at the 1979 congress.[110] The issue was the 'Marxist' label of the PSOE, opposed by its leader Felipe Gonzalez in his desire to capture the electoral centre ground. The battle was eventually won by Gonzalez, but only after he had resigned the party leadership and forced an extraordinary party congress.[111] Gonzalez was subsequently returned as leader with an 85 per cent vote, won the 1982 election, and, until 1986, had a reasonably free hand in running the party.

Even this brief discussion shows quite clearly that, overall, most of the main Spanish parties are prone to splits which can have a fundamental impact on the politics of coalition. On the right in particular, the situation has been very volatile, the 'parties' being in practice federations of factions (there were as many as 48 factions in the now defunct UCD on one estimate[112]). As a consequence parties are liable to fall apart and regroup on relatively little provocation.

SWEDEN

The existence of 'two-block' politics in Sweden has tended to operate, as in Norway, to maintain party solidarity. The level of support for the Social Democrats has tended to hover just below the majority threshold so that the three bourgeois parties—the Liberal, Conservative, and Centre (formerly Agrarian) parties—have needed to combine to evict the Social Democrats from office. This situation, together with the threshold for small parties in Swedish electoral law, has contributed to a remarkable stability in the Swedish party system. Accounts of coalitional behaviour in Sweden, therefore, lay very little stress on the potential for party splits.[113] Indeed, Strom and Bergman conclude very emphatically that the Swedish parties can be treated as unitary actors for coalitional purposes.

A more complex issue concerns the close interrelationship between interest groups and the party system. All accounts of Swedish politics lay very heavy stress on this quasi-corporatist style of policy making. This does not reproduce the situation that exists in Austria, with interest groups officially recognized as factions within parties, but it does mean that the process of intraparty decision making cannot be separated from that of dialogue between parties and interest groups. The extent, therefore, to which the Swedish parties are autonomous actors for coalitional purposes must be a matter of some doubt.[115]

As far as the Swedish coalition game is concerned, therefore, our conclusions can be relatively clear-cut. Tight party discipline and a stable party system mean that, in parliamentary terms, the parties can be treated as unitary actors for coalitional purposes. Strom, for example, concludes an analysis that applies also to Denmark and Norway with the remark that 'on the whole, the leaders of these parties clearly enjoy a very high degree of control over their respective organisations'.[116] The manner in which party politics and interest group politics intertwine, however, means that the autonomy of Swedish parties to make purely tactical coalitional arrangements is severely constrained. At the very least, actors outside the party system can be seen to have a particular importance in the politics of coalition in Sweden.

SWITZERLAND

The Swiss party system tends to be excluded from most analyses of coalitional politics despite the fact that it has always been a quite explicit coalition system. This is in part because it does not appear to have any coalition bargaining and in part because it is not a parliamentary democracy in the same sense as most other European systems, for the legislative Federal Assembly cannot withdraw confidence from the cabinet (Federal Council) during its four-year fixed term of office.[117] Since 1959 at least, Swiss coalition cabinets have been formed according to a 'magic' formula, which has given the Free Democrats two seats, the Christian Democrats two seats, the Social Democrats two seats, and the Swiss People's Party one seat. The result is a situation which 'bears little resemblance to classical and axiomatic models of parliamentary democracy'.[118] Instead, the system is one in which the 'ebbs and tides of party fortunes in winning seats in Parliament . . . are mere ripples on the surface of parliamentary life'.[119] Indeed, discussing the Swiss case, Steiner is forced to go back to the 1954–9 period to be able to draw the conclusion that 'coalition agreements are possible among Swiss parties'.[120] This phenomenal stability and the continuing grand coalition seems to have brought about a situation in which internal strains are relatively mild, mainly because it is possible for party discipline to be very lax with no consequent threat to government stability.[121] Certainly the incentives for the main parties to split are minimal when dissent can be allowed within them at little political cost.

There is some recent evidence of change, however. The 1987 election saw the steady consolidation of the Green movement's position. The Greens in Switzerland comprise two groups, a Green Party and a more radical Green Alternative. Between them, these parties moved forward from controlling seven of the 200 seats in 1983 to thirteen in 1987. Partly as a reaction, a Motorists' Party contested the 1987 Swiss election and won two seats, twice as many as the Communists.[122] With declining turnout and increasing voter volatility, party politics in Switzerland may be about to embark on a period of change which could result in the ending of the 'magic formula coalitions' and the re-emergence of normal coalition bargaining. Only then will we really be able to evaluate the interaction of intra- and interparty politics.

WEST GERMANY

West Germany has a superficially far 'simpler' party and coalition system than that to be found in many European states, but the existence of a regional tier of *Land* governments within the federal system complicates matters considerably.

The impact of federalism is evident, for example in the intraparty politics of the Free Democrats (FDP), a pivotal coalition actor. The FDP operates as a federation of *Land* parties, the balance of power among which determines strategy at national level. However, once the balance of power has been determined there is 'a strong tendency within the national FDP leadership to take decisions and then to present them to the party as a whole only for rubber stamping not for discussion. It was alleged at the time that the party's Praesidium never formally debated the change in coalition parties to the CDU/CSU in 1982.'[123] This is possible at least in part because 'there . . . appears to be a tendency amongst ordinary FDP membership to leave the party rather than stay and fight when a coalition decision is taken with which they disagree. It is estimated that 29,000 members left between 1969 and 1970 after the change to the SPD and roughly 8,000–9,000 left soon after the switch back to the Christian Democrats in 1982.'[124] Considering quite explicitly the question at hand, Broughton and Kirschner conclude that 'the FDP cannot be regarded as a unitary actor, but this doesn't really affect to any degree the coalitional strategy of the party'.[125]

The regional dimension is even stronger in its impact on the internal politics of the CDU/CSU. It is particularly difficult to decide whether the Christian Democrats constitute either one or two political entities for coalitional purposes. Many studies treat the CDU/CSU as a single actor throughout. Thus Hoffman-Lange argues that 'There are formally two independent Christian Democratic Parties, the CDU and its Bavarian 'sister party' the CSU . . . Though both differ somewhat in organisational structure and ideological appeal, it seems justified to treat them as a single party, particularly as they do not compete for votes.'[126] Klingemann concurs explicitly, and many other authors do so implicitly.[127] However, one recent edited volume on the German party system gives the CDU and CSU quite separate chapters.[128] In the same vein, Grande continually refers to the CDU, CSU, and FDP as three parties.[129] Irving, in a comprehensive treatment, also deals with the CDU and CSU as separate entities.[130]

Several episodes in the politics of coalition in West Germany have clearly highlighted the potential for the CDU and CSU to go their own ways, especially with the CSU under the leadership of Franz Josef Strauss. The most spectacular episode came in November 1976 when the CSU voted to leave the joint CDU/CSU parliamentary party in the wake of electoral failure to wrest power from the SPD/FPD coalition. The CSU had outperformed the CDU in the 1976 elections, and blamed lacklustre CDU campaigning for the failure to win an overall majority.

The decision was, however, reversed within three weeks, after it became clear that the CDU would move in to attack the CSU in Bavaria if the rift was not healed. This incident is highlighted by Norpoth[131] and discussed in some detail by Irving, who concludes that 'all the signs are that the marriage of convenience between the CDU and CSU will continue, even if at times the relationship is somewhat strained'.[132] Overall, there is no doubt that the CDU/CSU liaison creates the greatest ambiguity in the cast of characters taking part in coalitional politics in Germany. While, in the event, the CDU/CSU has gone into and out of government as a unit, the potential for separation is there, the party organizations and leadership structures remain distinct, and, in certain circumstances, it might well be more useful to treat it as a protocoalition rather than as a single party.

The Social Democrats (SPD) in Germany have also been deeply divided in recent times by 'virulent factionalism . . . nurtured in the traumatic period of the late 1960s when a neo-Marxist student generation demanded a greater say in policy-making within the SPD'.[133] On the one hand was the Young Socialists (Jusos) faction, comprising former student radicals with a strong emphasis on left-wing ideology. On the other hand was the party establishment, far more conservative and pragmatic in policy terms. At the local level this division led to 'deep cleavages and intense fratricide',[134] a situation that contributed to the break-up of the SDP/FDP coalition in 1983 and the subsequently increased difficulty that the SPD found in making coalition arrangements.

Overall, then the West German party system illustrates three distinct models. The most unusual case is that of the CDU/CSU, an electoral alliance that some treat as a single party, while others insist that it is two quite separate entities. In the FDP, we see a rather autocratic organization, and in the SPD a formally united party that became deeply divided by policy disputes between ideologically motivated activists and more pragmatic and office-oriented party hierarchs. We can see how the flexibility of the FDP's bargaining strategy, which is clearly a product of its internal structure, has enabled it to remain in office for a very long period of time despite being much smaller than the SPD or CDU/CSU. It has switched coalition partners back and forth without serious internal trauma, unlike the SPD, whose ability to do coalition deals appears to have declined with the increase of internal factionalism.

Locating Political Parties on Empirical Policy Scales

Not only much of coalition theory but also much of public debate in general tends to be couched in terms that refer to the various 'dimensions' of policy or ideology. Most notably, we hear of the socioeconomic left–right dimension. Also, however, we hear of a clerical vs. anti-clerical dimension, of a rural vs. urban dimension of centre vs. periphery dimensions, and so on. As we have seen, theorists of party competition tend to portray policy competition between parties as being conducted within a 'policy space' defined by an independent set of policy dimensions such as these. When we come to apply these theories to the real world, we must operationalize these policy dimensions in such a way as to allow us to place the actors at precise positions on them.

DIFFERENT SOURCES OF DATA ON PARTY POLICY

As we indicated in Chapter 3, there are essentially four methods of constructing empirical policy scales. The first relies on expert judgements; the second relies on the dimensional analysis of legislative behaviour; the third relies on the dimensional analysis of mass survey data; and the fourth relies on the dimensional analysis of the content of policy documents. The dimensional analysis of legislative behaviour seems to us, as we argue in Chapter 3, to be a tautologically inappropriate method of defining party policy positions as independent inputs to the bargaining process and we do not consider this method further. Of the other three methods, expert judgements are the most likely to be conditioned by historical experiences of coalitions, while mass attitudes reflected in surveys may be conditioned in the same way if voters assume that parties which go into government together share policy goals. The analysis of electoral policy documents, therefore, seems likely to provide the most genuinely independent 'fix' that we are likely to get on the policy positions of political parties.

We have gathered together a range of published empirical policy scales that relate to the coalition systems that we have discussed in this book and report these in Figures B.1–B.18 below. To ensure cross-national comparability, most of the information comes from nine basic sources. These have been supplemented for individual countries, however, where systematic empirical data on policy positions are sparse or where a particularly appropriate specific source suggests itself. The majority of the sources that we use are based directly on 'expert' judgements though these may in turn be based on other material. In addition, however, one source is based on a content analysis of party policy documents,[1] while two are based on the analysis of mass survey data.[2] A full list of the sources used in given at the end of this Appendix.

Expert Judgements

Early tests of coalition theories relied almost entirely on policy scales derived from expert judgements. Scales used by Taylor and Laver, de Swaan, and Dodd fall into this category.[3] The methods followed by Taylor and Laver and by Dodd were very similar, involving the collation of information from a range of published sources, listed in each case in bibliographies to their work. These authors bear a heavy, indeed a critical, responsibility for the manner in which this collation process resulted in specific policy scales. Taylor and Laver offer no more than a ranking of parties on one or more dimensions. Dodd offers a more precise position (at quasi-interval level). De Swaan, on the other hand, orders parties on his left–right scale

according to the share of the national income they wish to see redistributed by means of the national budget, military and police expenditures excepted. When this does not affect the ranking of the other actors, the criterion of nationalism will be added to place the Fascist parties. The preference of a party's cadre will be taken as indicative of the party's stand and, in the absence of such information, the judgement of parliamentary historians and other expert observers will be taken instead.[4]

He does not reveal the specific sources of this information, though he does provide a general bibliography for the book as a whole. Building on these approaches, Browne and Dreijmanis asked specifically commissioned country specialists, in their chapters on the various coalition systems, to provide a two-dimensional representation of the policy space in question, based on their own judgement.[5] The positions of the parties in each system on these left–right scales are calculated from the diagrams in the published book.

By far the most systematic analysis of expert judgements of positions on a left–right scale, however, can be found in the work of Morgan and of Castles and Mair.[6] Castles and Mair administered a questionnaire asking 'leading political scientists' to locate parties in 'their' systems on a left–right scale ranging from 'ultra-left' (0) through 'moderate left'

TABLE B.1. Expert judgements on the number of policy dimensions in European coalition systems, 1945–1973

Country	Percentage citing Left–right scale as primary scale	Percentage citing one of these scales				
		Religious/ anticlerical	Pro/anti system	Centre/ periphery	Cultural/ linguistic	Other
Belgium	64	18	0	0	33	5
Denmark	95	0	0	6	0	19
Finland	100	0	0	19	4	11
France (1946–58)	92	15	17	0	2	11
Iceland	92	0	0	0	0	21
Israel	62	28	0	0	0	28
Italy	83	20	12	12	0	9
Luxemburg	100	19	0	0	0	0
Netherlands	90	29	0	0	0	17
Norway	96	16	0	21	5	7
Sweden	95	0	0	11	0	11

Source: Adapted from Morgan, *The Modelling of Government Coalition Formation*, in the light of comments on pp. 459–60.

$(2\frac{1}{2})$, 'centre' (5), 'moderate-right' $(7\frac{1}{2})$, to 'ultra-right' (10). This results in a set of quite explicit left–right scales, shown in the Figures below. Morgan received 110 replies to a questionnaire mailed to a named list of specialists in particular systems, though often one specialist gave views on a number of systems, creating a considerable volume of data. Specialists were asked to place each of the parties in 'their' systems, at a specified time point, on up to three policy scales. These scales were then 'named' and weighted by the country specialists.[7]

Morgan's results are particularly useful, since they also give us information on the number of salient dimensions in each system analysed, as well as estimates of the positions of the parties on the left–right dimension. He concludes that the left–right dimension is overwhelmingly the most salient in each of the systems studied. The evidence for this is summarized in the first column of figures in Table B.1, which shows the proportions of country specialists who nominated the left–right dimension as the 'primary' scale in the system in question. Only in Belgium and Israel does the left–right scale not dominate overwhelmingly. (In both these cases a religious vs. secular dimension is important; in Belgium, an ethnic/linguistic dimension is also important.) The aggregate evaluations of Morgan's experts are reported in the Figures below.

Analysis of Manifestos

A major ECPR research project has analysed the content of most election manifestos of most European parties issued since the Second World War. The main report of this analysis is contained in a volume edited by Budge, Robertson, and Hearl.[8] These data have since been supplemented by an analysis of coalition government programmes in the same terms and re-analysed to generate a left–right dimension common to all ·of the coalition systems.[9] This forms the basis of the third interval-level scale shown in the Figures. The left–right scale is calculated by taking the proportion of the manifesto coded as dealing with 'right-wing themes' and subtracting the proportion dealing with 'left-wing themes'. The scale is shown in its raw form and thus has a substantive interpretation. A score of − 100 (or + 100) means that every sentence in the manifesto dealt with left- (or right-) wing themes; a score of 0 means that the treatment of left-wing themes was balanced by the treatment of right-wing themes. In practice, almost all manifestos scored in the range − 50 to + 50. The common substantive interpretation of these scales also means that party positions can be compared across systems.

Analyses of Mass Survey Data

Inglehart and Klingemann report their re-analysis of a series of Euro-barometer surveys in which respondents were asked: 'In political matters people talk of 'the Left' and 'the Right'. How would you place your views on this scale?' They were given a left–right scale with ten boxes in it and asked to indicate on it their own position. The authors report mean scores on this scale for different groups of party identifiers in each of the countries surveyed and these data are reported in the Figures below.[10] Sani and Sartori follow a broadly similar strategy on a rather different group of countries, and their data are also reported below.[11] Similar data were assembled for the 1987 Iceland Election Study (in a system for which no comparable scales are available) as well as responses to a question in which voters were asked to place the parties on a left–right scale; both sets of findings are reported for Iceland. Bruneau and Macleod, reporting on Portugal, also asked respondents to locate the parties rather than themselves on a left–right scale.[12]

DIFFERENCES BETWEEN SCALES

Our intention in this Appendix is simply and solely to provide a compendium of policy scales that may prove useful to students of the politics of coalition. We do not, therefore, set out to generate any 'scale of scales'. Some comments on the potential sources of difference between scales are, however, in order. These take three basic forms: differences may result from simple error, from differences of timescale, and from variations in the particular definition of 'party policy' implicit in each scale.

Error

Expert judgements, of course, may well be prone to error. This is especially the case for those studies in which the final collation of expert judgements is itself a matter for the judgement of a single author who will by no means be familiar with the intricacies of party politics in many of the coalition systems at issue. Such doubts about *reliability* must therefore overshadow the scales developed by Taylor and Laver, de Swaan, and Dodd, though none offers data at full interval level. (It is worth noting as a historical fact that the Taylor/Laver and de Swaan scales were developed simultaneously and entirely independently, yet correspond very closely indeed. Dodd, though publishing three years later, cites neither study and seems also to have developed his scales independently; his scales also correspond closely to the Taylor/Laver and de Swaan scales.) The surveys of experts by Morgan and by Castles and Mair, on the other hand, have the great advantage of spreading the risk of the unreliabilities and errors of expert judgement.

The notion of 'error' in relation to the manifesto or survey analyses relates more to the overall *validity* of using content analyses of party manifestos or self-placements of survey respondents on left–right scales, both the subject of major methodological debate that extends far beyond the scope of this work. (As far as reliability goes, however, the Inglehart/Klingemann and the Sani/Sartori scales, using the same basic method on different surveys conducted at rather different time points, have very similar results.)

Timescale

Each of the scales is compiled on the basis of a different timescale. The Taylor/Laver and de Swaan studies both dealt with the period 1945–71 and placed all parties in a fixed ordering on the left–right scale for the entire period. (Taylor and Laver applied different sets of saliency weights to the dimensions at different time points within the period.) The Browne and Dreijmanis scales are ambiguous on this matter, though the chapters were presumably written around 1980. The Morgan study deals with the period 1945–73. The Castles and Mair survey relates, implicitly, to a fixed time point, presumably around 1982. The Inglehart and Klingemann study explicitly deals with the position at September–October 1973. The Sani and Sartori study is based on various surveys taken over the 1973–9 period (see the original source for precise details).

Obviously, considerable movement in party policy positions has taken place since 1945. The manifesto-based scales can be calculated for each election and show such movement quite clearly.[13] The Laver and Budge scales reported here, however, are mean scores for every election contested by the party in question since the Second World War. Space constraints allow us to do no more, and this strategy allows at least a crude comparison of the results of manifesto-based scales with those of other policy scales constructed on a quite different basis. What is reported here, however, is a grossly simplified summary of the copious time series manifesto data which can be found in the original sources.

Variations in the time periods that form the point of reference for these studies, therefore, may account for differences between them. The political world studied by Castles and Mair in the early 1980s, after all, had moved on from that studied by Dodd in the early 1970s.

Definition of 'Party'

As our discussion in Chapter 2 illustrated, different sections of a party may have different views about the same thing, including party policy. In this context, it is not clear what 'experts' have in mind when asked to locate a 'party' on a left–right scale. Do they think of legislators, of leaders, of activists, of supporters, or of published policy documents? Different experts may think of different things and differ in their placements of the same party accordingly. The manifesto analysis rests on the firm ground of the published policy document. Even this, of course, is controlled by different levels of the hierarchy of different parties, but is at least the version of policy that is officially offered by the party to the electorate; in that sense it is a definitive statement of each party's electoral policy position. Similarly, both the Inglehart/Klingemann and Sani/Sartori scales are based on the self-location of party identifiers, explicitly dealing with the ideological position of the *electorate*. The Bruneau and Macleod study, however, together with others that follow the same strategy, asks voters to locate *parties* on a left–right scale. This generates the same ambiguity as can be found in the expert studies over what, precisely, are the objects that are being manipulated when 'parties' are located on a left–right scale.

When we deal with mass surveys and party policy documents, therefore, we know quite clearly what we are talking about. Differences between these scales, furthermore, may well have a very important substantive interpretation if they show that the policy put forward by party elites is not the same as that most favoured by party supporters. (This is another fascinating matter that unfortunately takes us well beyond our current terms of reference.) When we deal with expert judgements, on the other hand, we tend to get neat and tidy scales but scales that are none the less undermined by a certain degree of ambiguity. This ambiguity is almost certain to cause variation between scales and such variation is, obviously, quite impossible to interpret.

Presentation of Scales

Of the up to nine scales presented in the Figures below for each of the coalition systems under consideration, three are defined at ordinal level, and six at interval or quasi-interval level. Party positions on the six interval level scales are reported in the original units in which they were denominated. The diagrams, however, represent each scale in terms of a line of fixed length, in an attempt to produce some comparability between them. The ordinal scales simply rank the parties from left to right. The distances between parties, as these scales are laid out on the page, are not always equal. This is simply a device adopted to illustrate the extent to which ordinal and cardinal scales are mutually consistent (the Castles and Mair scale is taken as a baseline 'expert' scale). The precise distances used in the presentation of the ordinal scales, therefore, are not in any sense based upon the original sources.

B.1–B.18   LOCATING NATIONAL PARTIES ON POLICY SCALES:

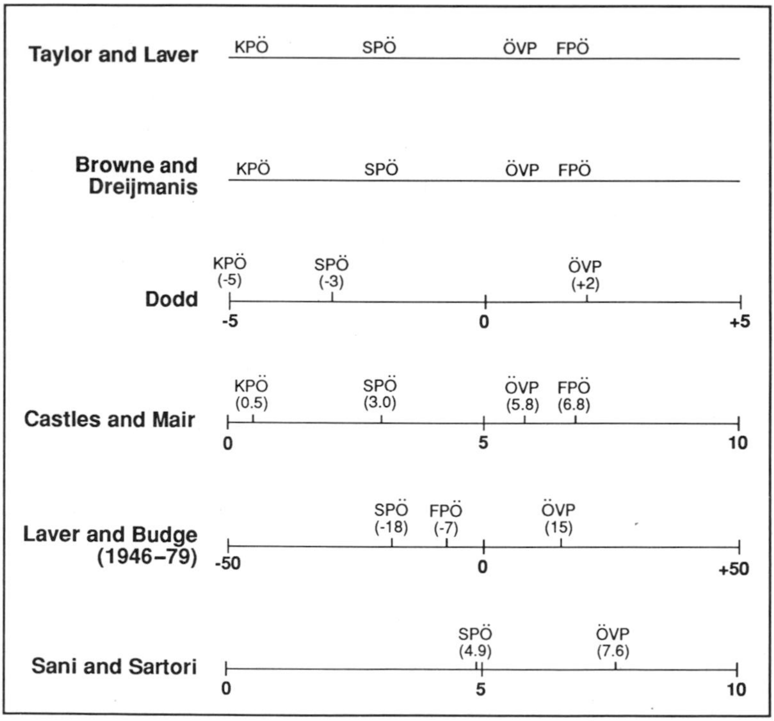

FIG. B.1. Austria

FPÖ: Freedom Party; KPÖ: Communists; ÖVP: People's Party; SPÖ: Socialists

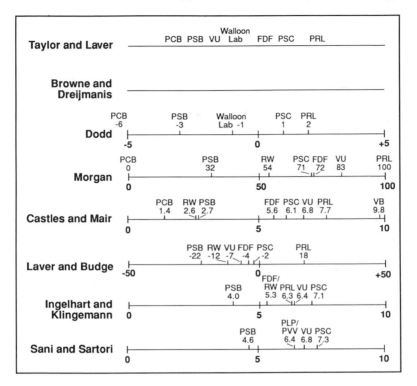

FIG. B.2. Belgium

FDF: Front des Francophones; PCB: Communists; PSB: Socialists; PSC: Christian Socials; RW: Rassemblement Wallon; VB: Vlammishebloc; VU: Volksunie

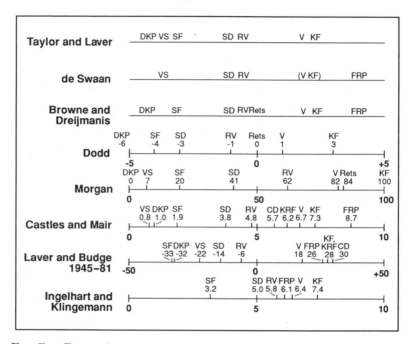

Fig. B.3. Denmark

CD: Centre Democrats; DKP: Communists; FRP: Freedom Party; KF: Conservatives; KRF: Christian People's Party; RV: Radicals; Rets: Justice Party; SD: Social Democrats; SF: Socialist People's Party; V: Liberals; VS: Left Socialists

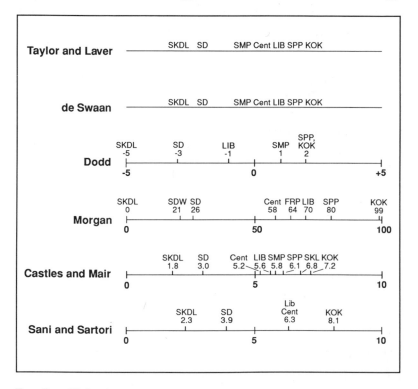

FIG. B.4. Finland

Cent: Centre; FRP: Finnish Rural Party; KOK: Conservatives; Lib: Liberal; SDW: Workers and Smallholders; SD: Social Democrats; SKDL: Communists; SPP: Swedish People's Party

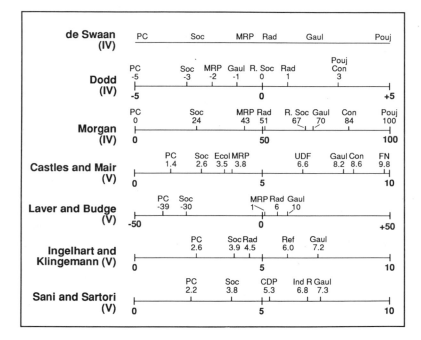

FIG. B.5. France

Con: Conservative (inc. CNIP); FN: National Front; Gaul: Gaullists; Ind R: Independent Republicans; MRP: Mouvement Republicain Populaire; Pouj: Poujadists; Rad: Radicals; Ref: Reformateurs; Soc: Socialists

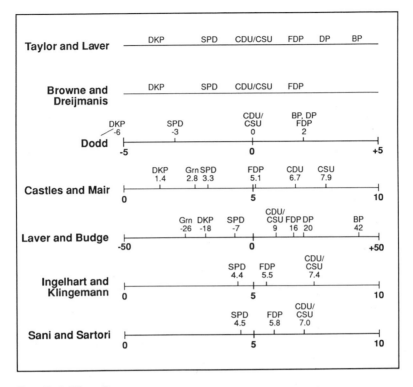

FIG. B.6. West Germany

CDU: Christian Democratic Union; CSU: Christian Social Union; BP: Refugee Party; DKP: Communists; DP: German Party; Grn: Greeens; SPD: Social Democrats

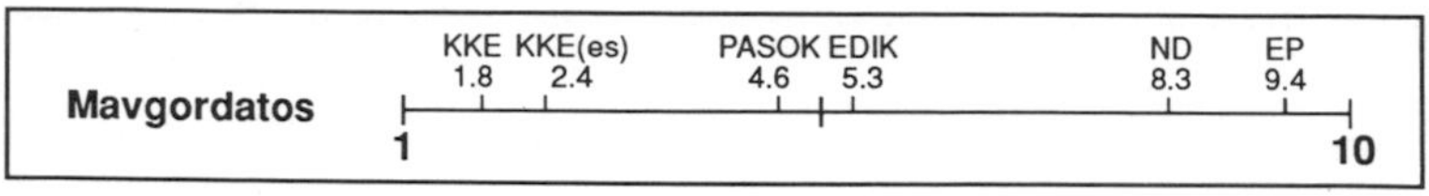

Mavgordatos	KKE 1.8	KKE(es) 2.4	PASOK 4.6	EDIK 5.3	ND 8.3	EP 9.4

FIG. B.7. Greece

ND: New Democracy; EDIK: Centre; EP: National Front; KKE: Communists; KKE(es): Eurocommunists; PASOK: Socialists

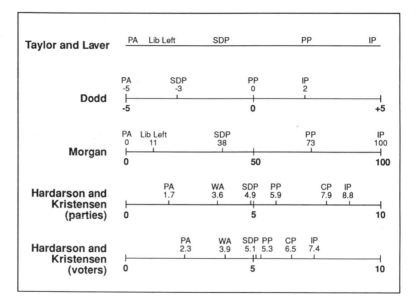

FIG. B.8. Iceland

CP: Citizens' Party; IP: Independence Party; PA: People's Alliance; PP: Progressive Party; SDP: Social Democratic Party; WA: Women's Alliance

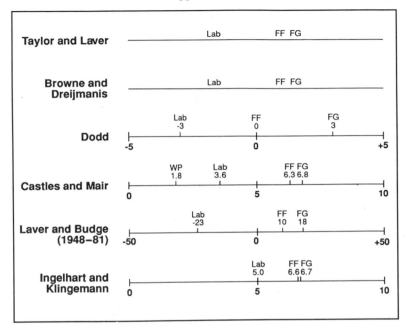

FIG. B.9. Ireland
FF: Fianna Fáil; FG: Fine Gael; Lab: Labour; WP: Workers' Party

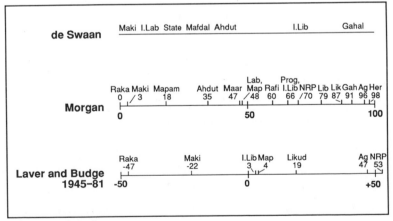

FIG. B.10. Israel
Ag: Agudat Israel; Gah: Gahal; Her: Herut; I Lib: Independent Liberals; Lib: Liberals; Lik: Likud; Maar: Maarach; Map: Mapai; NRP: National Religious Party; Prog: Progressives

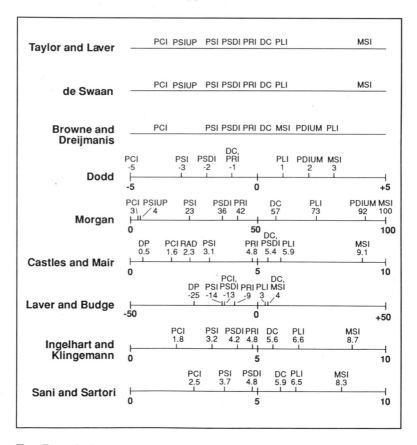

FIG. B.11. Italy

DC: Christian Democrats; DP: Proletarian Democrats; MSI: MSI; PCI: Communists; PRI: Republicans; PLI: Liberals; PSDI: Social Democrats; PSI: Socialists; PSIUP: Left Socialists; Rad: Radicals

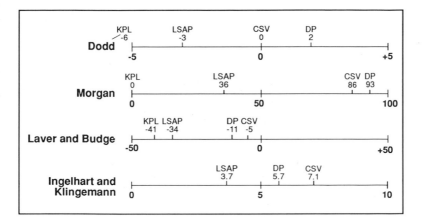

FIG. B.12. Luxemburg

CSV: Christian Socials; DP: Liberals; LSAP: Socialists; KPL: Communists

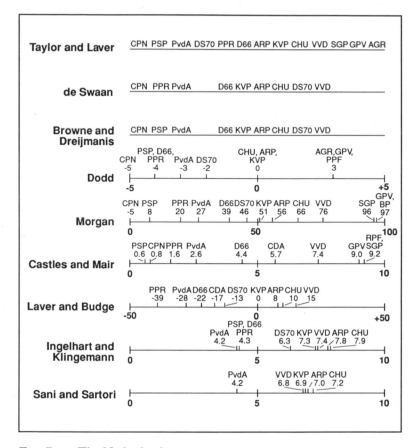

FIG. B.13. The Netherlands

ARP: Anti-Revolutionary Party; CDA: Christian Democratic Appeal; CHU: Christian Historical Union; CPN: Communists; D66: Democrats 66: DS70: Democratic Socialists 70; KVP: Catholic People's Party; PPR: Political Radicals; PSP: Pacifist Socialists; PvdA: Labour

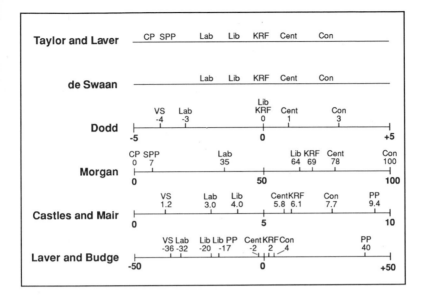

FIG. B.14. Norway

Cent: Centre; Con: Conservatives; KRF: Christian People's Party; Lab: Labour; Lib: Liberals; Lib PP: Liberal People's Party; PP: Progress Party; SPP: Socialist People's Party; VS: Left Socialists

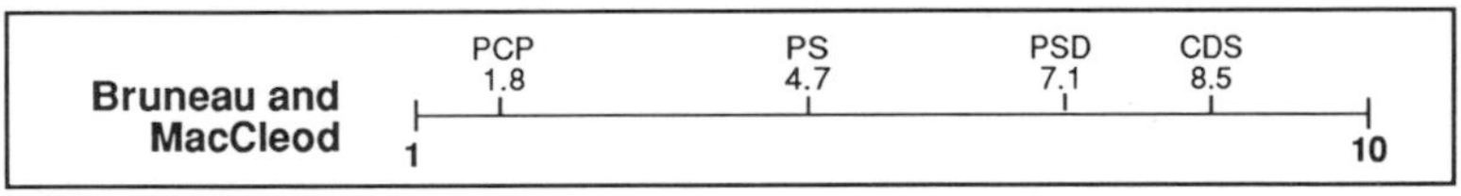

FIG. B.15. Portugal

CDC: Social Democratic Centre; PCP: Communists; PS: Socialists; PSD: Social Democrats

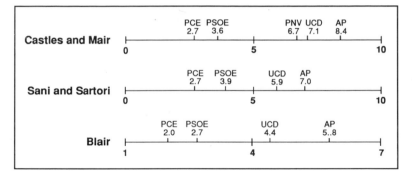

FIG. B.16. Spain

AP: Popular Alliance; PCE: Communists; PSOE: Socialists; UCD: Centre Democrats

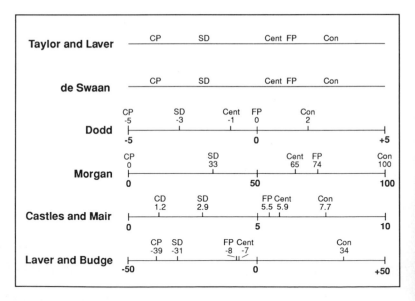

FIG. B.17. Sweden

Centre: Centre; CP: Communists; Con: Conservatives; FP: Liberals; SD: Social Democrats

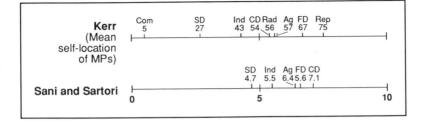

Fig. B.18. Switzerland

Ag: Agrarian; CD: Christian Democrats; Com: Communists; FD: Free Democrats; Ind: Independents; Rad: Radicals; Rep: Republicans; SD: Social Democrats

Sources for Scales shown in Figures B.1–B.18

A. Blair, 'The Emerging Spanish Party System: Is There a Model?', *West European Politics*, 1984, 7:4, 120–55.

E. C. Browne and J. Dreijmanis (eds.), *Government Coalitions in Western Democracies* (New York: Longman, 1982).

T. Bruneau and A. MacCleod, *Politics in Contemporary Portugal* (Boulder, Co: Lynne Rienner, 1986).

F. Castles and P. Mair, 'Left–Right Political Scales: Some Expert Judgements', *European Journal of Political Research*, 1984, 12, 83–8.

A. de Swaan, *Coalition Theories and Cabinet Formation* (Amsterdam: Elsevier, 1973).

L. C. Dodd, *Coalitions in Parliamentary Government* (Princeton: Princeton University Press, 1976).

O. Hardarson and G. Kristensen, 'The Icelandic Parliamentary Election of 1987', *Electoral Studies*, 1987, 6, 209–18.

R. Ingelhart and H.-D. Klingemann, 'Party Identification, Ideological Preference and the Left–Right Dimensions Among Western Pass Publics', in I. Budge, D. Robertson, and D. Hearl (eds.), *Ideology, Strategy and Party Change* (Cambridge: Cambridge University Press, 1987).

H. H. Kerr, 'The Swiss Party Systems: Steadfast and Changing', in H. Daalder (ed.), *Party Systems in Denmark, Austria, Switzerland, The Netherlands and Belgium* (London: Pinter, 1987).

M. Laver and I. Budge (eds.), *Party and Coalition Policy in Western Europe* (Cambridge: Cambridge University Press, 1991).

G. Mavgordatos, 'The Greek Party System: A Case of Limited but Polarised Pluralism', *West European Politics*, 1984, 7:4, 156–69.

M.-J. Morgan, 'The Modelling of Governmental Coalition Formation: A Policy-Based Approach with Interval Measurement' (University of Michigan PhD thesis, 1976).

G. Sani and G. Sartori, 'Polarization, Fragmentation and Competition in Western Democracies', in H. Daalder and P. Mair (eds.), *Western European Party Systems* (London and Beverly Hills: Sage, 1983).

M. Taylor and M. Laver, 'Government Coalitions in Western Europe', *European Journal of Political Research*, 1973, 1, 205–48.

Notes

PREFACE

1. For example, W. Riker, *The Theory of Political Coalitions* (New Haven: Yale University Press, 1962); A. de Swaan, *Coalition Theories and Cabinet Formation* (Amsterdam: Elsevier, 1973); L. C. Dodd, *Coalitions in Parliamentary Government* (Princeton: Princeton University Press, 1976).

1. THE POLITICS OF COALITION IN EUROPE

1. H. Kliemt and B. Schauenberg, 'Coalitions and Hierarchies: Some Observations on the Fundamentals of Human Co-operation', in M. Holler (ed.), *Coalitions and Collective Action* (Wurzburg: Physica, 1984), 9–32.
2. W. Riker, *The Theory of Political Coalitions* (New Haven: Yale University Press, 1962).

2. WHO PLAYS THE COALITION GAME?

1. This is the solution adopted, for example, by M. Taylor and M. Laver, 'Government Coalitions in Western Europe', *European Journal of Political Research*, 1 (1973), 205–48, in their original 'testing' of various coalition theories.
2. See, for example, H. Daalder, 'The Comparative Study of European Parties and Party Systems: An Overview', in H. Daalder and P. Mair (eds.), *Western European Party Systems* (London and Beverly Hills: Sage, 1983), 1–28; K. von Beyme, 'Coalition Government in Western Germany', in V. Bogdanor (ed.), *Coalition Government in Western Europe* (London: Heinemann, 1983), 16–37; G. Pridham, 'An Inductive Theoretical Framework for Coalitional Behaviour', in G. Pridham (ed.), *Coalitional Behaviour in Theory and Practice: An Inductive Model for Western Europe* (Cambridge: Cambridge University Press, 1986).

3. K. von Beyme, 'Governments, Parliaments and the Structure of Power within Political Parties', in Daalder and Mair (eds.), *Western European Party Systems*, pp. 341–5; von Beyme, 'Coalition government in Western Germany', pp. 25–6.

4. von Beyme, *Political Parties in Western Democracies* (Aldershot: Gower, 1984), p. 224.

5. Ibid., 313.

6. Ibid., 320.

7. H. Daalder, 'The Comparative Study of European Parties and Party Systems: An Overview', p. 21, emphasis in original.

8. E. Browne and J. Dreijmanis (eds.), *Government Coalitions in Western Democracies* (New York; Longman, 1982); V. Bogdanor (ed.), *Coalition Government in Western Europe*; Pridham (ed.), *Coalitional Behaviour in Theory and Practice*.

9. V. Bogdanor, 'Introduction', in Bogdanor (ed.), *Coalition Government in Western Europe*, p. 13.

10. R. Irving, *The Christian Democratic Parties of Western Europe* (London: Allen and Unwin, 1979), p. 58.

11. D. Arter, *Politics and Policy-Making in Finland* (Brighton: Wheatsheaf, 1987), p. 48.

12. M. Laver, 'Party Competition and Party System Change; The Interaction of Electoral Bargaining and Party Competition', *Journal of Theoretical Politics*, 1 (1989) 301–24.

13. T. Bruneau and A. MacCleod, *Politics in Contemporary Portugal* (Boulder: Lynne Rienner, 1986), p. 79.

14. G. Luebbert, *Comparative Democracy: Policy Making and Governing Coalitions in Europe and Israel* (New York: Columbia University Press, 1986).

15. D. Robertson, *A Theory of Party Competition* (London: Wiley, 1976).

16. K. Strom, 'Towards an Institutional Model of Competitive Party Behaviour', paper presented at ECPR Joint Sessions, Barcelona, 1985.

17. Luebbert, *Comparative Democracy*, p. 46.

18. Ibid., p. 52, emphasis added.

19. This is a solution explored by N. Frohlich, J. Oppenheimer, and O. Young, *Political Leadership and Collective Goods* (Princeton: Princeton University Press, 1971) and by M. Laver, *The Politics of Private Desires* (Harmondsworth: Pelican, 1981).

3. WHAT ARE THE STAKES?

1. M. Laver, *The Politics of Private Desires* (Harmondsworth: Pelican, 1981).

2. A. Downs, *An Economic Theory of Democracy* (New York: Harper and Row, 1987), p. 28.
3. W. Riker, *The Theory of Political Coalitions* (New Haven: Yale University Press, 1962), p. 39.
4. For example, by D. Austen-Smith and J. Banks, 'Elections, Coalitions and Legislative Outcomes', *American Political Science Review*, 88 (1988), 405–22.
5. A. de Swaan, *Coalition Theories and Cabinet Formation* (Amsterdam: Elsevier, 1973), p. 88.
6. J. Schlesinger, 'The Primary Goals of Political Parties: A Clarification of Positive Theory', *American Political Science Review*, 69 (1976), 840–9.
7. J. Bara, 'Coalition and Party Policy in Israel', in M. Laver and I. Budge (eds.), *Party and Coalition Policy in Western Europe* (Cambridge: Cambridge University Press, forthcoming).
8. A. de Swaan, 'The Netherlands: Coalitions in a Segmented Polity', in E. Browne and J. Dreijmanis (eds.), *Government Coalitions in Western Democracies* (New York: Longman, 1982), 227n.
9. E. Browne and M. Franklin, 'Aspects of Coalition Payoffs in European Parliamentary Democracies', *American Political Science Review*, 67 (1973), pp. 453–4.
10. For a discussion of the operation and expanding role of parastatal agencies, see C. Hood and G. Schuppert (eds.), *Delivering Public Services in Western Europe* (London: Sage, 1988).
11. S. Hellman, 'The Italian Communist Party between Berlinguer and the Seventeenth Congress', in R. Leonardi and R. Y. Nanetti (eds.), *Italian Politics: A Review, Volume I* (London: Pinter, 1986), p. 51.
12. A. Marradi, 'Italy: from "Centrism" to Centre–Left Coalitions', in Browne and Dreijmanis (eds.), *Government Coalitions in Western Democracies*, p. 39.
13. G. Pasquino, 'Sources of Stability and instability in the Italian Party System', *West European Politics*, 6:1 (1983), p. 101.
14. G. Pridham, 'An Inductive Theoretical Framework for Coalitional Behaviour', in G. Pridham (ed.), *Coalitional Behaviour in Theory and Practice: An Inductive Model for Western Europe* (Cambridge: Cambridge University Press, 1986), p. 215.
15. Ibid., p. 216.
16. R. Irving, *The Christian Democratic Parties of Western Europe* (London: Allen and Unwin, 1979), p. 65.
17. Pridham, 'An Inductive Theoretical Framework for Coalitional Behaviour', p. 215.
18. For a more detailed discussion, see M. Laver, 'Using Cluster Analysis to Model Coalition Formation in Policy Spaces of High

Dimensionality', in N. Schofield (ed.), *Coalition Theory and Coalition Government* (Dordrecht: Kluwer, 1990).

19. M. Taylor and M. Laver, 'Government Coalitions in Western Europe', *European Journal of Political Research*, 1 (1973), 205–48; de Swaan, *Coalition Theories and Cabinet Formation*, L. C. Dodd, *Coalitions in Parliamentary Government* (Princeton: Princeton University Press, 1976)

20. M.-J. Morgan, *The modelling of Governmental Coalition Formation: A Policy-Based Approach with Interval Measurement* (University of Michigan, PhD thesis, 1976); F. Castles and P. Mair, 'Left–Right Political Scales: Some Expert Judgements', *European Journal of Political Research*, 12 (1984), 83–8.

21. D. McCrea, *Parliament, Parties and Society in France 1946–58* (New York: St Martins, 1967).

22. I. Budge, I. Crewe, and D. Farlie (eds.), *Party Identification and Beyond: Representations of Voting and Party Competition* (London: Wiley, 1976).

23. K. Strom, 'Minority Govenments in Parliamentary Democracies: The Rationality of Non-Winning Cabinet Solutions', *Comparative Political Studies*, 17 (1984), 213–16.

24. De Swaan, *Coalition Theories and Cabinet Formation*, pp. 88–9.

25. N. B. Grossman, 'Party Distances and Coalition Governments: A New Model', in M. Holler (ed.), *Coalitions and Collective Action* (Wurzburg: Physica, 1984), pp. 134–5.

26. E. Browne and M. Franklin, 'Aspects of Coalition Payoffs in European Parliamentary Democracies', p. 454.

27. E. Browne and K. Feste, 'Qualitative Dimensions of Coalition Payoffs: Evidence for European Party Governments 1945–70', *American Behavioral Scientist*, 18 (1975), 530–56; I. Budge, 'A Preliminary Comparative Check of Links Between Party and Ministry in 22 Democracies', paper presented at the Workshop on Comparative Theory, ECPR Joint Sessions, Barcelona, 1985.

28. J. Schlesinger, 'On the Theory of Party Organisation', *Journal of Politics*, 46 (1984), 369–400; D. Wittman, 'Candidate Motivation: A Synthesis of Alternative Theories', *American Political Science Review*, 77 (1983), 142–57; R. Calvert, 'Robustness of the Multidimensional Voting Model: Candidate Motivations, Uncertainty and Convergence', *American Journal of Political Science*, 29 (1985), 69–95; H. Chappell and W. Keech, 'Policy Motivation and Party Differences in a Dynamic Spatial Model of Party Competition', *American Political Science Review*, 80 (1986), 881–99.

29. D. Austen-Smith and J. Banks, 'Elections, Coalitions and Legislative Outcomes'; Laver, 'Using Cluster Analysis to Model Coalition Formation'.

30. Ibid.
31. J. Schlesinger, 'The Primary Goals of Political Parties,' p. 845.
32. B. Grofman, 'A Dynamic Model of Protocoalition Formation in Ideological n-space', *Behavioural Science*, 27 (1982), 77–90; M. Laver and J. Underhill, 'The Bargaining Advantages of Combining with Others', *British Journal of Political Science*, 12 (1982), 75–90.
33. Austen-Smith and Banks, 'Elections, Coalitions and Legislative Outcomes', pp. 409–10, emphasis in original.
34. Schlesinger, 'The Primary Goals of Political Parties'.

4. HOW DO YOU WIN?

1. K. Strom, *Minority Government and Majority Rule* (Cambridge: Cambridge University Press, 1989).
2. V. Herman and J. Pope, 'Minority Governments in Western Democracies', *British Journal of Political Science*, 3 (1973), 191–212; M. Taylor and M. Laver, 'Government Coalitions in Western Europe', *European Journal of Political Research*, 1 (1973), 205–48; K. Strom, 'Minority Governments in Parliamentary Democracies: The Rationality of Non-Winning Cabinet Solutions', *Comparative Political Studies*, 17 (1984), 199–227; Strom, *Minority Government and Majority Rule*; G. Luebbert, *Comparative Democracy: Policy Making and Governing Coalitions in Europe and Israel* (New York: Columbia Unversity Press, 1986).
3. Taylor and Laver, 'Government Coalitions in Western Europe'; Herman and Pope, 'Minority Govenments in Western Democracies'; L. C. Dodd, *Coalitions in Parliamentary Government* (Princeton: Princeton University Press, 1976); A. Lijphart, 'Power Sharing versus Majority Rule: Patterns of Cabinet Formation in Twenty Democracies', *Government and Opposition*, 16 (1981), 395–413; K. Strom, 'Minority Governments in Parliamentary Democracies: The Rationality of Non-Winning Cabinet Solutions'; Strom, *Minority Government and Majority Rule*.
4. Herman and Pope, 'Minority Governments in Western Democracies', p. 195.
5. Ibid.
6. Ibid.
7. Ibid., p. 196.
8. Ibid., p. 197.
9. Ibid.
10. Taylor and Laver, 'Government Coalitions in Western Europe'.
11. Ibid., p. 232.

12. Strom, 'Minority Governments in Parliamentary Democracies'; Strom, *Minority Government and Majority Rule*; Luebbert, *Comparative Democracy*.
13. Strom, 'Minority Governments in Parliamentary Democracies', pp. 209, 211.
14. Ibid., p. 211.
15. Ibid., p. 212, emphasis in original.
16. Ibid., p. 212.
17. Luebbert, *Comparative Democracy*.
18. Ibid., p. 42.
19. Ibid., p. 31.
20. Ibid., p. 68.
21. Ibid., pp. 44, 41–2.
22. K. Strom, 'Deferred Gratification and Minority Governments in Scandinavia', *Legislative Studies Quarterly*, 11 (1986), 583–605.
23. I. Budge and M. Laver, 'Office Seeking and Policy Pursuit in Coalition Theory', *Legislative Studies Quarterly*, 11 (1985), 485–506.
24. Ibid., p. 488.
25. Strom, 'Minority Governments in Parliamentary Democracies'; Strom, *Minority Government and Majority Rule*.
26. Taylor and Laver, 'Government Coalitions in Western Europe', p. 233.
27. Luebbert, *Comparative Democracy*.
28. Ibid., p. 72.
29. Ibid., p. 79.
30. Ibid., p. 80.
31. Ibid., p. 73.

5. WHO GETS IN?

1. W. Riker, *The Theory of Political Coalitions* (New Haven: Yale University Press).
2. J. von Neumann and O. Morgenstern, *Theory of Games and Economic Behaviour* (Princeton: Princeton University Press, 1953).
3. M. Taylor and M. Laver, 'Government Coalitions in Western Europe', *European Journal of Political Research*, 1 (1973), 205–48.
4. Riker, *The Theory of Political Coalitions*.
5. W. Gamson, 'A Theory of Coalition Formation', *American Sociological Review*, 26 (1961), 373–82.
6. M. Leiserson, 'Factions and Coalitions in One-Party Japan: An

Interpretation Based on the Theory of Games', *American Political Science Review*, 62 (1968), 70–87.

7. E. Browne, *Coalition Theories: A Logical and Empirical Critique* (London: Sage (Professional Papers in Comparative Politics), 1973); Taylor and Laver, 'Government Coalitions in Western Europe'; A. de Swaan, *Coalition Theories and Cabinet Formation* (Amsterdam: Elsevier, 1973).

8. A. de Swaan and R. Mokken, 'Testing Coalition Theories: The Combined Evidence', in L. Lewin and E. Vedung (eds.), *Politics and Rational Action* (Dordrecht: Reidel, 1980), p. 680.

9. M. Franklin and T. Mackie, 'Reassessing the Importance of Size and Ideology for the Formation of Governing Coalitions in Parliamentary Democracies', *American Journal of Political Science*, 28 (1984), 671–92.

10. M. Leiserson, *Coalitions in Politics* (Yale University, PhD thesis, 1966); R. Axelrod, *Conflict of Interest* (Chicago: Markham, 1970); de Swaan, *Coalition Theories and Cabinet Formation*.

11. Taylor and Laver, 'Government Coalitions in Western Europe'; de Swaan, *Coalition Theories and Cabinet Formation*; Franklin and Mackie, 'Reassessing the Importance of Size and Ideology'.

12. E. Browne, D. Gleiber, and C. Mashoba, 'Evaluating Conflict of Interest Theory: Western European Cabinet Coalitions, 1945–80', *British Journal of Political Science*, 14 (1984), 1–32.

13. M. Taylor, 'On the Theory of Government Coalition Formation', *British Journal of Political Science*, 2 (1972), 1–73.

14. Taylor and Laver, 'Government Coalitions in Western Europe'.

15. D. Austen-Smith and J. Banks, 'Elections, Coalitions and Legislative Outcomes', *American Political Science Review*, 82 (1988), 405–22.

16. Ibid., p. 407.

17. Ibid., p. 413.

18. G. Luebbert, *Comparative Democracy: Policy Making and Governing Coalitions In Europe and Israel* (New York: Columbia University Press, 1986).

19. Ibid., p. 49.

20. Ibid., p. 52.

21. Ibid., p. 64.

22. De Swaan, *Coalition Theories and Cabinet Formation*, p. 88, emphasis added.

23. Ó. Grimsson, 'Iceland: A Multilevel Coalition System', in E. Browne and J. Dreijmanis (eds.), *Government Coalitions in Western Democracies* (New York: Longman, 1982); H. Paloheimo, *Governments in Democratic Capitalist States, 1950–1983* (Turku, Finland: University of Turku, 1984).

24. M. Laasko and R. Taagepura, 'Effective Number of Parties: A Measure with Applications to West Europe', *Comparative Political Studies*, 12 (1979), 3–27.
25. D. Hearl, 'Luxemburg', in. M. Laver and I. Budge (eds.), *Party and Coalition Policy in Western Europe* (forthcoming).
26. K. Krehbiel, 'Spatial Models of Legislative Choice', *Legislative Studies Quarterly*, 3 (1988), 259–319.
27. R. McKelvey, 'Intransitivities in Multidimensional Voting Models and Some Implications for Agenda Control', *Journal of Economic Theory*, 12 (1976), 472–82.
28. C. Plott, 'A Notion of Equilibrium and its Possibility under Majority Rule', *American Economic Review*, 57 (1967), 787–806; J. Sloss, 'Stable Outcomes and Majority Rule Voting Games', *Public Choice*, 15 (1973), 19–48; G. H. Kramer, 'On a Class of Equilibrium Conditions for Majority Rule', *Econometrica*, 41 (1973), 285–97; McKelvey, 'Intransitivities in Multidimensional Voting Models'; McKelvey, 'General Conditions for Global Intransitivities in Formal Voting Models', *Econometrica*, 47 (1979), 1085–111; L. Cohen, 'Cyclic Sets in Multidimensional Voting Models', *Journal of Economic Theory*, 20 (1979), 1–12; L. Cohen and S. A. Matthews, 'Constrained Plott Equilibria, Directional Equilibria and Global Cycling Sets', *Review of Economic Studies*, 47 (1980), 975–86; S. A. Matthews, 'Pairwise Symmetry Conditions for Voting Equilibria', *Journal of Game Theory*, 9 (1980), 141–56; Matthews, 'Local Simple Games in Public Choice Mechanisms', *International Economic Review*, 23 (1982), 623–45; N. Schofield, 'Instability of Simple Dynamic Games', *Review of Economic Studies*, 45 (1978), 575–94; Schofield, 'Generic Properties of Simple Bergson–Samuelson Welfare Functions', *Journal of Mathematical Economics*, 7 (1980), 175–92; Schofield, 'Generalised Bargaining Sets for Cooperative Games', *International Journal of Game Theory*, 7 (1978), 183–99; Schofield, 'Generic Instability of Majority Rule', *Review of Economic Studies*, 50 (1983), 696–705; Schofield, 'Existence of a Structurally Stable Equilibrium for a Non-Collegial Voting Rule', *Public Choice*, 51 (1986), 267–84; R. McKelvey and N. Schofield, 'Structural Instability of the Core', *Journal of Mathematical Economics*, 15 (1986), 555–91.
29. Schofield, 'Generic Instability of Majority Rule'.
30. N. Schofield, *Choice and Democracy* (Heidelberg: Springer, 1985).
31 K. Shepsle, 'Institutional Arrangements and Equilibrium in Multidimensional Voting Models', *American Journal of Political Science*, 23 (1979), 27–60; A. Denzau and R. Mackay, 'Structure Induced Equilibrium and Perfect Foresight Expectations', *American Journal*

of Political Science, 25 (1981), 762–79; K. Shepsle and B. Weingast, 'Structure Induced Equilibrium and Legislative Choice', *Public Choice*, 37 (1981), 503–19; Shepsle and Weingast, 'The Institutional Foundations of Committee Power', *American Political Science Review*, 81 (1987), 85–104.

32. Denzau and Mackay, 'Structure Induced Equilibrium'; D. Baron and J. Ferejohn, *Bargaining in Legislatures* (Stanford University, unpublished manuscript, 1987); T. Gilligan and K. Krehbiel, 'Collective Decisision Making and Standing Committees: An Informational Rationale for Restrictive Amendment Procedure', *Journal of Law, Economics and Organisations*, 3 (1987), 287–335.

33. J. Enelow and M. Hinich, 'Voting One Issue at a Time; The Question of Voter Forecasts', *American Political Science Review*, 27 (1983), 435–45; Enelow and Hinich, 'Voter Expectations in Multi-stage Voting Systems: An Equilibrium Result', *American Journal of Political Science*, 27 (1983), 820–70.

34. R. McKelvey and N. Schofield, 'Generalised Symmetry Conditions at a Core Point', *Econometrica*, 55 (1987), 923–33; Schofield, 'Existence of A Structurally Stable Equilibrium for a Non-Collegial Voting Rule'.

35. Krehbiel, 'Spatial Models of Legislative Choice'.

36. Shepsle, 'Institutional Arrangements and Equilibrium in Multi-dimensional Voting Models'.

37. McKelvey and Schofield, 'Generalised Symmetry Conditions at a Core Point'; Schofield, 'Existence of A Structurally Stable Equilibrium for a Non-Collegial Voting Rule'.

38. Schofield, 'Existence of a Structurally Stable Equilibrium for a Non-Collegial Voting Rule', p. 282. See also N. Schofield, S. Feld, and B. Grofman, 'The Core and the Stability of Group Choice in Spatial Voting Games', *American Political Science Review*, 82 (1988), 195–211.

39. M. Holmstedt and T.-L. Schou, 'Sweden', in I. Budge, D. Robertson, and D. Hearl (eds.), *Ideology, Strategy and Party Change* (Cambridge: Cambridge University Press, 1987).

40. McKelvey and Schofield, 'Generalised Symmetry Conditions at a Core Point'.

41. Schofield, Feld, and Grofman, 'The Core and the Stability of Group Choice in Spatial Voting Games'.

42. M. Laver, 'Using Cluster Analysis to Model Coalition Formation in Policy Spaces of High Dimensionality', in N. Schofield (ed.), *Coalition Theory and Coalition Government* (Dordrecht: Kluwer, 1990).

43. D. Hearl, 'Luxemburg 1945–82: Dimensions and Strategies', in

Budge, Robertson, and Hearl (eds.), *Ideology, Stategy and Party Change*.

44. M. Slater and A. Mastropaolo, 'Italy', in M. Laver and I. Budge (eds.), *Party and Coalition Policy in Western Europe*; K. Dittrich, 'The Netherlands 1946–81', in Budge, Robertson, and Hearl (eds.), *Ideology, Strategy, and Party Change*.

45. Laver, 'Using Cluster Analysis to Model Coalition Formation'; Laver and Budge (eds.), *Party and Coalition Policy in Western Europe*.

46. B. Grofman, 'A Dynamic Model of Protocoalition Formation in Ideological n–Space', *Behavioural Science*, 27 (1982), 77–90.

47. Laver, 'Using Cluster Analysis to Model Coalition Formation'.

48. Ibid.

49. This approach is implemented empirically by the authors of the country chapters in Laver and Budge (eds.), *Party and Coalition Policy in Western Europe*.

50. Laver and Budge (eds.), *Party and Coalition Policy in Western Europe*.

6. WILL IT LAST?

1. P. Warwick, 'Models of Cabinet Stability: A Preliminary Evaluation', paper presented at the annual meeting of the American Political Science Association, Washington, DC, 1988.

2. A. Lijphart, 'Measures of Cabinet Durability: A Conceptual and Empirical Evaluation', *Comparative Political Studies*, 17:2 (1984), 265–79.

3. L. C. Dodd, *Coalitions in Parliamentary Government* (Princeton: Princeton University Press, 1976).

4. E. Browne, D. Gleiber, and C. Mashoba, 'Evaluating Conflict of Interest Theory', *British Journal of Political Science*, 14 (1984), p. 7; Browne, Frendreis, and Gleiber, 'Contending Models of Cabinet Stability: Rejoinder', *American Political Science Review*, 82 (1988), p. 933; K. Strom, 'Party Goals and Government Performance in Parliamentary Democracies', *American Political Science Review*, 79 (1985), p. 741.

5. M. Taylor and M. Laver, 'Government Coalitions in Western Europe', *European Journal of Political Research*, 1 (1973), p. 214; Warwick, 'Models of Cabinet Stability', p. 8.

6. M. Duverger, *Political Parties* (London: Methuen, 1954); J. Blondel, 'Party Systems and Patterns of Government in Western Democracies', *Canadian Journal of Political Science*, 1 (1968), 180–203.

7. D. Rae, *The Political Consequences of Electoral Laws* (New Haven: Yale University Press, 1971); D. Rae and M. Taylor, *The Analysis of Political Cleavages* (New Haven: Yale University Press, 1970); M. Laasko and R. Taagepura, 'Effective Number of Parties: A Measure with Applications to West Europe', *Comparative Political Studies*, 12 (1979), 3–27; N. Schofield, 'Stability of Coalition Governments in Western Europe', *European Journal of Political Economy*, 3 (1987), 555–91.

8. G. Sartori, *Parties and Party Systems: A Framework for Analysis* (Cambridge: Cambridge University Press, 1976).

9. Dodd, *Coalitions in Parliamentary Government*; Sartori, *Parties and Party Systems*.

10. K. Strom, 'Minority Governments in Parliamentary Democracies: The Rationality of Non-Winning Cabinet Solutions', *Comparative Political Studies*, 17 (1984), 199–227; Strom, 'Party Goals and Government Performance in Parliamentary Democracies'; Strom, *Minority Government and Majority Rule* (Cambridge: Cambridge University Press, 1989).

11. Ibid.

12. Strom, 'Party Goals and Government Performance in Parliamentary Democracies'.

13. Ibid., p. 748.

14. G. King, J. Alt, N. Burns, and M. Laver, *A Unified Model of Cabinet Dissolution in Parliamentary Democracies* (American Journal of Political Science, forthcoming).

15. M. Laver, 'Dynamic Factors in Government Coalition Formation', *European Journal of Political Research*, 2 (1974), 259–70; Dodd, *Coalitions in Parliamentary Government*; D. Sanders and V. Herman, 'The Stability and Survival of Governments in Western Democracies', *Acta Politica*, 12 (1977), 346–77; P. Warwick, 'The Durability of Coalition Governments in Parliamentary Democracies', *Comparative Political Studies*, 11 (1979), 465–98; Warwick, 'Models of Cabinet Stability'.

16. King *et al.*, *A Unified Model of Cabinet Dissolution in Parliamentary Democracies*.

17. Sanders and Herman, 'The Stability and Survival of Governments in Western Democracies'; Warwick, 'The Durability of Coalition Governments in Parliamentary Democracies'; Warwick, 'Models of Cabinet Stability'.

18. Schofield, 'Stability of Coalition Governments in Western Europe'.

19. Ibid., p. 588.

20. Dodd, *Coalitions in Parliamentary Government*.

21. Schofield, 'Stability of Coalition Governments in Western Europe'.

22. E. Browne, J. Frendreis, and D. Gleiber, 'The Process of Cabinet Dissolution: An Exponential Model of Duration and Stability in Western Democracies', *American Journal of Political Science*, 30 (1986), pp. 628–9.

23. Ibid., pp. 643–4.

24. K. Strom, 'Contending Models of Cabinet Stability', *American Political Science Review*, 82 (1988), 930–41.

25. King *et al.*, *A Unified Model of Cabinet Dissolution in Parliamentary Democracies*.

7. WHO GETS WHAT?

1. Ó. Grímsson, 'Iceland: A Multilevel Coalition System', in E. Browne and H. Dreijmanis (eds.), *Government Coalitions in Western Democracies* (New York: Longman, 1982), pp. 174–5.

2. Ibid., p. 175.

3. A. Marradi, 'Italy: From "Centrism" to Centre–Left Coalitions', in Browne and Dreijmanis (eds.), *Government Coalitions in Western Democracies*, pp. 65–6.

4. E. Browne and M. Franklin, 'Aspects of Coalition Payoffs in European Parliamentary Democracies', *American Political Science Review*, 67 (1973), p. 457; W. Gamson, 'A Theory of Coalition Formation', *American Sociological Review*, 26 (1961), 373–82.

5. E. Browne and J. Frendreis, 'Allocating Coalition Payoffs by Conventional Norm: An Assessment of the Evidence for Cabinet Coalition Situations', *American Journal of Political Science*, 24 (1980), 753–68.

6. Ibid.

7. Browne and Franklin, 'Aspects of Coalition Payoffs in European Parliamentary Democracies', p. 460*n*.

8. N. Schofield and M. Laver, 'Bargaining Theory and Portfolio Payoffs in European Coalition Governments 1945–83', *British Journal of Political Science*, 15 (1985), 143–64.

9. M. Davis and M. Maschler, 'Existence of Stable Payoff Configurations for Cooperative Games' and B. Peleg, 'Existence Theorem for the Bargaining Set', both in M. Shubik (ed.), *Essays in Mathematical Economics in Honor of Oskar Morgenstern* (Princeton: Princeton University Press, 1967); N. Schofield, 'Generalised Bargaining Sets for Cooperative Games', *International Journal of Game Theory*, 7 (1978), 183–99; N. Schofield and M. Laver, 'Bargaining Theory and Portfolio Payoffs in European Coalition Governments 1945–83'.

10. Schofield and Laver, 'Bargaining Theory and Portfolio Payoffs', pp. 155–8.
11. Ibid., p. 159.
12. I. Budge, D. Robertson, and D. Hearl (eds.), *Ideology, Strategy and Party Change* (Cambridge: Cambridge University Press, 1987).
13. Schofield and Laver, 'Bargaining Theory and Portfolio Payoffs'.
14. L. C. Dodd, *Coalitions in Parliamentary Government* (Princeton: Princeton University Press, 1976).
15. Browne and Franklin, 'Aspects of Coalition Payoffs in European Parliamentary Democracies', p. 468.
16. E. Browne and K. Feste, 'Qualitative Dimensions of Coalition Payoffs: Evidence for European Party Governments 1945–70', *American Behavioral Scientist*, 18 (1975), 530–56.
17. J. Dreijmanis, 'Austria: The "Black"–"Red" Coalitions', in Browne and Dreijmanis (eds.), *Government Coalitions in Western Democracies*, p. 252.
18. Browne and Feste, 'Qualitative Dimensions of Coalition Payoffs', p. 534.
19. Ibid., p. 533.
20. Browne and Franklin, 'Aspects of Coalition Payoffs in European Parliamentary Democracies'.
21. Browne and Feste, 'Qualitative Dimensions of Coalition Payoffs', p. 547.
22. I. Budge, 'A Preliminary Comparative Check on Links Between Party and Ministry in 22 Democracies', paper presented at the Workshop on Comparative Theory, ECPR Joint Sessions, Barcelona, 1985.
23. Ibid., p. 9.
24. Ibid.
25. Ibid., p. 10.
26. Ibid.
27. Browne and Dreijmanis (eds.), *Government Coalitions in Western Democracies*.
28. Ibid.
29. O. Seliktar, 'Israel: Fragile Coalitions in a New Nation', in Browne and Dreijmanis (eds.), *Government Coalitions in Western Democracies*, 309.
30. M. Laver and I. Budge (eds.), *Party and Coalition Policy in Western Europe* (forthcoming)
31. Marradi, 'Italy: From "Centrism" to Centre–Left Coalitions', p. 60.
32. C. Rallings, 'The Influence of Election Programmes: Britain and Canada 1945–1979', in Budge *et al.* (eds.), *Ideology, Strategy and Party Change*.

33. R. Hofferbert and H.-D. Klingemann, 'Coalitions and Cookie Jars: The Policy Impact of Party Programs and Government Declarations in Germany', paper presented at Conference of Party Manifesto Research Group, Palermo, Italy, December 1987.

34. M. Laver and A. Byrne, 'The Relationship between Party and Coalition Policy in Europe: An Empirical Analysis', in Laver and Budge (eds.), *Party and Coalition Policy in Western Europe*.

35. Browne and Franklin, 'Aspects of Coalition Payoffs in European Parliamentary Democracies'.

36. Ibid., p. 454.

37. E. Browne and K. Feste, 'Qualitative Dimensions of Coalition Payoffs: Evidence for European Party Governments 1945–70', *American Behavioral Scientist*, 18 (1975); Budge, 'A Preliminary Comparative Check on Links between Party and Ministry'.

38. Laver and Byrne, 'The Relationship between Party and Coalition Policy in Europe'.

8. COALITIONS IN A CONSTRAINED REAL WORLD

1. K. von Beyme, 'Governments, Parliaments and the Structure of Power within Political Parties', in H. Daalder and P. Mair (eds.), *Western European Party Systems* (Beverly Hills and London: Sage, 1983), p. 342.

2. Ibid., p. 343.

3. G. Pridham, 'An Inductive Theoretical Framework for Coalitional Behaviour', in G. Pridham (ed.), *Coalitional Behaviour in Theory and Practice: An Inductive Model for Western Europe* (Cambridge: Cambridge University Press, 1986), p. 2.

4. G. Pridham, 'Italy's Party Democracy', in G. Pridham (ed.), *Coalitional Behaviour in Theory and Practice: An Inductive Model for Western Europe*, (Cambridge: Cambridge University Press, 1986), p. 211.

5. J. de Jong and B. Pijnenburg, 'The Dutch Christian Democratic Party and Coalitional Behaviour in The Netherlands', in Pridham (ed.), *Coalitional Behaviour in Theory and Practice*, p. 150.

6. C. Rudd, 'Coalition Formation and Maintenance in Belgium', in Pridham (ed.), *Coalitional Behaviour in Theory and Practice*, p. 117.

7. J. Fitzmaurice, 'Coalitional Theory and Practice in Scandinavia' in Pridham (ed.), *Coalitional Behaviour in Theory and Practice*, p. 259.

8. J. Dreijmanis, 'Austria: The "Black"–"Red" Coalitions', p. 257.

9. M. Laver and M. Higgins, 'Coalition or Fianna Fáil? The Politics

of Inter-Party Government in Ireland', in Pridham (ed.), *Coalitional Behaviour in Theory and Practice*, p. 171.

10. K. Shepsle, 'Institutional Arrangements and Equilibrium in Multidimensional Voting Models', *American Journal of Political Science*, 23 (1979), 27–60.

11. M. Slater and A. Mastropaolo, 'Italy 1946–79: Ideological Distances and Party Movements', in Budge, Robertson, and Hearl (eds.), *Ideology, Strategy and Party Change*; Slater and Mastropaolo, 'Italy', in Laver and Budge (eds.), *Party and Coalition Policy in Western Europe*.

12. Rudd, 'Coalition Formation and Maintenance in Belgium', p. 122.

13. Ibid.

14. Ibid., pp. 122–3.

15. D. Rae, *The Political Consequences of Electoral Laws* (New Haven: Yale University Press, 1971), p. 179.

16. P. Personan and A. Thomas, 'Coalition Formation in Scandinavia', in V. Bogdanor (ed.), *Coalition Government in Western Europe* (London: Heinemann, 1983).

17. G. King, J. Alt, N. Burns, and M. Laver, *A Unified Model of Cabinet Dissolution in Parliamentary Democracies* (American Journal of Political Science, forthcoming).

18. J. Vis, 'Coalition Government in a Constitutional Monarchy: The Dutch Experience', in Bogdanor (ed.)., *Coalition Government in Western Europe*.

19. Ibid., p. 160.

20. Ibid., p. 161.

21. B. Grofman, N. Noveillo, and P. Straffin, 'A New Model of Coalition Formation in which One Party is Asked to Form a Government', paper presented at Conference on European Cabinet Coalition Formation, Fiesole, Italy, 1987; D. Austen-Smith and J. Banks, 'Elections, Coalitions and Legislative Outcomes', *American Political Science Review*, 82 (1988), 405–22.

22. Ibid.

23. J. Clemens, *Polls, Politics and Populism* (Aldershot: Gower, 1983).

APPENDIX A. THE UNITARY ACTOR STATUS OF POLITICAL PARTIES IN EUROPEAN COALITION SYSTEMS

1. P. Gerlich, 'Consociationalism to Competition: The Austrian Party System since 1945', in H. Daalder (ed.), *Party Systems in Denmark, Austria, Switzerland, The Netherlands and Belgium* (London: Pinter, 1987), p. 83.

2. Ibid.
3. J. Dreijmanis, 'Austria: The "Black"–"Red" Coalitions', in E. Browne and J. Dreijmanis (eds.), *Government Coalitions in Western Democracies* (New York: Longman, 1982), p. 241.
4. Ibid., pp. 243–4; see also C. Haerpfer, 'Austria', in I. Crewe and D. Denver (eds.), *Electoral Change in Western Democracies* (Beckenham: Croom Helm, 1985); F. Horner, 'Austria 1945–78', in I. Budge, D. Robertson, and D. Hearl (eds.), *Ideology, Strategy and Party Change* (Cambridge: Cambridge University Press, 1987).
5. W. Müller, 'Conservatism and the Transformation of the Austrian People's Party', in B. Girvin (ed.), *The Transformation of Contemporary Conservatism* (London and Beverly Hills: Sage, 1988).
6. Horner, 'Austria 1945–78', p. 272.
7. Gerlich, 'Consociationalism to Competition', p. 86.
8. For an account of this process see W. Dewachter, 'Changes in a Particratie: The Belgian System from 1944 to 1986', in Daalder (ed.), *Party Systems in Denmark, Austria, Switzerland, The Netherlands and Belgium*, pp. 287–8.
9. Ibid. For a chronology and discussion of this process, combined with general accounts of the Belgian party system, see J. Fitzmaurice, *The Politics of Belgium: Crisis and Compromise in a Plural Society* (London: Hurst, 1983), pp. 144–84; A. Mughan, 'The Failure of Conservative Politics in Belgium', in Z. Layton-Henry (ed.), *Conservative Politics in Western Europe* (London: Macmillan, 1982); Mughan, 'Accommodation or Defusion in the Management of Linguistic Conflict in Belgium?', *Political Studies*, 31 (1983), 434–51; Mughan, 'Belgium', in Crewe and Denver (eds.), *Electoral Change in Western Democracies*; Dewachter, 'Changes in a Particratie'.
10. L. de Winten, 'Belgium: Democracy of Oligarchy?' in M. Gallagher and M. Marsh (eds.), *Candidate Selection in Comparative Perspective* (London: Sage, 1988), p. 28.
11. C. Rudd, 'Coalition Formation and Maintenance in Belium', in G. Pridham (ed.), *Coalitional Behaviour in Theory and Practice: An Inductive Model for Western Europe* (Cambridge: Cambridge University Press, 1986).
12. Ibid., p. 129.
13. Ibid., p. 29.
14. Ibid., p. 133.
15. De Winten, 'Belgium: Democracy or Oligarchy?', p. 29.
16. Dewachter, 'Changes in a Particratie', p. 325.
17. For a discussion of this see Mughan, 'Accommodation or Defusion in the Management of Linguistic Conflict in Belgium?', p. 446 and

W. Dewachter and E. Clijsters, 'Belgium: Political Stability Despite Coalition Crises', in Browne and Dreijmanis (eds.), *Government Coalitions in Western Democracies*, p. 198.

18. Dewachter and Clijsters, 'Belgium: Political Stability Despite Coalition Crises', p. 198, emphasis added.

19. Dewachter, 'Changes in a Particratie', p. 299.

20. M. Pederson, 'The Danish "Working Multiparty System"': Breakdown or Adoption?', in Daalder (ed.), *Party Systems in Denmark, Austria, Switzerland, The Netherlands and Belgium*.

21. K. Miller, *Government and Politics in Denmark* (Boston: Houghton Mifflin, 1968), pp. 87–92.

22. J. Fitzmaurice, 'Coalitional Theory and Practice in Scandinavia', in Pridham (ed.), *Coalitional Behaviour in Theory and Practice*.

23. Pederson, 'the Danish "Working Multiparty System"'.

24. For brief discussions of this see P. Pesonan and A. Thomas, 'Coalition Formation in Scandinavia', in V. Bogdanor (ed.), *Coalition Government in Western Europe* (London: Heinemann, 1983), p. 73, and A. Thomas, 'Denmark: Coalitions and Minority Governments' in Browne and Dreijmanis (eds.), *Government Coalitions in Western Democracies*, p. 114.

25. Pederson, 'The Danish "Working Multiparty System"', p. 37.

26. Ibid., pp. 14–15.

27. Fitzmaurice, 'Coalitional Theory and Practice in Scandinavia', p. 274.

28. Pederson, 'The Danish "Working Multiparty System"', p. 49.

29. D. Arter, *Politics and Policy-Making in Finland* (Brighton: Wheatsheaf, 1987), p. 48.

30. For brief accounts of this see P. Nyholm, 'Finland: A Probabilistic View of Coalition Formation', in Browne and Dreijmanis (eds.), *Government Coalitions in Western Democracies*, p. 72; N. Elder, A. Thomas, and D. Arter, *The Consensual Democracies: The Government and Politics of the Scandinavian States* (Oxford: Martin Robertson, 1982), p. 84.

31. Nyholm, 'Finland: A Probabilistic View of Coalition Formation', p. 72; Elder *et al.*, *The Consensual Democracies?*, p. 94.

32. Elder *et al.*, *The Consensual Democracies?*, p. 85.

33. G. Grunberg, 'France', in Crewe and Denver (eds.), *Electoral Change in Western Democracies*.

34. V. Lauber, 'Change and Continuity in French Conservatism 1944–86', in Girvin (ed.), *The Transformation of Contemporary Conservatism*.

35. For an account of this see A. Werth, *De Gaulle* (Harmondsworth: Penguin, 1965).

36. D. McCrea, *Parliament, Parties and Society in France 1946–58* (New York: St Martins, 1967).

37. Browne and Dreijmanis (eds.), *Government Coalitions in Western Democracies*; Bogdanor (ed.), *Coalition Government in Western Europe*; Pridham (ed.), *Coalitional Behaviour in Theory and Practice*.

38. It was not considered by E. Browne and M. Franklin, 'Aspects of Coalition Payoffs in European Parliamentary Democracies', *American Political Science Review*, 67 (1973), 453–69; M. Taylor and M. Laver, 'Government Coalitions in Western Europe', *European Journal of Political Research*, 1 (1973), 205–48; A. de Swaan, *Coalition Theories and Cabinet Formation* (Amsterdam: Elsevier, 1973); L. C. Dodd, *Coalitions in Parliamentary Government* (Princeton: Princeton University Press, 1976); N. Schofield, *Choice and Democracy* (Heidelberg: Springer, 1985); or G. Luebbert, *Comparative Democracy: Policy Making and Governing Coalitions in Europe and Israel* (New York: Columbia University Press, 1986).

39. P. Cerny, 'Democratic Socialism and the Tests of Power', *West European Politics*, 6:3 (1983), p. 202.

40. C. Lyrintsis, 'Political Parties in Post-Junta Greece: A Case of Bureaucratic Clientelism?', *West European Politics*, 7 (1984), p. 106.

41. Ibid., p. 108.

42. P. Diamandouros, 'Transition to and Consolidation of Democratic Politics in Greece 1974–83: Tentative Assessment', *West European Politics*, 7:2 (1984), p. 67.

43. K. Featherstone and D. Katsoudas, 'Change and Continuity in Greek Voting Behaviour', *European Journal of Political Research*, 13 (1985), 27–40; S. Tsokon, Mark C. Shelley II, and Betty Dobratz, 'Some Correlates of Partisan Preference in Greece, 1980: A Discriminant Analysis', *European Journal of Political Research*, 13 (1986), 441–63.

44. C. Lyrintsis, 'The Power of Populism: The Greek Case', *European Journal of Political Research*, 15 (1987), p. 668.

45. K. Featherstone, 'The Greek Socialists in Power', *West European Politics*, 6:3 (1983), p. 283.

46. Ó. Hardarson and G. Kristensen, 'The Icelandic Parliamentary Election of 1987', *Electoral Studies*, 6 (1987), p. 22.

47. G. Arnason, 'Fluidity in Icelandic Politics: The Election of April 1987', *West European Politics*, 11:1 (1988), 122–5; I. Norderval, 'Party and Legislative Participation among Scandinavian Women', *West European Politics*, 8 (1985), pp. 75–6.

48. R. Tomasson, 'Iceland', in V. McHale (ed.), *Political Parties of Europe* (Westport: Greenwood, 1983), p. 526.

49. Ó. Grímsson, 'Iceland: A Multilevel Coalition System', in Browne

and Dreijmanis (eds.), *Government Coalitions in Western Democracies*, p. 46.

50. Ibid., p. 148, emphasis added.
51. Ó. Hardarson, 'Iceland', in G. Delury (ed.), *World Encyclopedia of Political Systems and Political Parties* (New York: Facts on File, 1983), p. 432, emphasis added.
52. Hardarson and Kristensen, 'The Icelandic Parliamentary Election of 1987), p. 220.
53. J. Madely, 'The Politics of Hyper-Inflation: Iceland's Election', *West European Politics*, 7 (1984), p. 126.
54. Hardarson and Kristensen, 'The Icelandic Parliamentary Election of 1987', pp. 226–7; Arnason, 'Fluidity in Icelandic Politics'.
55. Hardarson and Kristensen, 'The Icelandic Parliamentary Election of 1987', pp. 223, 229.
56. The internal workings of the Irish parties are described in some detail by M. Gallagher, *The Irish Labour Party in Transition 1957–81* (Dublin: Gill and Macmillan, 1982); Gallagher, *Political Parties in the Republic of Ireland* (Dublin: Gill and Macmillan, 1985); and P. Mair, *The Changing Irish Party System* (London: Pinter, 1987).
57. M. Laver, M. Higgins, 'Coalition or Fianna Fáil? The Politics of Inter-Party Government in Ireland', in Pridham (ed.), *Coalitional Behaviour in Theory and Practice*, pp. 104–7.
58. M. Laver, M. Marsh, and R. Sinnott, 'Patterns of Party Support', in M. Laver, P. Mair, and R. Sinnott (eds.), *How Ireland Voted: The General Election of February 1987* (Swords: Poolbeg, 1987).
59. Laver and Higgins, 'Coalition or Fianna Fáil?', p. 187.
60. See Gallagher, *The Irish Labour Party in Transition 1957–81* for an account of the impact on internal Labour Party politics of discussions of coalition arrangements with Fine Gael.
61. There is no better evidence of this, from the perspective of Fianna Fáil, than the ability of party leader C. J. Haughey to commit to a coalition after the 1989 election, in the face of severe opposition at many levels of the party.
62. J. Bara, 'Israel 1949–81', in Budge, Robertson, and Hearl (eds.), *Ideology, Strategy and Party Change*, p. 115.
63. Ibid., pp. 114–15.
64. S. Hellman, 'The Italian Communist Party between Berlinguer and the Seventeenth Congress', in R. Leonardi and R. Y. Nanetti (eds.), *Italian Politics: A Review, Volume I* (London: Pinter, 1986), p. 55.
65. D. Wertman, 'Italy: Local Involvement and Central Control', in Gallagher and Marsh (eds.), *Candidate Selection in Comparative Perspective*, pp. 152–3.
66. G. Pridham, 'Party Politics and Coalition Government in Italy', in Bogdanor (ed.), *Coalition Government in Western Europe*, p. 222.

67. F. Spotts and T. Wieser, *Italy: A Difficult Democracy* (Cambridge: Cambridge University Press, 1986), p. 8.
68. Ibid., p. 9.
69. R. Irving, *The Christian Democratic Parties of Western Europe* (London: Allen and Unwin, 1979), p. 58.
70. G. Pridham, 'Italy's Party Democracy and Coalitional Behaviour', in Pridham (ed.), *Coalitional Behaviour in Theory and Practice*, p. 222.
71. Wertman, 'Italy: Local Involvement and Central Control', p. 152.
72. G. Pasquino, 'Sources of Stability and Instability in the Italian Party System', *West European Politics*, 6:1 (1983), p. 97.
73. Ibid.
74. S. Tarrow, 'Introduction', in Leonardi and Nanetti (eds.), *Italian Politics: A Review, Volume I*, p. 3; Pridham, 'Italy's Party Democracy and Coalitional Behaviour', p. 222.
75. G. Pasquino, 'Modernity and Reforms: The PSI between Political Entrepreneurs and Gamblers', *West European Politics*, 9:1 (1986), p. 12.
76. This process is charted briefly by A. Marradi, 'Italy: From "Centrism" to Centre–Left Coalitions', in Browne and Dreijmanis (eds.), *Government Coalitions in Western Democracies*.
77. Pasquino, 'Sources of Stability and Instability in the Italian Party System', p. 105.
78 Wertman, 'Italy: Local Involvement and Central Control', p. 158.
79. D. Hine, 'The Italian General Election of 1987', *Electoral Studies*, 6 (1987), 267–70.
80. D. Hearl, 'Luxemburg 1945–82: Dimensions and Strategies', in Budge, Robertson, and Hearl (eds.), *Ideology, Strategy and Party Change*, pp. 254–7.
81. V. McHale (ed.), *Political Parties of Europe*, p. 624.
82. M. Hirsch, 'The 1984 Luxemburg Election', *Electoral Studies*, 4 (1985), 116–18.
83. See especially A. de Swaan, 'The Netherlands: Coalitions in a Segmented Polity', in Browne and Dreijmanis (eds.), *Government Coalitions in Western Democracies*; J. de Jong and B. Pijnenburg, 'The Dutch Christian Democratic Party and Coalitional Behaviour in The Netherlands', in Pridham (ed.), *Coalitional Behaviour in Theory and Practice*. For other recent accounts of Dutch coalitional politics, see J. Vis, 'Coalition Government in a Constitutional Monarchy: The Dutch Experience' and K. Gladdish, 'Coalition Government and Policy Options in The Netherlands', both in Bogdanor (ed.), *Coalition Government in Western Europe*; K. Dittrich, 'The Netherlands 1946–81' in Budge, Robertson, and

Hearl (eds.), *Ideology, Strategy and Party Change*; and H. Daalder, 'The Dutch Party System: From Segmentation to Polarisation— and then?', in Daalder (ed.), *Party Systems in Denmark, Austria, Switzerland, The Netherlands and Belgium*.

84. Daalder, 'The Dutch Party System', p. 214.
85. De Jong and Pijnenburg, 'The Dutch Christian Democratic Party and Coalitional Behaviour in The Netherlands'.
86. R. Koole and M. Leijenaar, 'The Netherlands: The Predominance of Regionalism', in Gallagher and Marsh (eds.), *Candidate Selection in Comparative Perspective*, p. 205.
87. de Jong and Pijnenburg, 'The Dutch Christian Democratic Party and Coalitional Behaviour in The Netherlands', p. 165.
88. Daalder, 'The Dutch Party System', p. 215.
89. Koole and Leijenaar, 'The Netherlands: The Predominance of Regionalism', pp. 200–1.
90. See P. Lucardie, 'Conservatism in The Netherlands: Fragments and Fringe Groups', in Girvin (ed.), *The Transformation of Contemporary Conservatism* for an analysis of the position of the VVD and the small Christian parties.
91. Koole and Leijenaar, 'The Netherlands: The Predominance of Regionalism', pp. 197–200.
92. B. Sarlvik, 'Coalition Politics and Policy Output in Scandinavia: Sweden, Denmark and Norway', in Bogdanor (ed.), *Coalition Government in Western Europe*.
93. K. Strom, 'Deferred Gratification and Minority Governments in Scandinavia', *Legislative Studies Quarterly*, 11:4 (1986), p. 589; Fitzmaurice, 'Coalitional Theory and Practice in Scandinavia', p. 274.
94. H. Valen, 'Norway: Decentralisation and Group Representation', in Gallagher and Marsh (eds.), *Candidate Selection in Comparative Perspective*, p. 231.
95. K. Strom and J. Leipart, 'Norway: Policy Pursuit and Coalition Avoidance', in Laver and Budge (eds.), *Party and Coalition Policy in Western Europe* (forthcoming).
96. Ibid.
97. T. Gallagher, 'Goodbye to Revolution: The Portuguese Election of July 1987', *West European Politics*, 11:1 (1988), 139–45.
98. T. Bruneau and A. MacCleod, *Politics in Contemporary Portugal* (Boulder: Lynne Rienner, 1986), pp. 60–4.
99. Gallagher, 'Goodbye to Revolution'.
100. Bruneau and MacCleod, *Politics in Contemporary Portugal*, p. 79.
101. T. Gallagher, 'Twice Choosing the Unexpected: The Portuguese

Elections of 1985 and 1986', *West European Politics*, 9:4 (1986), 233–7.

102. See, however, J. Capo, 'Party Coalitions in Spain 1977–82', in Pridham (ed.), *Coalitional Behaviour in Theory and Practice*.

103. See J. Amodia, 'Union of the Democratic Centre', in D. Bell (ed.), *Democratic Politics in Spain* (London: Pinter, 1983) for a discussion of the formation of the UCD; R. Cotarelo and L. L. Nieto, in 'Spanish Conservatism 1976–87', *West European Politics*, 11:2 (1988), 80–95, go so far as to claim that the UCD 'was the result of the fusion of 48 pre-existing parties'.

104. See Amodia, 'Union of the Democratic Centre'; J. Marcus, 'The Triumph of Spanish Socialism: The 1983 Election', *West European Politics*, 6:3 (1983), 281–6; Capo, 'Party Coalitions in Spain 1977–82' for an account of this process of splitting.

105. Marcus, 'The Triumph of Spanish Socialism', p. 253.

106. Cotarelo and Nieto, 'Spanish Conservatism 1976–87', pp. 86–7.

107. Ibid., p. 81.

108. Marcus, 'The Triumph of Spanish Socialism', p. 284.

109. D. Bell, 'The Spanish Communist Party in Transition', in Bell (ed.), *Democratic Politics in Spain*.

110. See D. Share, 'Two Transitions: Democratisation and the Evolution of the Spanish Left', *West European Politics*, 8:1 (1985), 83–103, for a detailed account of the internal politics of the PSOE.

111. Elizabeth Nash, 'The Spanish Socialist Party Since Franco', in Bell (ed.), *Democratic Politics in Spain*.

112. Cotarelo and Nieto Lourdes, 'Spanish Conservatism 1976–87'.

113. See especially Personan and Thomas, 'Coalition Formation in Scandinavia'; Sarlvik, 'Coalition Politics and Policy Output in Scandinavia'; and Strom, 'Deferred Gratification and Minority Governments in Scandinavia'.

114. K. Strom and T. Bergman, 'Sweden: Social Democratic Dominance in a Unidimensional Party System', in Laver and Budge (eds.), *Party and Coalition Policy in Western Europe*.

115. See especially Sarlvik, 'Coalition Politics and Policy Output in Scandinavia' for a discussion of party–interest group relations in Sweden.

116. Strom, 'Deferred Gratification and Minority Governments in Scandinavia', p. 589.

117. J. Steiner, 'Switzerland: "Magic Formula" Coalitions', in Browne and Dreijmanis (eds.), *Coalition Governments in Western Democracies*, p. 316.

118. H. Kerr, 'The Swiss Party System: Steadfast and Changing', in Daalder (ed.), *Party Systems in Denmark, Austria, Switzerland, The Netherlands and Belgium*, p. 124.

119. Ibid., p. 128.
120. Steiner, 'Switzerland: "Magic Formula" Coalitions', p. 327.
121. Kerr, 'The Swiss Party System', p. 138.
122. I. Papadopoulos, 'The Swiss Election of 1987: A "Silent Revolution" behind Stability', *West European Politics*, 11:3 (1988), 146–9.
123. D. Broughton and E. Kirchner, 'The FDP and Coalitional Behaviour in the Federal Republic of Germany', in Pridham (ed.), *Coalitional Behaviour in Theory and Practice*, p. 86.
124. Ibid.
125. Ibid.
126. U. Hoffman-Lange, 'Changing Coalitional Preferences among West German Parties', in Pridham (ed.), *Coalitional Behaviour in Theory and Practice*, p. 45*n*.
127. H.-D. Klingemann, 'Election Programmes in West Germany', in Budge, Robertson, and Hearl (eds.), *Ideology, Strategy and Party Change*; and see, for example, M. Schmidt, 'Two Logics of Coalition Policy: The West German Case' and von Beyme, 'Coalition Government in Western Germany', both in Bogdanor (ed.), *Coalition Government in Western Europe*; von Beyme, *The Political System of the Federal Republic of Germany* (Aldershot: Gower, 1983).
128. R. Livingston (ed.), *West German Political Parties: CDU, CSU, FDP, SDP, The Greens* (Washington, DC: American Institute for Contemporary German Studies, 1986).
129. E. Grande, 'Neoconservatism and Conservative–Liberal Economic Policy in West Germany', *European Journal of Political Research*, 15 (1987), 281–96.
130. Irving, *The Christian Democratic Parties of Western Europe*.
131. H. Norpoth, 'The German Federal Republic: Coalition Government at the Brink of Majority Rule', in Browne and Dreijmanis (eds.), *Coalition Governments in Western Democracies*.
132. Irving, *The Christian Democratic Parties of Western Europe*, p. 161.
133. G. Braunthal, 'The West German Social Democrats: Factionalism at the Local Level', *West European Politics*, 7:1 (1984), p. 61.
134. Ibid.

APPENDIX B. LOCATING POLITICAL PARTIES ON EMPIRICAL POLICY SCALES

1. M. Laver and I. Budge (eds.), *Party and Coalition Policy in Western Europe* (forthcoming).

2. R. Inglehart and H.-D. Klingemann, 'Party Identification, Ideological Preference and the Left–Right Dimensions among Western Pass Publics', in I. Budge, I. Crewe, and D. Farlie (eds.), *Party, Identification and Beyond: Representations of Voting and Party Competition* (London: Wiley, 1976); G. Sani and G. Sartori, 'Polarization, Fragmentation and Competition in Western Democracies', in H. Daalder and P. Mair (eds.), *Western European Party Systems* (London and Beverly Hills: Sage, 1983).

3. M. Taylor and M. Laver, 'Government Coalitions in Western Europe', *European Journal of Political Research*, 1 (1973), 205–48; L. C. Dodd, *Coalitions in Parliamentary Government* (Princeton: Princeton University Press, 1976).

4. A. de Swaan, *Coalition Theories and Cabinet Formation* (Amsterdam: Elsevier, 1973), p. 42.

5. E. C. Browne and J. Dreijmanis (eds.), *Government Coalitions in Western Democracies* (New York: Longman, 1982).

6. F. Castles and P. Mair, 'Left–Right Political Scales: Some Expert Judgements', *European Journal of Political Research*, 12 (1984), 83–8.

7. For a very detailed discussion of the survey instrument and other issues, see M.-J. Morgan, 'The Modelling of Governmental Coalition Formation: A Policy-Based Approach with Interval Measurement' (University of Michigan, PhD thesis, 1976).

8. I. Budge, D. Robertson, and D. Hearl (eds.), *Ideology, Strategy and Party Change* (Cambridge: Cambridge University Press, 1987).

9. Laver and Budge (eds.), *Party and Coalition Policy in Western Europe*.

10. Inglehart and Klingemann, 'Party Identification, Ideological Preference and the Left–Right Dimensions', pp. 253–5.

11. Sani and Sartori, 'Polarization, Fragmentation and Competition in Western Democracies'.

12. T. Bruneau and A. MacCleod, *Politics in Contemporary Portugal* (Boulder: Lynne Rienner, 1986).

13. Budge, Robertson, and Hearl (eds.), *Ideology, Strategy and Party Change*; Laver and Budge (eds.), *Party and Coalition Policy in Western Europe*.

Bibliography

Aldrich, John H., 'A Downsian Spatial Model with Party Activism', *American Political Science Review*, 77 (1983), 974–90.

Antonian, Armen and Wall, Irwin, 'The French Communists under François Mitterrand', *Political Studies*, 33 (1985), 254–73.

Arnason, Gudmundur, 'Fluidity in Icelandic Politics: The Election of April 1987', *West European Politics*, 11:1 (1988), 122–5.

Arter, David, *Politics and Policy-Making in Finland* (Brighton: Wheatsheaf, 1987).

Austen-Smith, David and Banks, Jeffrey, 'Elections, Coalitions and Legislative Outcomes', *American Political Science Review*, 82 (1988), 405–22.

Axelrod, Robert, *Conflict of Interest* (Chicago: Markham, 1970).

Baron, David, and Ferejohn, John, *Bargaining in Legislatures* (Stanford University, unpublished manuscript, 1987).

Bell, David (ed.), *Democratic Politics in Spain* (London: Pinter, 1983).

Blair, Antonio, 'The Emerging Spanish Party System: Is There a Model?' *West European Politics*, 7:4 (1984), 120–55.

Blondel, Jean, 'Party Systems and Patterns of Government in Western Democracies', *Canadian Journal of Political Science*, 1 (1968), 180–203.

Bogdanor, Vernon (ed.), *Coalition Government in Western Europe* (London: Heinemann, 1983).

Bradley, Ian, *Breaking the Mould? The Birth and Prospects of the Social Democratic Party* (Oxford: Martin Robertson, 1981).

Braunthal, Gerard, 'The West German Social Democrats: Factionalism at the Local Level', *West European Politics*, 7:1 (1984), 47–64.

Browne, Eric, *Coalition Theories: a Logical and Empirical Critique* (London: Sage (Professional Papers in Comparative Politics), 1973).

Browne, Eric, C. and Dreijmanis, John (eds.), *Government Coalitions in Western Democracies* (New York: Longman, 1982).

Browne, Eric and Feste, Karen, 'Qualitative Dimensions of Coalition Payoffs: Evidence for European Party Governments 1945–70', *American Behavioral Scientist*, 18 (1975), 530–56.

Browne, Eric and Franklin, Mark, 'Aspects of Coalition Payoffs in European Parliamentary Democracies', *American Political Science Review*, 67 (1973), 453–69.

Browne, Eric and Frendreis, John, 'Allocating Coalition Payoffs by Conventional Norm: An Assessment of the Evidence for Cabinet Coalition Situations', *American Journal of Political Science*, 24 (1980), 753–68.

Browne, Eric, Frendreis, John, and Gleiber, Dennis, 'An Events Approach to the Problem of Cabinet Stability', *Comparative Political Studies*, 17 (1984) 167–97.

Browne, Eric, Frendreis, John, and Gleiber, Dennis, 'The Process of Cabinet Dissolution: An Exponential Model of Duration and Stability in Western Democracies', *American Journal of Political Science*, 30 (1986), 625–50.

Browne, Eric, Frendreis, John, and Gleiber, Dennis, 'Contending Models of Cabinet Stability: Rejoinder', *American Political Science Review*, 82 (1988), 930–41.

Browne, Eric, Gleiber, Dennis, and Mashoba, Carolyn, 'Evaluating Conflict of Interest Theory: Western European Cabinet Coalitions, 1945–80', *British Journal of Political Science*, 14 (1984), 1–32.

Bruneau, Thomas and MacCleod, Alex, *Politics in Contemporary Portugal* (Boulder: Lynne Rienner, 1986).

Budge, Ian, 'A Preliminary Comparative Check on Links Between Party and Ministry in 22 Democracies', paper presented at the Workshop on Comparative Theory, ECPR Joint Sessions, Barcelona, 1985.

Budge, Ian, Crewe, Ivor, and Farlie, Dennis, (eds.), *Party Identification and Beyond: Representations of Voting and Party Competition* (London: Wiley, 1976).

Budge, Ian and Laver, Michael, 'Office Seeking and Policy Pursuit in Coalition Theory', *Legislative Studies Quarterly*, 11 (1985), 485–506.

Budge, Ian, Robertson, David, and Hearl, Derek, (eds.), *Ideology, Strategy and Party Change* (Cambridge: Cambridge University Press, 1987).

Butler, David (ed.), *Coalitions in British Politics* (London: Macmillan, 1978).

Calvert, Randall, 'Robustness of the Multidimensional Voting Model: Candidate Motivations, Uncertainty and Convergence', *American Journal of Political Science*, 29 (1985), 69–95.

Castles, Francis and Mair, Peter, 'Left–Right Political Scales: Some Expert Judgements', *European Journal of Political Research*, 12 (1984), 83–8.

Cerny, Philip, 'Democratic Socialism and the Tests of Power', *West European Politics* 6:3 (1983), 197–215.

Chappell, Henry and Keech, William, 'Policy Motivation and Party Differences in a Dynamic Spatial Model of Party Competition', *American Political Science Review*, 80 (1986), 881–99.

Clemens, John, *Polls, Politics and Populism* (Aldershot: Gower, 1983).

Cohen, Linda, 'Cyclic Sets in Multidimensional Voting Models', *Journal of Economic Theory*, 20 (1979), 1–12.

Cohen, Linda and Matthews, S. A. 'Constrained Plott Equilibria, Directional Equilibria and Global Cycling Sets', *Review of Economic Studies* 47 (1980) 975–86.

Cotarelo, Ramon and Nieto, Lourdes Lopez, 'Spanish Conservatism 1976–87', *West European Politics*, 11:2 (1988), 80–95.

Cox, Gary, *The Efficient Secret* (Cambridge: Cambridge University Press, 1987).

Crewe, Ivor and Denver, David (eds.), *Electoral Change in Western Democracies* (Beckenham: Croom Helm, 1985).

Daalder, Hans, 'Cabinets and Party Systems in Ten Smaller European Democracies', *Acta Politica*, 6 (1971), 282–303.

Daalder, Hans (ed.), *Party Systems in Denmark, Austria, Switzerland, The Netherlands and Belgium* (London: Pinter, 1987).

Daalder, Hans and Mair, Peter (eds.), *Western European Party Systems* (Beverly Hills and London: Sage, 1983).

de Swaan, Abram, *Coalition Theories and Cabinet Formation* (Amsterdam: Elsevier, 1973).

Delury, George (ed.), *World Encyclopedia of Political Systems and Political Parties* (New York: Facts on File, 1983).

Denzau, Arthur and Mackay, Robert, 'Structure Induced Equilibrium and Perfect Foresight Expectations', *American Journal of Political Science*, 25 (1981), 762–79.

Diamandouros, P. Nikiforos, 'Transition to and Consolidation of Democratic Politics in Greece 1974–83: Tentative Assessment', *West European Politics* 7:2 (1984), 50–71.

Dodd, L. C., *Coalitions in Parliamentary Government* (Princeton: Princeton University Press, 1976).

Downs, Anthony, *An Economic Theory of Democracy* (New York: Harper and Row, 1987).

Duverger, Maurice, *Political Parties* (London: Methuen, 1954).

Eckstein, Harry, *The Evaluation of Political Performance: Problems and Dimensions* (Beverly Hills and London: Sage, 1971).

Edmondson, Ricca, *Rhetoric in Sociology* (London: Macmillan, 1984).

Elder, Neil, Thomas, Alastair, and Arter, David, *The Consensual Democracies? The Government and Politics of the Scandinivan States* (Oxford: Martin Robertson, 1982).

Enelow, James and Hinich, Melvin, 'Voter Expectations in Multistage Voting Systems: An Equilibrium Result', *American Journal of Political Science*, 27 (1983), 820–70.

Enelow, James and Hinich, Melvin, 'Voting One Issue at a Time: The Question of Voter Forecasts', *American Political Science Review*, 77 (1983), 435–45.

Featherstone, Kevin, 'The Greek Socialists in Power', *West European Politics*, 6:3 (1983) 237–50.

Featherstone, Kevin and Katsoudas, Dimitas, 'Change and Continuity in Greek Voting Behaviour', *European Journal of Political Research*, 13 (1985), 27–40.

Fitzmaurice, John, *The Politics of Belgium: Crisis and Compromise in a Plural Society* (London: Hurst, 1983).

Franklin, Mark and Mackie, Tom, 'Reassessing the Importance of Size and Ideology for the Formation of Governing Coalitions in Parliamentary Democracies', *American Journal of Political Science* 28 (1984), 671–92.

Frohlich, Norman, Oppenheimer, Joe, and Young, Oran, *Political Leadership and Collective Goods* (Princeton: Princeton University Press, 1971).

Gallagher, Michael, *The Irish Labour Party in Transition 1957–81* (Dublin: Gill and Macmillan, 1982).

Gallagher, Michael, *Political Parties in the Republic of Ireland* (Dublin: Gill and Macmillan, 1985).

Gallagher, Michael, and Marsh, Michael (eds.), *Candidate Selection in Comparative Perspective* (London: Sage, 1988).

Gallagher, Tom, 'Twice Choosing the Unexpected: The Portuguese Elections of 1985 and 1986', *West European Politics*, 9:4 (1986), 233–7.

Gallagher, Tom, 'Goodbye to Revolution: The Portuguese Election of July 1987', *West European Politics* 11:1 (1988), 139–45.

Gamson, William, 'A Theory of Coalition Formation', *American Sociological Review*, 26 (1961), 373–82.

Gilligan, Thomas, and Krehbiel, Keith, 'Collective Decision Making and Standing Committees: An Informational Rationale for Restrictive Amendment Procedure', *Journal of Law, Economics and Organisations*, 3 (1987) 287–335.

Girvin, Brian (ed.), *The Transformation of Contemporary Conservatism* (London and Beverly Hills: Sage, 1988).

Grande, Edgar, 'Neoconservatism and Conservative–Liberal Economic Policy in West Germany', *European Journal of Political Research*, 15, (1987), 281–96.

Grofman, Bernard, 'A Dynamic Model of Protocoalition Formation in Ideological n-space', *Behavioural Science*, 27 (1982), 77–90.

Grofman, Bernard, Noviello, Nicholas, and Straffin, Phillip, 'A New Model of Coalition Formation in Which One Party is Asked to Form a Government', paper presented at Conference on European Cabinet Coalition Formation, Fiesole, Italy, 1987.

Hardarson, Olafur and Kristensen, Gunnar, 'The Icelandic Parliamentary Election of 1987', *Electoral Studies*, 6 (1987), 209–18.

Herman, Valentine, and Pope, John, 'Minority Governments in Western

Democracies', *British Journal of Political Science*, 3 (1973), 191–212.

Hine, David, 'The Italian General Election of 1987', *Electoral Studies*, 6 (1987), 267–70.

Hirsch, Mario, 'The 1984 Luxemburg Election', *Electoral Studies*, 4 (1985), 116–18.

Hirschman, Albert, *Exit, Voice and Loyalty* (Cambridge, MA: Harvard University Press, 1970).

Hofferbert, Richard and Klingemann, Hans-Dieter, 'Coalitions and Cookie Jars: The Policy Impact of the Party Programs and Government Declarations in Germany', paper presented at Conference of Party Manifesto Research Group, Palermo, Italy, December 1987.

Holler, Manfred (ed.), *Coalitions and Collective Action* (Wurzburg: Physica, 1984).

Hood, Christopher and Gunnar Folke Schuppert, *Delivering Public Services in Western Europe* (Beverly Hills and London: Sage, 1988).

Irving, R. E. M., *The Christian Democratic Parties of Western Europe* (London: Allen and Unwin, 1979).

King, Gary, Alt, James, Burns, Nancy, and Laver, Michael, *A Unified Model of Cabinet Dissolution in Parliamentary Democracies* (American Journal of Political Science, forthcoming).

Kramer, G. H., 'On a Class of Equilibrium Conditions for Majority Rule', *Econometrica*, 41 (1973), 285–97.

Krehbiel, Keith, 'Spatial Models of Legislative Choice', *Legislative Studies Quarterly*, 3 (1988), 259–319.

Laasko, M. and Taagepura, R., 'Effective Number of Parties: A Measure with Applications to West Europe', *Comparative Political Studies*, 12 (1979), 3–27.

Laver, Michael, 'Dynamic Factors in Government Coalition Formation', *European Journal of Political Research*, 2 (1974), 259–70.

Laver, Michael, *The Politics of Private Desires* (Harmondsworth: Pelican, 1981).

Laver, Michael, 'Party Competition and Party System Change: The Interaction of Electoral Bargaining and Party Competition', *Journal of Theoretical Politics*, 1 (1989), 301–25.

Laver, Michael and Budge, Ian (eds.), *Party and Coalition Policy in Western Europe* (forthcoming).

Laver, Michael, Mair, Peter, and Sinnott, Richard (eds.), *How Ireland Voted: The General Election of February 1987* (Swords: Poolbeg Press, 1987).

Laver, Michael, Rallings, Colin, and Thrasher, Michael, 'Coalition Theory and Local Government Coalition Payoffs in Britain', *British Journal of Political Science*, 17 (1987), 501–9.

Laver, Michael and Underhill, John, 'The Bargaining Advantages of Combining with Others', *British Journal of Political Science*, 12 (1982), 75–90.

Layton-Henry, Zig (ed.), *Conservative Politics in Western Europe* (London: Macmillan, 1982).

Leiserson, Michael, *Coalitions in Politics* (Yale University, PhD thesis, 1966).

Lieserson, Michael, 'Factions and Coalitions in One-Party Japan: An Interpretation Based on the Theory of Games', *American Political Science Review*, 62 (1966), 70–87.

Leonardi, Robert and Nanetti, Raffaella Y. (eds.), *Italian Politics: A Review, Volume I* (London: Pinter, 1986).

Lewin, L. and Vedung, E. (eds.), *Politics and Rational Action* (Dordrecht: Reidel, 1980).

Lijphart, Arend, 'Power Sharing versus Majority Rule: Patterns of Cabinet Formation in Twenty Democracies', *Government and Opposition*, 16 (1981), 395–413.

Lijphart, Arend, 'Measures of Cabinet Durability: A Conceptual and Empirical Evaluation', *Comparative Political Studies*, 17: 2 (1984), 265–79.

Livingston, Robert (ed.), *West German Political Parties: CDU, CSU, FDP, SPD, The Greens* (Washington, DC: American Institute for Contemporary German Studies, 1986).

Luebbert, Gregory, *Comparative Democracy: Policy Making and Governing Coalitions in Europe and Israel* (New York: Columbia University Press, 1986).

Lyrintsis, Christos, 'Political Parties in Post-Junta Greece: A Case of Bureaucratic Clientelism?', *West European Politics*, 7:2 (1984), 99–118.

Lyrintsis, Christos, 'The Power of Populism: The Greek Case', *European Journal of Political Research*, 15 (1987), 667–86.

McCrea, Duncan, *Parliament, Parties and Society in France 1946–58* (New York: St Martins, 1967).

McHale, Vincent (ed.), *Political Parties in Europe* (Westport: Greenwood, 1983).

McKelvey, R. D., 'Intransitivities in Multidimensional Voting Models and some Implications for Agenda Control', *Journal of Economic Theory*, 12 (1976), 472–82.

McKelvey, R. D., 'General Conditions for Global Intransitivities in Formal Voting Models', *Econometrica*, 47 (1979), 1085–111.

McKelvey, Richard D., Ordeshook, Peter, and Winer, Michael, 'The Competitive Solution for N-person Games without Transferable Utility, with an Application to Committee Games', *American Political Science Review*, 72 (1978), 599–615.

McKelvey, R. D. and Schofield, Norman, 'Structural Instability of the Core', *Journal of Mathematical Economics*, 15 (1986), 555–91.

McKelvey, R. D. and Schofield, Norman, 'Generalised Symmetry Conditions at a Core Point', *Econometrica*, 55 (1987), 923–33.

Madely, John, 'The Politics of Hyper-Inflation: Iceland's Election', *West European Politics*, 7 (1984), 124–7.

Mair, Peter, *The Changing Irish Party System* (London: Pinter, 1987).

Marcus, Jonathan, 'The Triumph of Spanish Socialism: The 1983 Election', *West European Politics* 6:3 (1983), 281–6.

Matthews, S. A., 'Pairwise Symmetry Conditions for Voting Equilibria', *Journal of Game Theory*, 9 (1980), 141–56.

Matthews, S. A., 'Local Simple Games in Public Choice Mechanisms', *International Economic Review*, 23 (1982), 623–45.

Mavgordatos, George, 'The Greek Party System: A Case of Limited but Polarised Pluralism', *West European Politics*, 7:4 (1984) 156–69.

Miller, Kenneth, *Government and Politics in Denmark* (Boston: Houghton Mifflin, 1968).

Morgan, Michael-John, 'The Modelling of Governmental Coalition Formation: A Policy-Based Approach with Interval Measurement.' (University of Michigan, PhD thesis, 1976).

Mughan, Anthony, 'Accomodation or Defusion in the Management of Linguistic Conflict in Belgium?', *Political Studies*, 31 (1983), 434–51.

Norderval, Ingunn, 'Party and Legislative Participation among Scandinavian Women', *West European Politics* 84 (1985), 71–89.

Paloheimo, Heikki, *Governments in Democratic Capitalist States 1950–1983* (Turku, Finland: University of Turku), 1984).

Papadopoulos, Ioannis, 'The Swiss Election of 1987: A "Silent Revolution" behind Stability', *West European Politics*, 11:3 (1988), 146–9.

Pasquino, Gianfranco, 'Sources of Stability and Instability in the Italian Party System', *West European Politics*, 6:1 (1983), 93–110.

Pasquino, Gianfranco, 'Modernity and Reforms: The PSI between Political Entrepreneurs and Gamblers', *West European Politics*, 9:1 (1986), 120–41.

Penniman, Howard R. (ed.), *Britain at the Polls, 1979* (Washington, DC: American Enterprise Institute, 1981).

Plott, Charles, 'A Notion of Equilibrium and its Possibility under Majority Rule', *American Economic Review*, 57 (1967), 787–806.

Pridham, Geoffrey (ed.), *Coalitional Behaviour in Theory and Practice: An Inductive Model for Western Europe* (Cambridge: Cambridge University Press, 1986).

Rae, Douglas, *The Political Consequences of Electoral Laws* (New Haven: Yale University Press, 1971).

Rae, Douglas and Taylor, Michael, *The Analysis of Political Cleavages* (New Haven: Yale University Press, 1970).

Riker, William, *The Theory of Political Coalitions* (New Haven: Yale University Press, 1962).

Riker, William, 'Implications of the Disequilibrium of Majority Rule for the Study of Institutions', *American Political Science Review*, 74 (1980), 432–46.

Riker, William, *Liberalism Against Populism: A Confrontation Between the Theory of Democracy and the Theory of Social Choice* (San Francisco: Freeman, 1982).

Riker, William, *The Art of Political Manipulation* (New Haven: Yale University Press, 1986).

Robertson, David, *A Theory of Party Competition* (London: Wiley, 1976).

Sanders, David and Herman, Valentine, 'The Stability and Survival of Governments in Western Democracies', *Acta Politica*, 12 (1977), 346–77.

Sartori, Giovanni, *Parties and Party Systems: A Framework for Analysis* (Cambridge: Cambridge University Press, 1976).

Schlesinger, Joseph A., 'The Primary Goals of Political Parties: A Clarification of Positive Theory', *American Political Science Review*, 69 (1976), 840–9.

Schlesinger, Joseph A., 'On The Theory of Party Organisation', *Journal of Politics*, 46 (1984), 369–400.

Schofield, Norman, 'Instability of Simple Dynamic Games', *Review of Economic Studies*, 45 (1978), 575–94.

Schofield, Norman, 'Generalised Bargaining Sets for Cooperative Games', *International Journal of Game Theory*, 7 (1978) 183–99.

Schofield, Norman, 'Generic Properties of Simple Bergson–Samuelson Welfare Functions', *Journal of Mathematical Economics*, 7 (1980), 175–92.

Schofield, Norman, 'Generic Instability of Majority Rule', *Review of Economic Studies*, 50 (1983), 696–705.

Schofield, Norman, *Choice and Democracy* (Heidleberg: Springer, 1985).

Schofield, Norman, 'Existence of a Structurally Stable Equilibrium for a Non-Collegial Voting Rule', *Public Choice*, 51 (1986), 267–84.

Schofield, Norman, 'Stability of Coalition Governments in Western Europe', *European Journal of Political Economy*, 3 (1987), 555–91.

Schofield, Norman (ed.), *Coalition Theory and Coalition Government* (Dordrecht: Kluwer, 1989).

Schofield, Norman and Laver, Michael, 'Bargaining Theory and Portfolio Payoffs in European Coalition Governments 1945–83, *British Journal of Political Science*, 15 (1985), 143–64.

Schofield, Norman, Feld, Scott, and Grofman, Bernard, 'The Core and the Stability of Group Choice in Spatial Voting Games', *American Political Science Review*, 82 (1988), 195–211.

Share, Donald, 'Two Transitions: Democratisation and the Evolution of the Spanish Left', *West European Politics*, 8:1 (1985), 83–103.

Shepsle, Kenneth, 'Institutional Arrangements and Equilibrium in Multidimensional Voting Models', *American Journal of Political Science*, 23 (1979), 27–60.

Shepsle, Kenneth and Weingast, Barry, 'Structure Induced Equilibrium and Legislative Choice', *Public Choice*, 37 (1981), 503–19.

Shepsle, Kenneth and Weingast, Barry, 'The Institutional Foundations of Committee Power', *American Political Science Review*, 81 (1987), 85–104.

Shubik, Martin (ed.), *Essays in Mathematical Economics in Honor of Oskar Morgenstern* (Princeton: Princeton University Press, 1967).

Sloss, J., 'Stable Outcomes and Majority Rule Voting Games', *Public Choice*, 15 (1973), 19–48.

Spotts, Frederic and Wieser, Theodar, *Italy: A Difficult Democracy* (Cambridge: Cambridge University Press, 1986).

Strom, Kaare, 'Minority Governments in Parliamentary Democracies: The Rationality of Non-Winning Cabinet Solutions', *Comparative Political Studies*, 17 (1984), 199–227.

Strom, Kaare, 'Towards an Institutional Model of Competitive Party Behaviour', paper presented at ECPR Joint Sessions, Barcelona, 1985.

Strom, Kaare, 'Party Goals and Government Performance in Parliamentary Democracies', *American Political Science Review*, 79 (1985), 738–54.

Strom, Kaare, 'Deferred Gratification and Minority Governments in Scandinavia', *Legislative Studies Quarterly*, x:4 (1986), 583–605.

Strom, Kaare, 'Contending Models of Cabinet Stability', *American Political Science Review*, 82 (1988), 930–41.

Strom, Kaare, *Minority Government and Majority Rule* (Cambridge: Cambridge Univeristy Press, 1990.)

Strom, Kaare and Leipart, Jorn, 'Ideology, Strategy and Party Competition in Postwar Norway', *European Journal of Political Research*, 17 (1989), 263–88.

Taylor, Michael, 'On the Theory of Government Coalition Formation', *British Journal of Political Science*, 2 (1972), 361–73.

Taylor, Michael and Laver, Michael, 'Government Coalitions in Western Europe', *European Journal of Political Research*, 1 (1973), 205–48.

Tsokou, Starroula, Shelley, Mack C. II, and Dobratz, Betty, 'Some Correlates of Partisan Preference in Greece, 1980: A Discriminant Analysis', *European Journal of Political Research*, 13 (1986), 441–63.

von Beyme, Klaus, *The Political System of the Federal Republic of Germany* (Aldershot: Gower, 1983).

von Beyme, Klaus, *Political Parties in Western Democracies* (Aldershot: Gower, 1984).

von Neumann, I. and Morgenstern, O., *Theory of Games and Economic Behaviour* (Princeton; Princeton University Press, 1953).

Warwick, Paul, 'The Durability of Coalition Governments in Parliamentary Democracies', *Comparative Political Studies*, 11 (1979), 465–98.

Warwick, Paul, 'Models of Cabinet Stability: A Preliminary Evaluation', paper presented at the annual meeting of the American Political Science Association, Washington, DC, 1988.

Werth, Alexander, *De Gaulle* (Harmondsworth: Penguin, 1965).

Wittman, Donald, 'Candidate Motivation: A Synthesis of Alternative Theories', *American Political Science Review*, 77 (1983), 142–57.

Index